D0201312

# The Essay

NCTE Editorial Board: Colette Daiute, Hazel Davis, Bobbi Fisher, Keith Gilyard, Brenda Greene, Gail Hawisher, Ronald Jobe, Richard Luckert, Karen Smith, Chair, ex officio, Marlo Welshons, ex officio

**College Section Committee**

James L. Hill, Albany State College, Georgia, Chair

Frank Madden, Westchester Community College, Valhalla, New York, Assistant Chair

Pat Belanoff, SUNY—Stony Brook

Theresa Enos, University of Arizona, Tucson

Jeanette Harris, University of Southern Mississippi, Hattiesburg

Dawn Rodrigues, Kennesaw State College, Marietta, Georgia

Cynthia Selfe, Michigan Technological University, Houghton

Tom Waldrep, University of South Carolina, Columbia

Collett Dilworth, East Carolina University, Greenville, North Carolina

Louise Smith, University of Massachusetts, Boston, ex officio

Miriam Chaplin, Rutgers University, Camden, New Jersey, Executive Committee Liaison

Miles Myers, NCTE Staff Liaison

# The Essay

## Theory and Pedagogy for an Active Form

**PAUL HEILKER**

Virginia Tech

National Council of Teachers of English
1111 W. Kenyon Road, Urbana, Illinois 61801-1096

Grateful acknowledgment is made to the publisher for permission to reprint the following: "Mellow" from *Collected Poems* by Langston Hughes. Copyright 1994 by the estate of Langston Hughes. Reprinted by permission of Alfred A. Knopf, Inc.

Editor: Peter Feely

Cover Design: Doug Burnett

Interior Design: Doug Burnett

NCTE Stock Number 15845-3050

© 1996 by the National Council of Teachers of English. All rights reserved. Printed in the United States of America.

It is the policy of NCTE in its journals and other publications to provide a forum for the open discussion of ideas concerning the content and the teaching of English and the language arts. Publicity accorded to any particular point of view does not imply endorsement by the Executive Committee, the Board of Directors, or the membership at large, except in announcements of policy, where such endorsement is clearly specified.

## Library of Congress Cataloging-in-Publication Data

Heilker, Paul, 1962–
    The essay : theory and pedagogy for an active form / Paul Heilker.
       p.     cm.
    Includes bibliographical references and index.
    ISBN 0-8141-1584-5 (pbk.)
    1. English language—Rhetoric—Study and teaching. 2. Essay—Authorship—Study and Teaching. 3. Academic writing—Study and teaching. I. Title.
PE1404.H396 1996
808.4'07—dc20                                         96-2669
                                                      CIP

# Contents

———————

For anyone like myself, who—having recognized that the struggle
and search for knowledge, wisdom, and truth will never end—
cannot understand what is so wrong with being confused and
uncertain, what is so bad about changing one's mind.

# Acknowledgments

I would like to thank every person I have spoken with about this project since its inception in 1991 and thank my students for their willingness to take a risk for the sake of learning and growing. I would especially like to thank Gary Tate for his insights, guidance, encouragement, and criticism, Winifred B. Horner, Jim W. Corder, and Neil Daniel for their enthusiastic endorsement and cogent critiques of this work, Claudia Knott for her generous help in concluding my research, Aileen Murphy for her unwavering support, and Eli Heilker for being such an inspiration. Without each of these people, my thinking and writing—*my life*—would have remained impoverished and this book would not exist.

# Introduction

This book presents itself in such a level-headed fashion that readers might miss the affront implicit in what it asks. Its claim, after all, sounds so sensible: the essay, as it was originally practiced, is a perfect complement to the thesis/support form mandated in most composition classrooms, and as such needs to be taught at least as much as its counterpart. Consequently, we need a more tightly focused, "rehabilitative" theory of the essay. As a corrective to the teacherly habit of referring to virtually all normal school writing as *essays*—a practice that has rendered the word ambiguous to the point of being practically meaningless—Paul Heilker argues that it is better to envision the essay as a distinctive textual form identifiable by three major ingredients: skepticism, anti-scholasticism, and an alternative mode of arrangement or organization (*chrono-logic*). These characteristics are not the result of some idiosyncratic rereading stemming from the author's private aesthetics. Rather, by examining the origins of the essay, its earliest practice by Montaigne and the first English essayists, the work of twentieth-century theorists of the form, and the essays of contemporary writers, Heilker has found these three major elements to be present throughout the genre's history.

Nonetheless, Heilker's call for a new way of teaching and writing student essays makes significant demands, for in rehabilitating the essay we are also challenged to rehabilitate the very nature of the academy. When we realize this means more than some minor fixing, that it implies nothing less than profoundly rethinking what it means to teach and learn within an academy, this business of reconceptualizing the essay becomes something more than just a "compositional" matter.

To be sure, this book will be most helpful for those in composition studies. Heilker's legwork has resulted in his amassing an impressive amount of material on the nature of the essay, all of it aimed toward articulating, once and for all, what an essay is and how it differs from, say, the academic argument or feature article. Although volumes have been written about the essay, and we have numerous anthologies featuring the "best" examples of the form, attempts to define the genre have been more impressionistic than helpful. As we advance through Heilker's research, however, we quickly begin to hear the voices and echoes that he has heard, to see the obvious parallels between authorial motives, and by the end of the book the nature of the essay, which has eluded so many attempts at delineation, seems almost obvious. Heilker's definition is *not* obvious, but the thoroughness with which he has collected his evidence makes it seem so.

Heilker's rehabilitative project has the important effect of rendering our professional vocabulary a little more precise, no small accomplishment in a field with more than its share of jargon. Distinguishing between the thesis/support form and the essay eliminates the need to continue using terms like *personal writing* and *expressive discourse*, terms which conjure affinities with the language of greeting cards and therapy sessions and whose demise is overdue. Since the idea of the essay presented here always assumes at least some degree of introspection, any insistence on "being personal" would identify the writer as naive and/or self-indulgent. As a result, teachers of writing might find it more worthwhile to limit themselves to, perhaps, three basic categories of writing: *arguments* (traditional thesis/support forms, lab reports, technical writing, agitprop, and any text intended ultimately to sell a point), *essays* (in Heilker's rehabilitative sense, which could mean any text written ultimately to show an author's process of discovery), and *exercises* (any text made en route to larger writing endeavors, to develop a particular skill, or simply assist one's thinking, like "in-class writing").

But the most exciting implications for this "new traditional" portrayal of the essay are to be found in those three ingredients Heilker has isolated: the form's "profound epistemological skepticism" and "transgressive anti-scholasticism," which are conveyed within an "anti-Ciceronian chrono-logic." Each pose a major challenge to our fundamental understanding of the relationship between teachers, students, and the academy.

Skepticism is not the same as cynicism, although the two are often conflated. Skeptics are doubtful because everywhere one looks there are those selling their version of the truth as the only version of the truth. The skeptic, respectful of the idea of truth, is disturbed by the countless claims for single world views that ultimately seek not to enlighten but convert. The skeptic's battle with phonies and charlatans is really a fight against missionary fervor and its disrespect for others to arrive at truths by their own paths. Of course, skeptics can be consumed by skepticism, thus unwittingly falling prey to the very myopia they once distrusted. But when this happens the skeptic really turns into a cynic. Cynics are those who have given up. The cynic's energies are consumed with writing off everything as hopelessly mediated or hopelessly irrelevant or hopelessly poisonous. The cynic has been beaten, and can respond with no gesture other than a fashionable sneer (or smile—it's hard to tell the difference now) and a throwing up of the hands. Cynicism is the culture's operative condition as we enter the 21st century, and it requires virtually no effort to obtain.

Skepticism, on the other hand, is hard to come by in academia or anywhere else for that matter. It requires faith in something; it implies hope: one tests the atmosphere, finds things amiss, raises questions, and generally aims to improve by articulating doubt and exposing uncertainties. Skepticism is another word for *critical thinking*, which is the art of saying "no." Traditionalists and progressives alike have always claimed that they want their students to be critical thinkers, but few really mean it. Permissible skepticism is largely tokenistic.

But what if genuine skepticism were encouraged in the classroom? That would mean respecting students enough to give them the tools to question everything, even—especially—if it resulted in the student's creating newer tools to replace those favored by the teacher. To want students to constantly question the tenets of the beliefs presented to them is to want students to argue with everything: other students, the teacher, the curriculum, the university, the works. It is to give permission to students to disrupt the "educational process" by halting it in its tracks, asking difficult and embarrassing questions of the teachers and administrators. Most of all, it would mean encouraging students to act on those questions, to *go* someplace with them. To teach the essay in Heilker's rehabilitative sense is to promote skeptical thinking: no casual suggestion, given the intensely hierarchical, deeply political nature of the academy.

After skepticism, the second quality is no less exciting and risky in its ramifications. Anti-scholasticism can be seen as a need to seek answers outside the limited palette of ideas sanctioned within the classroom, the department, the discipline, the academy itself. It acknowledges that better answers often lie elsewhere, that the very nature of "answers" can elsewhere be radically different from those obtainable within the system. It does not promote the pejorative relativism that sees all truths as interchangeable, but rather recognizes that there are multiple truths for multiple localities, and that to experience additional truths one must sometimes travel outside the academic walls, leaving behind one's most comfortable paradigms. To permit anti-scholasticism is to admit up front that academia is incomplete. It is to take the university off of its hill and situate it on a more horizontal playing field where it becomes simply one church among many. For a university to condone anti-scholasticism would require serious weakening of the academic ego. It would require that the making of meaning would take precedence above self-promotion.

Finally, what Heilker calls the essay's *chrono-logic* represents a fundamental openness to diverse, nontraditional forms and logics. Instead of an artist carefully balancing the elements of his or her composition in some "timeless" space of perfect harmony, the essayist is someone working with found art and chance. The ideas that evolve are incorporated into the composition *as* they evolve, and it is okay, in fact, desirable, if it doesn't look like it is retrospectively balanced together in any classical, symmetrical presentation. This *chrono-logic* is another way of saying "receptiveness to *other* forms traditionally impermissible in the academy." It is to recognize that chaos itself is a shifting web of formal systems, and that virtually any presentation of materials might now be considered utterly complete in its randomness and fragmentation. To embrace this different logic of presentation of materials is to say that no one logic is sufficient. If we push this idea to its limits, the doorway of potentiality for composition blows wide open. If chrono-logic is acceptable, what about other unconventional, "disruptive" logics? What if, say, one person's "otherly" logical sense requires that sentences be abandoned mid-sentence? What if the presentation of meaning no longer takes the shape of prose, but is presented in some distinctly other kind of visual arrangement on the page? Why stick with written text, for that matter? Why couldn't an essay be any performance of inquisitiveness, whether live or re-created with music, video, or CD-ROM?

An embracing of *chrono-logic* need not end with an appreciation of writers whose train of thought moves more unpredictably than those with a more Ciceronian training. To accept chrono-logic is to admit *any* logic that erupts and evolves within the compositional time-space of the essay. The essay now becomes a locus for critical investigation where distinctions between prose and poetry, fiction and fact, performance and text might no longer matter much. The rehabilitative/rehabilitated essay is not supposed to look Montaigne-ish or like something from *The New Yorker*. It is expected, if we take these characteristics to their limits, to look like something we have never seen before. To prevent this from happening would be to deny the very skeptical, anti-scholastic attributes that also define the form.

What Heilker has done is to identify, carefully and with ample support, the three historical characteristics that give the essay its unique nature. And the question before us now is: given that we all have our endpoints of permissibility, how willing are we to explore the logical extensions of those characteristics?

One movement toward answering that question comes in the last section of the book, where Heilker reiterates and pursues the idea of the essay as not a noun, but a verb. Heilker insists that the essay must not be thought of as a static entity, a carefully framed object intended for the reader's passive, after-the-fact reflection. Echoing similar conclusions from other writers, Heilker shows us that the essay is not a form, but a force, not an abstract writ large, but an active display. The essay is movement, "kineticism incarnate" he calls it, and taking this idea seriously has great repercussions.

We all know the problem with arguments, be they classically constructed or taking the form of two people yelling in the street: nothing usually happens, except that people get angry and maybe hurt each other. Certainly some arguments can and do result in change for the better, but these are in the minority. And rarely does an argument by itself instigate profound, necessary change, for change is often the product of numerous unpredictable forces coming into alignment as much by chance as by intention.

Consider, specifically, the academic argument, the thesis/support paper that takes a stand, defines its terms, assembles evidence, and anticipates counterarguments. Thinking things through according to this logic obviously has its benefits; there is nothing inherently wrong about instructing someone on how to sculpt such a presentation. But it is wrong to make unjustifiable claims for such a form—to insist that the academic argument is the highest example of intellectual thought, and that the bulk of academic activity must evolve around the perpetuation of such a formula. And this is wrong for the simple reason that such thinking and the objects produced by such thought rarely ever *do* anything.

The research paper, the exam question, the master's thesis, the dissertation, the professional article, the scholarly book—these are almost never expected to be catalysts for real change. They are primarily icons, badges signifying our entry into some level of the academic hierarchy. They are not even ritual exercises in the tribal sense of the word, for most tribal ritualistic display is profoundly suffused with meaning or magic. The hundreds of thousands of academic arguments made every semester by students and their teachers far too often amount to little more than a complex distraction for all involved. Far too often, the business of making academic arguments (and it *is* a business) amounts to somnambulistic displays of imitation, exercises in inconsequentiality. And students know it—no matter whether they get As or Fs: at the end of the semester their papers remain in the boxes outside faculty offices, dead objects with no purpose, no function.

Perhaps—we hope—through the course of writing their papers their thinking evolved, changed, got more analytical and complex, and this is why it can still be valuable to teach the thesis/support form. But this is not how most of us teach argumentation; if it was, we would seldom be concerned in evaluating where the topic sentence appeared, whether or not the works cited followed MLA style, how appropriately the student cited sources, and other functions of custom. We would be more concerned with the activity than the final garb if we admitted that, no matter how polished that final garb, it almost never performs any measurable function of real consequence. In class, we point out to each other where a certain argument "breaks down," question the organization behind its delivery, the logic of its claims. But we almost never ask, "How has this changed your life? What does this argument *do*? Okay, if/since it has done that, what do we do now?"

Because Heilker's rehabilitative theory considers the essay an activity, we are returned to the possibility of learning as a catalytic force, and the success of any academic endeavor being judged not by how well it indoctrinates, but how it changes the life of the student. The rehabilitated essay is an extremely *located* enterprise, grounded in time, a work in progress (as is all life). Its demand is not to formally conclude (die), but rather to move, and to stay on the move: to *go* somewhere and hopefully infect others with the need to follow. Heilker's book ends by pointing toward a literacy of action.

To embrace the rehabilitated essay is not to promote any of the essayists cited in Heilker's work as better models, but to take the ideas which predicated their activity and keep those ideas alive in our work. I envision this book producing two generalized and opposite reactions in its readers—one reductive, the other radical. The reductive response would be to promote a certain type of essay as a better model for student writing. Instead of academic arguments, we would encourage more introspective, "familiar" essays, more wandering, "personalized" musings on the death of relatives, animals, the weather, fishing, big issues, and so forth. This would be no accomplishment, and it is *not* what Heilker has in mind. The other response to this book would be to take what the rehabilitated essay stands for seriously, and to cultivate skepticism, anti-scholastic thinking, and alternative forms of presentation in our work, in our play, in the classroom, outside the classroom. This is no small challenge. It is precisely the kind of challenge educators need to tackle head on.

—Derek Owens
St. John's University

# This Is *Not* an Essay

*OR*

## An Apology (of Sorts)

What follows is *not* an essay. Indeed, what follows can be considered an arch example of writing in the thesis/support form, even though this is exactly the form I will soon be sharply criticizing. In fact, ironically, I will shortly be using the thesis/support form to attack the thesis/support form. I wish to emphasize that this choice of form is a highly self-conscious and difficult authorial decision. I chose to present this text in the thesis/support form, despite all the attendant risks and limitations I discuss in Chapter 1, for three main reasons. First, as Jim W. Corder has pointed out to me on several occasions, the forcefully argued thesis/support form *is* the established, traditional, expected genre for scholarly texts. It is not simply more difficult to get essays published in scholarly arenas; on the rare occasions that they do appear, Corder notes, they are always seen as being "less than." An essay is perceived to be less rigorous, less scholarly, less serious, less important, less intellectually demanding to compose, and less worthy of respect and interest than the traditional thesis-driven texts that comprise the vast majority of professional scholarship. In short, I wanted this text to be taken seriously, so I put it in a "serious" form. Second, as Winifred B. Horner has reminded me on several occasions, the readers of scholarly texts are usually operating within a specific and tremendously demanding economy of reading, one which offers them very little reading time in concert with a difficult, often abstract, textual content. She notes that we usually just do not have the time that is needed to follow the unhurried, exploratory, sometimes meandering development of essays. The thesis/support form's familiarity and schematic nature, however, allows us to rapidly and efficiently digest large amounts of abstract material in a small amount of time. In other words, I have chosen to present this text in a thesis/support form because I want it to be read by my often harried colleagues. And third, I have chosen to present this text in a thesis/support form because it is, in the final analysis, simply *not* an essay. It is, rather, an argument. Employing Kurt Spellmeyer's useful distinction, I would like to note that what follows is not "writing as a means of achieving understanding," but rather "writing as a demonstration of understanding." In sum, what follows was not written so that I might *come to know*, but rather so that I might *show what I know*.

Moreover, I wish to make it clear from the outset that I am *not* advocating that we displace thesis/support writing from the center of academic discourse and composition pedagogy and replace it with the essay. Rather, I am arguing that we need to problematize students' understanding of the thesis/support form (and thus improve their performance in it) by including the essay as an alternative, supplementary form in composition instruction.

'Nuff said, I hope.

# Chapter 1

# The Need for an Alternative Form in Composition Instruction

## *OR*

## The Emperor Has No Clothes

Thesis statement. Topic sentences. Supporting details. The unholy trinity of composition instruction. This trio of god terms in composition instruction has been worshiped by legions of composition teachers and has thus left its indelible stamp on the thinking and writing of generations of students. Indeed, the traditional thesis/support form continues to dominate college composition instruction and our students' thinking. A quick survey of 29 recent composition handbooks and rhetorics (Appendix A) reveals a litany consistently intoning that the thesis statement is a necessary part of the ritual, an indispensable part of effective writing, "the key to writing a successful college [paper]" (Crews and Schor 5). The thesis is presented to students as occupying a crucial textual position. It is, they are told: "the bedrock . . . upon which you will build your paper" (O'Hare and Memering 69); "the keystone of your [paper]" (Kirszner and Mandell 43); "the weightiest part of your paper" (Guth 67); "something on which to focus everything else you have to say" (Neeld 44); "the critical moment," the sentence that "gives meaning to all of the others in the paper" (Kurilich and Whitaker 22); "the essence of what you discuss" (Troyka 38); and "the heart of the [paper] . . . the core . . . the one thing you have to say"

(Rawlins 84). The thesis statement is also portrayed as performing a number of critical functions. Students are told that it is a necessity for shaping a topic (Barnet and Stubbs 26), an essential strategy for both shaping a draft (Kennedy and Kennedy 469) and cuing the reader (Axelrod and Cooper 400), a "main method" of organizing "a tight and easy-to-follow paper" (Hairston and Ruszkiewicz 41), a requirement for "transforming writing into a demonstration of learning" (Gere 53), and "a promise to the readers" (Lunsford and Connors 22) or "a contract" that the writer has "a serious responsibility to honor" (Mann and Mann 24). Moreover, students learn that the thesis statement has talismanic properties, that it has the power to "control and unify the whole paper" (Gebhardt and Rodrigues 54), to introduce and summarize "the entire paper" by putting the central idea "into a nutshell" (Leggett, Mead, and Kramer 362), to embody "a clear, definite, one-sentence answer" to the writer's "basic question" (Heffernan and Lincoln 41), to point "you in a specific direction, helping you to stay on track and out of tempting byways" (Reinking and Hart 26), and to restrict "the scope of the [paper] to manageable limits," and so prevent the paper "from trying to do too many things" (Fergenson 33). Our worship of the thesis/support form's various mystical attributes, institutionalized in these sacred texts of our classrooms and drilled into our students through their catechism, seems to have blinded us, however, because the thesis/support god is not all-powerful, not all-fulfilling. It is, rather, inadequate from developmental, epistemological, ideological, and feminist rhetorical perspectives.

First, the thesis/support form, once learned, works to actually thwart students' development. As David W. Chapman has said, "Most students have internalized this form to such a degree that it has become the 'default drive' for expository writing," the automatically and unthinkingly invoked routine ("Forming" 73). Similarly, in a longitudinal case study, Russel K. Durst found that while students had some difficulties in learning the form in secondary school, "once they had mastered it, they tended to rely on the thesis/support structure almost exclusively in their English critical writing." Overall, Durst says, 90 percent of the student texts in his sample were organized this way, students using the thesis/support form to structure literary analyses, autobiographical, informative, and argumentative compositions, and even writing outside of English class (86). Despite their differing degrees of mastery of the form, the students in this study "were almost totally faithful to the thesis/support [form] in their high school English writing, using it in virtually all of their [papers] from ninth grade on" (89).

Durst's findings remind me of Brad, a student in one of my junior-level, elective composition classes at Colorado State University some years ago. Despite my repeated protestations, no matter how atypical I tried to make the assignments, no matter whether the goal of the paper was remembering, problem solving, or even exploring, Brad struggled to formulate for each of his texts succinct and unambiguous thesis statements supported by three reasons, sometimes jamming ideas together, sometimes lopping off the most interesting thoughts from his working drafts in order to precisely fill in and fit his five-paragraph forms. Perhaps he thought me crazy; perhaps he thought he would dissolve if he deviated from what had always worked in the past; regardless, it was a long semester for us both. Brad would have fit in quite well with the students in Durst's study, because the thesis/support format in his sample of student writing was, he says,

> so rigid and formulaic that students were often able to simply "slot in" points, which took their shape and plan from the overall structure. Helpful at first, these structures may eventually have limited their further development. . . . What the . . . students seemed to need most was a loosening of some of the formal constraints, the scaffolds they had come to rely on at the global level, to lead them toward other, more heuristic forms of writing. (102)

Besides being the uncritically and automatically invoked template for producing text, the scaffolding of the thesis/support form that allows students to simply and mechanically organize information reveals a second way this form limits students' development: by closing rather than opening their minds. This closing process begins by requiring students to repeatedly narrow and focus their topics (often to the point of inconsequentiality) in order to find a "workable" thesis, one that is straightforward (often to the point of being obvious, incontestable, or clichéd) and has clear supporting reasons. Next, this form works to close students' minds by requiring them to keep an "objective" distance from the narrowed and focused topics they eventually choose. At least half of their experience, the subjective part, is off limits as they attempt to develop the topics they have chosen in expository prose. Students in my composition classes, for instance, have been convinced that they can only use "I" in their "personal" writing, like journals, diaries, or letters, never in their "serious" or transactional "school" writing, a conviction I find difficult to change. Likewise, the thesis/support form works to close students' minds by urging them to use one and only one of the many voices at their disposal throughout the length of their texts: the objective, "scientific" voice, the one that is, in many ways, the most "not I." As this preference for a single voice implies, the thesis/support form also closes students' minds by encouraging them to view their subject from a single, static perspective. Their position relative to their subject matter should remain immobile; altering that position—changing their minds—is strongly discouraged. Finally, as William Zeiger has noted, the thesis/support form closes rather than opens students' minds because it works "to stop inquiry rather than to start it." This form, he says, creates "a logically exclusive, linear progression to a predetermined end" which serves to "move the reader to one and only one conclusion." In short, he says, the thesis/support form does not operate to help a writer learn about a given idea, but instead functions "to fix it in certainty" ("Exploratory" 456). The thesis/support form, it seems, is inherently paradoxical: it begins with where it has already ended; it introduces the topic with its conclusion; it opens with airtight closure.

In addition to actually restricting students' development in a number of ways, the thesis/support form is inadequate because it also embodies what I see as an overly simplistic positivistic epistemology, one at odds with the assumptions of social constructionist thought that I and many other contemporary composition teachers have embraced. According to James A. Berlin, in a positivistic epistemology and corresponding rhetoric:

> Truth is prior to language, is clearly and distinctly available to the person who views it in the proper spirit, and is ultimately communicable in clear and distinct terms. Disagreement has always to do with faulty observation, faulty language, or both, and never is due to the problematic and contingent nature of truth. (*Reality* 11)

Berlin says that truth, in this view, is determined through induction, through the collection of sensory data to arrive at generalizations; thus, the observer's job is to be as objective as possible and then to describe his/her discoveries in transparent language that captures the original experience and reproduces it in the minds of the audience (*Reality* 8). Berlin says that in this corresponding rhetoric the main goals of writing instruction are the training of students in patterns of arrangement and surface-level correctness, with special emphasis on the forms of exposition. Most important, he maintains that in this epistemological/rhetorical complex, "all truths are regarded as certain, readily available to the correct method of investigation" (*Reality* 9).

In stark contrast to this perspective, however, it has been my experience that the "truths" in each of the various spheres of my life (emotional, spiritual, familial, intellectual, professional, political, and so on) have been anything but "certain," especially in the innumerable areas where these spheres intersect and conflict. Indeed, each of these "truths" has been slippery and elusive, embroiled in continual disagreement and contradiction, defying all my attempts to pin it down and thus settle the matter once and for all, no matter how scrupulously I examine or try to articulate the matter at hand.

It seems clear that the thesis/support form (in its attempts to fix truth in certainty and to declare a definite and singular reality, one that is knowable from a single, immobile point-of-view and completely re-presentable in correctly used language forms) embodies a positivistic epistemology and rhetoric that runs counter to the social epistemology and rhetoric espoused by many contemporary thinkers, a view which sees truth and reality as, at best, multiple, provisional, and tentative. In this view, truth and reality arise, as Berlin says, from "a transaction that involves all elements of the rhetorical situation: interlocutor, audience, material reality, and language," with the interlocutor, audience, and material world all being conceived of as verbal constructs (*Reality* 16). According to Berlin, in social epistemic rhetoric:

> All truths arise out of dialectic, out of the interaction of individuals within discourse communities. Truth is never simply "out there" in the material world or the social realm, or simply "in

here" in a private and personal world. It emerges only as the three—the material, the social, and the personal—interact, and the agent of mediation is language. (*Reality* 16–17)

Seen from the complexities of the social epistemic perspective, the thesis/support form seems woefully simplistic and inadequate. While the world is a complex and problematic web of perplexities, the thesis/support form keeps offering our students the same simple, straightforward, and insufficient answers. Our pedagogical reliance on this form suggests to students that they need only know how to use a single tool, that their mastery of one simple and easy procedure will allow them to "fix" the infinite variety of interconnected problems they will face in the world.

In much the same way that it is epistemologically reductive, the thesis/support form is also ideologically misleading. Berlin has argued that one's "rhetoric can never be innocent, can never be a disinterested arbiter of the ideological claims of others because it is always already serving certain ideological claims," its very discursive structure favoring "one version of economic, social, and political arrangements over others" ("Ideology" 477). The thesis/support form makes the opposite claim in its convention of "objectivity" on the part of the writer. This convention makes the implicit ideological claim that the author can, and indeed should, be "un-ideological," disinterested, removed from the sociopolitical structures operating in his or her environment. Perhaps this is why my students often think they can successfully write on topics about which they do not care. Perhaps this is why they have to be trained to choose topics in which they are interested. The incredibly tight discursive structure of the thesis/support form makes the additional ideological claim that the complexities of the world's problems and issues are not problematic after all—not a complex web of interconnections that need to be addressed from multiple perspectives in a collaborative dialogue—but really rather neat, "slottable," and solvable in a very short space using a single point of view and formulaic thinking, a procedure that will leave one with no bothersome loose ends. Again, it presents the students with a conceptual tool box that has only one tool in it, but also with the guarantee that this one tool is all they will ever need to deal with the problems they will encounter. Furthermore, as Keith Fort contends, the thesis/support form serves the ideological function of mystifying the nature of authority and making students blindly revere and replicate existing hierarchical power structures in society. According to Fort, our "unconscious need to believe in the reality of a transcendent authority" is at odds with our "conscious belief that such authority cannot exist," and so we have evolved the thesis/support form "in large part as a strategy that will seem to solve this contradiction" (633). Fort says that since we accept that the scientific method has the power to define reality, we accept authority if it seems to be based on impersonal scientific observation. In the thesis/support form, he says, "the technique of 'hidden omniscience' . . . allows subjective interpretation to be presented in such a way that it does not appear to be dependent on the mind of a fallible human being" (634). The thesis/support form not only masks the nature of authority in this manner but also conditions our attitudes toward that mystified authority. Fort maintains that our insistence on the standard thesis/support form conditions students to think in terms of authority and hierarchy. In the thesis/support form, he writes, "is found the same manifestation of the 'proper' attitudes toward authority that would be found in almost any of the institutions in our society." In this way, he concludes, composition teachers "may be doing as much as anyone to inculcate the attitude that generates [our] hierarchical and competitive society" (635). Fort asks us to consider to what extent our teaching of the traditional thesis/support form, our replication of the status quo operating in composition instruction, may lead to our students' unquestioning replication of an oppressive status quo in society outside the classroom. To what extent, we might wonder, does our teaching of this form lead students into an unconscious buttressing of the societal pyramid that has rich, young, able-bodied, highly educated, scientific, white, Christian, business-minded, materialistic, type-A males at the top and everyone else somewhere below them, trying to assimilate those values and become "empowered"? In obvious contrast to these hegemonic implications, Berlin says that social epistemic rhetoric, through its claim that arguments from transcendent truth are impossible since all arguments arise in ideology, inevitably functions to offer an explicit critique of economic, political, and social arrangements and to support economic, social, political, and cultural democracy ("Ideology" 489–90).

Finally, in addition to being developmentally, epistemological-ly, and ideologically inadequate, the thesis/support form's mandated use of rational, linear, agonistic, masculine rhetoric is frequently derided by many, myself included, who instead promote an oppos-ing and complementary intuitive, associative, holistic, feminine rhetoric. Thomas J. Farrell, expressing notions that are generally accepted in feminist studies, says that thinking in the masculine mode is "framed, contained, . . . preselected, and packaged," while writing in this mode tends to accentuate the boundaries between writer and subject and writer and audience, emphasizing explicit-ness and a need for closure (910). In contrast, Farrell writes, the "indirection" of the feminine mode "tries to simulate how one might actually reason to a conclusion" (909) and "seems to proceed without a readily recognizable plan" since the thinking in the femi-nine mode is open-ended and generative, the ideas less processed and controlled than in the male mode. Writing in the feminine mode, he says, tends to obfuscate the boundaries between writer and subject and writer and audience, and to emphasize "indirection," implicitness, and an openness "useful in reconciling differences" (910). Likewise, discussing the French feminist perspective, Clara Juncker has said that feminine writing knows "no boundaries, no beginnings and endings, instead reaching toward . . . infinite desire and inconclusion" (426), that it overflows with multiplicity, simul-taneity, and ruptures "that defy phallogocentric notions of coher-ence and meaning" (427). What French feminists seek to liberate, Juncker says, is "the tortured voice of the (wo)man imprisoned" in phallogocentric sign systems (428). I think it important to note, though, that "man," too, is likewise tightly constrained within these sign systems, as unable as "woman" to use these alternate means of thinking and development, as unable to speak this taboo rhetoric or use these marginalized voices. While I thus agree with Juncker that teachers of writing must allow women students "to speak in foreign tongues" (431), I would add that we must also allow the men to adopt "foreign tongues." Hence, I concur with Juncker's assessment that we must disrupt and dislocate the dominant order of masculine academic discourse in order to allow for a multiplicity of discourses, for multiple kinds of writing in academia, so that we might "enable student writers to (re)invent themselves and to inscribe *differance* in(side) academia" (434). I would add, however, that we need to do this in order to liberate both the women *and* the men in our classes, in order for both the female and male students to have the opportunity to rhetorically reinvent themselves. My intent in including "man" in this "feminist" agenda is not to trivialize the efforts of feminists nor to masculinely appropriate and thus domesticate feminine discourse. All I am asserting is that "man," too, has become entrapped in patriarchal discourse. I fully acknowledge that feminists' perceptions of being shackled by masculine discourse and their desire to be free of it are legitimate, more urgent than "man's" could be; I agree that "woman" has been and still is far more victimized by phallogocentric language than "man." Pamela J. Annas, for instance, has written of how the imperial reign of the masculine thesis/support form extends even into the realm of women's studies, creating a dilemma for those teaching writing in these classes. "We have been trained to teach expository writing in a particular way—one which values writing that is defended, linear, and 'objective,'" she says, and thus many writing classes in women's studies are ironically designed "to teach the use of abstract, logical, and impersonal rather than sensual, contextual, and committed language" (360). Annas ultimately argues for a blending of feminine and masculine forms, for a bringing together of "the personal and the political, the private and the public" (370) in writing that can be "rigorous without sacrificing subjectivity" (361). Such a writing, I believe, would be a boon to both "woman" *and* "man," allowing both our female and male students the possibility of rhetorically reinventing themselves.

The notion of blending personal and public, feminine and masculine forms in writing may work to assuage the rage that some feminists rightly feel. As Jane Tompkins says, "The public-private dichotomy, which is to say the public-private *hierarchy*, is a founding condition of female oppression. I say to hell with it" (168). Tompkins, summarizing an unspecified lecture by Allison Jaggar, has argued that Western epistemology

> is shaped by the belief that emotion should be excluded from the
> process of attaining knowledge. Because women in our culture are
> not simply encouraged but *required* to be the bearers of emotion,
> which men are culturally conditioned to repress, an epistemology
> which excludes emotions from the process of attaining knowledge
> radically undercuts women's epistemic authority. (170)

In this way, she says, women have been socialized from birth to feel and act in ways that automatically exclude them from participating in our culture's most valued activities.

The blending of personal and public, feminine and masculine forms in writing may also function to fill the affective void experienced by many men, a loss and emptiness some have attempted to fill recently by joining the "men's movement." While the public-private dichotomy/hierarchy that Tompkins decries is a foundation of male domination and female oppression, it nevertheless comes with an awfully big price tag for men: it cuts them off from half of their being. This dichotomy/hierarchy requires men to deny and throw away half their nature, half their resources, half their potential: their emotional, affective selves. Through the use of the public-private schism, men have dominated women but cut themselves in two in the process. Like Tompkins, I say to hell with it.

While we may curse it, the public-private dichotomy/hierarchy nonetheless remains in place, exerting its powerful influence. As women attempt to participate in our culture's most highly valued knowledge-creating activities, the public-private schism places them in a difficult situation. Tompkins believes that it is ineffectual for women's thinking to adopt "the impersonal, technical vocabulary of the epistemic ideology it seeks to dislocate" (170), to adopt the half of the dichotomy that men retained and still wield, which puts her in a political predicament: "to adhere to the conventions is to uphold a male standard of rationality that militates against women being recognized as culturally legitimate sources of knowledge. To break with the conventions is to risk not being heard at all" (170–71). Thus, Tompkins seeks a discourse that will allow for more "Fluidity, flexibility, versatility, mobility," the ability to move "from one thing to another without embarrassment, . . . turning, weaving, bending, unbending, moving in loops and curves," because in the academy, women "all speak the father tongue, which is impersonal, while decrying the fathers' ideas" (174). She wants to be able to speak more often in her professional academic life in what Ursula LeGuin calls "the mother tongue" rather than the "father tongue":

> The dialect of the father tongue that you and I learned best in college . . . only lectures. . . . Many believe this dialect—the expository and particularly scientific discourse—is

the *highest* form of language, the true language, of which all other uses of words are primitive vestiges. . . . It is the language of thought that seeks objectivity.

The essential gesture of the father tongue is not reasoning, but distancing—making a gap, a space, between the subject or self and the object or other. . . . The father tongue is spoken from above. It goes one way. No answer is expected, or heard.

. . . The mother tongue, spoken or written, expects an answer. It is conversation, a word the root of which means "turning together." The mother tongue is language not as mere communication, but as relation, relationship. It connects. . . . Its power is not in dividing but in binding. . . . (qtd. in Tompkins 173–74)

What Tompkins wants for her professional academic life is what I want for all women and men, both in and out of academia, as well: the freedom to speak in the mother tongue. In this way, each will regain what it has been denied for so long. Finally, like Fort, Tompkins decries the father tongue's "authority effect," its "implicit deification of the speaker," because "authoritative" discourse like the thesis/support form ignores "the human frailty of the speaker, his body, his emotions, his history," ignores "the moment of intercourse with the reader—acknowledgement of the other person's presence, her feelings, her needs," and ultimately "speaks as though the other person weren't there" (175–76). The father tongue is a less-than-fully human discourse. It excises much of what makes us human: our fallibility, interdependence, and feelings. Our students need at least the option of exercising a more fully human discourse.

Thus, the thesis/support form is inadequate to the developmental, epistemological, ideological, and feminine (and thus more fully human) rhetorical needs of both students and instructors in the contemporary composition classroom. Some alternative form is clearly needed to address the weaknesses of the thesis/support form and meet these pressing theoretical and pedagogical needs.

The *essay*, as distinguished from the thesis/support form, is a form that can meet these various needs, that can truly foster students' continued development, embody the complexities of social epistemology, offer students an ideological counterpractice, and incorporate a more fully human rhetoric. However, as W. Ross Winterowd says, "if the essay is to serve as the kind of writing through which students realize their full potential as liberally educated beings, they, and we, need an expanded conception of what the essay is and what it can do" (146). Both instructors and students in the contemporary composition class need to rethink and rehabilitate the essay, to (re)turn to the earliest conception and practice of the genre, to (re)turn to the Montaignean, exploratory essay.

# Chapter 2

# Montaigne and the Early English Essay

## *OR*

## Back to the Future, Part One

### ORIGINS OF THE ESSAY

While it is a common notion that Montaigne "invented" the modern essay with the publication of his *Essais* in 1580, a number of scholars have traced the genealogy of the genre back to earlier periods and writers and have uncovered a complex matrix of relationships among the essay and other prose forms, while others have worked to situate the birth of the essay within the context of larger cultural developments.

Although the quality of their accounts sometimes seems to border on the capricious and dubious, scholars have presented a remarkable array of possible literary ancestors for Montaigne and the essay. As with any family history, there are surely some inaccuracies; but, also like any family history, these stories of the essay's origins probably contain some measure of truth at their cores. Because of their varying levels of veracity, these stories combine to offer us a colorful (if questionable) portrait of the essay's misty life before Montaigne.

Many argue, including Phillip Lopate, that "Essays go back at least to classical Greece and Rome" (1). Bonamy Dobrée, for instance, asserts that the essay, "a friendly, personal, informal piece of writing about anything you like, has existed from at least as early as the gay writings of Lucian in the second century B.C." (7). Dobrée's comment is illuminating, because while his conception of the essay is too broad to be of much critical power, many of the other commentators discussed below, in order to invoke the ancestors that he or she does, must also often work from notions of the essay that are no less plastic, sweeping, and idiosyncratic than Dobrée's. William J. Dawson and Coningsby W. Dawson, for instance, even go so far as to contend that the essay derives, in part, from the Chokhmah or wisdom literature of the Hebrews, such as the books of Proverbs, Ecclesiastes, the Wisdom of Jesus the Son of Sirach, and the Wisdom of Solomon (4). Most people who maintain that the form has origins earlier than Montaigne stay within the confines of classical Greek and Roman literature, however. For instance, the influence of Ciceronian (and thus ultimately Platonic) dialogue on the formation of the essay has been noted by both Charles E. Whitmore (555) and Arthur Christopher Benson, the latter writing that Montaigne "owed a great deal of his inspiration to Cicero, who treated . . . abstract topics in a conversational way," and to Plato, "whose dialogues undoubtedly contain the germ of . . . the essay" (51) and "would be essays but for the fact that they have a dramatic colouring" (52). Indeed, Georg Lukács asserts that Plato was "the greatest essayist who ever lived or wrote," the "greatest master of the form" (13). In contrast, O. B. Hardison Jr. contends that Plutarch was Montaigne's "principle guide and mentor," his *Moralia* embodying the prototype of short compositions on topics of general interest (13), while Réda Bensmaïa notes that scholars have also invoked Pliny, the *Meditations* of Marcus Aurelius, and the *Confessions* of Saint Augustine as the source of the essay (90). In the unpublished dedication intended for the 1612 edition of his essays, Sir Francis Bacon points to yet another predecessor as the source of the essay, saying "The word is late, but the thing is ancient. For Seneca's *Epistles to Lucilius*, if one mark them well, are but Essays—That is dispersed meditations, though conveyed in the form of epistles" (100). J. C. Guy Cherica also invokes Seneca, but then circles us back to Cicero, arguing that "the essay had already come into existence, as a literary genre, in Antiquity" in such works as Seneca's *Epistulae Morales* and Cicero's *De Amicitia* and *Cato Maior (De Senectute)* (152), since these texts display characteristics present

in the modern essay: lack of formalism, conversational tone, meditative mood, use of digressions for illustration and argumentation,
integration of form and content, and use of the reflective mood as a
process of individualization (153).

In moving from a consideration of the essay's relationships to
authors before Montaigne to an examination of its kinship with
earlier prose forms, we can see a noticeable leap in the general quality of critical precision, credibility, and agreement. The connection
between the epistle or letter and the essay, for example, has been
noted by several other commentators besides Bacon and Cherica.
Whitmore traces the roots of the essay back past Montaigne to the
beginnings of modern prose literature in Italian humanism, to "the
Latin letter which the humanists revived after the example of the
younger Seneca" (554); Wilbert Lorne MacDonald likewise claims
there is "a very close connection between the classical 'epistola' and
the essay of Montaigne, Cornwallis, and Bacon" (2); and Shirley
Brice Heath maintains that the "features of both the context and
text of letters bear close resemblance to those outlined by Michel de
Montaigne." Even though English essayists from Bacon forward
contributed their own features to lists of attributes of the essay, she
says, "all seemed to hold the view that both the letter and the essay
said much about both writer and context" (6).

While this set of commentary strongly suggests an essay-letter
connection, another group of critics, including Richard M.
Chadbourne, have convincingly argued that the essay has a close
kinship with the journal, the commonplace book, and other similar
forms (136). Graham Good, for instance, asserts that Montaigne
developed the *essai* "in relation and reaction to . . . the compendium
of sayings" (1), while H. V. Routh says that "the mere habit of keeping common-place books was bound sooner or later to end in the
publication of essays" (143), noting that in many cases Montaigne's
*Essais* "first came into existence as marginalia in books" (31).
Dawson and Dawson likewise contend that the essay "made its earliest appearance not as a single effort, but as a passage interpolated in
a larger work, as a reflection, or side remark, of the author upon the
events which he has been narrating" (5). Whitmore, too, stresses the
influences on the essay of the journal or diary (556) and "the commentary—a conveniently inclusive term for any collection of observations which did not pretend to the formality of a treatise" (555).

While some scholars point to the specific influences of the letter or journal forms on the essay, others try to locate the essay within a dense network of relationships to other forms, a move that gives us a more complex rendering of the essay's possible history but that sacrifices critical precision, credibility, and agreement in the process and thus ironically dilutes the move's attempt at increased explanatory power. For instance, while Chadbourne mentions the essay's relation to "kindred forms" such as the character, portrait, and aphorism (136), Heath states that literary historians, editors of essay collections, and essayists themselves "consistently agree that the form has evolved from conversation through letter- and journal-writing" (4) through an "intertwined trail of inner individual experience, conversation, letter, long narrative, essay, and literary letter-reading" (5). To further muddle the matter, MacDonald delineates the links he finds between the essay and still more "allied forms," such as the apophthegm, the maxim, the conduct book, the meditation, contemplation, and sermon, the character, and the anatomy (72–115).

Oddly enough, the most enlightening, the most powerfully explanatory discussions of the essay's origins, are those that have attempted to place these various generic genealogies into the even larger and more complex contexts of cultural developments, that try to flesh out even more fully the milieu from which Montaigne's *Essais* emerged. Robert Lane Kauffman, for example, asserts that the essay ultimately requires explanation in terms of "comprehensive cultural phenomena, such as the whole development of humanist thought, the rise of print-culture, and . . . the new scientific epistemology" ("Theory" 9). Michael L. Hall offers one such explanation, convincingly arguing that the essay emerged in the late 1500s and early 1600s "as a product of the Renaissance 'idea' of discovery and in response to it" ("Emergence" 73). Within a brief span of time, he says, astronomers challenged and overthrew the centuries-old and seemingly unassailable model of an ordered universe, while explorers altered "the face of the earth itself." This spirit of discovery extended beyond the sciences, manifesting itself as "a new mode of thought and discourse" that closely examined received opinions in "a search for inward truths as well as outward," manifesting itself as the essay, "a new genre written in a new style of prose" ("Emergence" 74–75). In this new spirit, Hall writes

> Truth in any realm is no longer something acquired by assimi-
> lating received views, but something which one must seek out
> for oneself and experience, like an explorer charting new lands.
> The key word in this discussion, it seems to me, is "experience,"
> and it applies to inward journeys of self-discovery as well as to
> ventures of outward-bound exploration. . . . [T]he essay provided
> a kind of prose composition particularly suited to the examina-
> tion of conventional wisdom, the exploration of received opin-
> ion, and the discovery of new ideas and insights—a kind of writ-
> ten discourse which allowed the author to think freely outside
> the constraints of established authority and traditional rhetori-
> cal forms. ("Emergence" 78)

In short, Hall argues, the earliest essayists all wrote in response to
the idea of discovery, in response "to the notion that the world was
in flux and that knowledge was no longer fixed by authority but in
a state of transition" ("Emergence" 89), an idea seconded by several
critics. Good concurs, for instance, asserting that the essay "emerges
between the old and the new learning, rejecting the old method of
uncritically accumulated commentary, but also refusing the systematic ambitions of the new science" (3). It is in this spirit that
Montaigne excuses himself in "Of Repentance," noting his "refrain"
of "sincere and complete submission"; he says, "I speak as an ignorant inquirer. . . . I do not teach, I tell" (612). Thus, Montaigne's
characteristic skepticism "was not based on the fear of not finding
confirmation of what he believed or felt he had to believe," Cherica
says, "but on the acknowledgment of the insufficiency of his own
knowledge and its uncertainty" (128). Here, I believe, lies our first
potent and useful generalization about the nature of the essay: the
essay is epistemologically skeptical, a manifestation of the spirit of
discovery at work in an uncertain universe, an exploration of a
world in flux that leaves old, inadequate orders behind in its quest
for new ideas, new insights, and new visions of the truth.

Kurt Spellmeyer's and Thomas Newkirk's accounts persuasively
posit the birth of the essay as a result of an intellectual shift similar
to the advent of the spirit of discovery in the late sixteenth and
early seventeenth centuries: the attack upon scholasticism. Newkirk
believes that Montaigne created the essay as a challenge to the
scholastic tradition, as a challenge to "the most basic beliefs . . . of
the academic specialists of his day," and as a challenge to "their

nominalism, their belief that the world consisted of fixed entities that can be named and categorized with precision" (11). Montaigne, we know, believed the world to be a much more problematic place. In "Of Repentance," he maintains that

> The world is but a perennial movement. All things in it are in constant motion—the earth, the rocks of the Caucasus, the pyramids of Egypt—both with the common motion and with their own. Stability itself is nothing but a more languid motion. (610)

Like the spirit of discovery, which rejected the unassailable model of the universe it received from tradition as inadequate, anti-scholasticism also scrutinized the fixity and stability of the conventional wisdom and opinion it inherited, interrogating the idea of authority itself and challenging its bases of categorization and specialization. According to Spellmeyer, the essay arose as Montaigne's attempt

> to repair precisely that fragmentation of experience—into grammar, logic, theology, rhetoric, and so forth—which characterized scholastic discourse, and which arose from still another fragmentation, between the "high" language of the court and college and the "low" language of the street and home. (262)

Montaigne, in "Of Repentance," prides himself on being the first author to overcome this fragmentation, on being the first to communicate with readers "by my entire being, as Michel de Montaigne, not as a grammarian or a poet or a jurist" (611). From Montaigne's anti-scholastic perspective, Spellmeyer says, the inherently specialized and mutually exclusive conventional branches of learning obscured both the complexity and coherence of real life (262); thus, he vigorously "opposed the assertion that any particular language, community, or worldview could define absolutely the boundaries of human experience" (268). Against the systematic impersonality, exclusionary purity, abstractness, and discrimination of scholastic discourse, Montaigne advocated "the central position of the author-as-speaker, at once subject and object in discourse" and championed a textual form that, "at the risk of imprecision and incongruity," offered "a 'coming-together' of dissonant perspectives in order to restore the lived world," according to Spellmeyer (263). By these means, Montaigne could maintain that

> At least I have one thing according to the rules: that no man
> ever treated a subject he knew and understood better than I do
> the subject I have undertaken; and that in this I am the most
> learned man alive. Secondly, that no man ever penetrated more
> deeply into his material, or plucked its limbs and consequences
> cleaner, or reached more accurately and fully the goal he had set
> for his work. ("Of Repentance" 611)

Thus, "Through a discourse that transgresses the propriety of discrete communities and challenges the unconditional priority of method itself," Spellmeyer says, "Montaigne points to a greater experiential and linguistic commonality," one that "cannot be recovered except through transgression" (268). And through such acts of textual transgression, Chapman writes, Montaigne "takes on all problems of human experience . . . and gives a form, however uncertain and temporary it may be, to these ideas" ("The Essay" 109). Hence, I believe, we arrive at a second major and productive generalization: the essay operates in opposition to the scholastic delineation of experience into discrete disciplines and their respective discourses, offering instead a transgressive and more inclusive discourse that temporarily brings together contrasting and incongruous points of view in an attempt to more fully and deeply address whole problems of human existence.

The late sixteenth and early seventeenth centuries' anti-scholasticism, its general cultural reaction against received intellectual and discursive norms, manifested itself in a more specific literary/rhetorical movement, the rise of anti-Ciceronian prose style, a shift that also strongly influenced the birth of the essay. Morris Croll has said that those who utilized an anti-Ciceronian or "baroque" style rejected the artificial symmetry, polish, and order of "Ciceronian" style, adopting instead an irregular, spontaneous style they felt was more appropriate to the skeptical bent of their thought. Croll states that, in their writing, anti-Ciceronian reformers sought "to portray, not a thought, but a mind thinking" (210). Ted-Larry Pebworth concurs, contending that these stylists sought to give the impression that, as writers, they were "essentially secretaries of their minds in motion." They therefore embraced or created genres appropriate to this goal: "Lengthy and overtly rhetorical forms gave way to briefer, more loosely constructed ones, the essay among them," he says (18). This rhetorical aim, the representation of the movements of the author's mind, is readily apparent in Montaigne, who remarks that "My style and my mind alike go roaming" ("Of Vanity" 761) and "we go hand in hand and at the same pace, my book and I" ("Of Repentance" 611–12). Thus, I believe, we come to our third important generalization: the essay rejects the norms of traditional composition in an effort to better represent movements of the writer's skeptical mind that cannot be effectively portrayed using Ciceronian rhetoric.

# MONTAIGNE

The various generic and cultural origins discussed in the last section intersect in the career and writings of Montaigne, who, by all accounts, is the creator of the modern essay. My purpose in the present section is not to undertake a detailed study of Montaigne's works. I intend, rather, to demonstrate how Montaigne's thinking about and practice of essay writing manifest two of my three generalizations about the essay (that it is an epistemologically skeptical exploration and a rejection of the traditional rhetorical norms) through his use of what I call *chrono-logic* to order and organize his compositions.

Bensmaïa notes that we stand at the end of a long tradition that gives us Montaigne as a writer who could not control his subject, confusedly organized his material, haphazardly threw together his work, and, not finding an appropriate form with which to present his ideas, created a genre "in which caprice, improvisation, and the arbitrary and impulsive ('irresponsible') linking of ideas seems to be the rule" (xxx). W. Wolfgang Holdheim agrees, writing that Montaigne's practice seems

> to establish the essay as the very quintessence of dispersion and inconsistency. . . . An apparently unguided play of digressions and associations, his essays . . . lack thematic discipline and even logic, for they seem to jump from theme to theme, and refuse to recognize any hierarchy of importance among subjects; as a result it is often impossible to relate any one essay to a particular subject at all. (20)

But these inherited images of both the man and his work are misleading. They only *seem* to be the case. Because rather than being confused, haphazard, inconsistent, or unguided, Montaigne, through his essays, was actually working with a clear purpose toward a specific goal: the promulgation of radical thinking and writing. The essay, rather than being confused, haphazard, inconsistent, or unguided, is better understood as a calculated, "rebellious response to the rigidity of the dogmatic tracts which preceded it" (Joeres and Mittman 18). As Holdheim says, Montaigne formulated the essay quite deliberately as "an antigenre" to flaunt the discursive prescriptiveness he inherited from a rationalistic rhetorical tradition (20). He asserts that Montaigne is

> engaged in an *Abbau* of his tradition (the term has lately been translated as "deconstruction"). It is an active deconstruction in the genuine sense: a clearing away of rubbish, of reified sedimentations, so that issues may once again be laid bare in their concreteness. His radical presentation of discontinuity is very much a reaction against uncritically accepted accumulations of continuity; his insistence on the uniquely diverse and particular is directed against a too exclusive concern with universals. (21)

In other words, Montaigne does not seek to portray universality, stability, and continuity (or "being") and thus replicate the authority of the tradition he is working within, but rather seeks to portray uniqueness, mutability, and discontinuity ("passing") and thus skeptically undermine the authority of the tradition he is working against. With this aim in mind we can better appreciate why Montaigne writes

> I cannot keep my subject still. It goes along befuddled and staggering, with a natural drunkenness. I take it in this condition, just as it is at the moment I give my attention to it. I do not portray being: I portray passing. Not the passing from one age to another, or, as the people say, from seven years to seven years, but from day to day, from minute to minute. My history needs to be adapted to the moment. I may presently change, not only by chance, but also by intention. This is a record of various and changeable occurrences, and of irresolute and, when it so befalls, contradictory ideas: whether I am different myself, or whether I take hold of my subjects in different circumstances and aspects. ("Of Repentance" 610–11)

Edwin M. Duval has carefully explicated the ironically precise and methodical manner in which Montaigne began his deconstruction of his tradition. In examining the first three chapters of the *Essais* of 1580, Duval found that Montaigne repeatedly followed the norms of the classical rhetorical *dispositio* to perfection, only to intentionally shatter that perfection with a willfully transgressive final sentence, paragraph, or page. In "A Consideration of Cicero," his last paragraph "opens a large breach in the tight and airless form of the rhetorical argument, thereby undercutting the compositional convention according to which the entire chapter has been so meticulously articulated" (274); until its conclusion, "Of Friendship" has also "conformed perfectly to the standard *dispositio* of classical rhetoric," but then "the absolute closure which has been guaranteed by the strictest adherence to both the general esthetic and the particular norms of classical composition, is violated and utterly destroyed by one superfluous sentence" in Montaigne's conclusion (278); and in "Of Glory," "Montaigne no sooner arrives at the final moment of stability and rest then he speaks again to destroy the formal perfection of all that has preceded" (282). Duval concludes that Montaigne's "anti-Ciceronian 'open-form' is the result of a willful and internally motivated violence against the ideal perfection of a form which belies the message it contains" (283) and that it was "the iconoclastic destruction of the schoolboy's sanctioned *dispositio* in the earliest chapters of the *Essais* that led Montaigne ultimately to his revolutionary new subject and manner—to the discovery of the 'moi' and the invention of the 'essai'" (287).

Following his meticulous undoing of the classical *dispositio* form, Montaigne developed a different method of arrangement for his new manner of writing, one he claimed was "accidental" and based on "fortune." Perhaps as a result of their radical departure from the expected norms of rhetorical composition, these texts *did* strike their author as being ordered purely by chance. For many years, and for the same reason, they have apparently struck many other readers the same way. Hence, we have inherited the notions of Montaigne as confused, capricious, and arbitrary, and of his essays as unguided, inconsistent, and illogical. Nonetheless, I would argue that the arrangement of Montaigne's essays is not based on chance, fortune, or accident, but only seemingly so. Rather, their arrangement is the result of Montaigne's simply (albeit radically) substituting one kind of logic for another: essayistic chrono-logic for the *dispositio's* classical, formal logic. His essays are not illogical or alogical, but simply *differently* logical: they follow the remarkably rigid and rigorous logic of time (first this, then this, then this, then this . . .), although he does not seem to recognize it. In "Of Friendship," for instance, Montaigne asks, "And what are these things of mine, in truth, but grotesques and monstrous bodies, pieced together of diverse members, without definite shape, having no order, sequence or proportion other than accidental?" (135). In their radical contrast to the two-millenia-long tradition from which they deviate, these things may indeed have seemed grotesque and monstrous to their author, having only an accidental shape or order. But I believe they *do* have a definite shape, order, sequence, and proportion, one dictated by chrono-logic. Likewise, in "Of Books," Montaigne says, "I have no other marshal but fortune to arrange my bits." Though he sees his marshal as fate, luck, or destiny, it is really the inescapable linearity of time that marshals his thoughts and arranges his texts. For, as he continues, "As my fancies present themselves, I pile them up; now they come pressing in a crowd, now dragging single file. I want people to see my natural and ordinary pace, however off track it is" (297). He echoes this idea in "Of the Resemblance of Children to Fathers," saying, "I want to represent the course of my humors, and I want people to see each part at its birth" (574).

It is not chance or caprice that allows Montaigne to pile up his fancies as they present themselves or to represent the course of his humors, but rather an arrangement based on the linearity of time. Take, for instance, the essay "Of Drunkenness." The arrangement of the text suggests that as each idea presents itself to Montaigne, so he presents it to the reader. As each thought leads inevitably into another (first this, then this, then this, then this . . .), so Montaigne leads the reader through the text. The most obvious thoughts in "Of Drunkenness" are, in order: the variety and inequality of vices (244); the confusion of the ordering, measuring, or ranking of sins (244–45); the baseness of the vice of drunkenness since it causes "the worst condition of man," his loss of knowledge and control of himself; the abilities of wine to "uncork" our most intimate secrets (245) and to render us comatose; the ancients' penchant for heavy drinking (246–47); drunkenness as "a less malicious and harmful" vice than others; a delicate palate as a liability for a good drinker; the need to "make our daily drinking habits more expansive and vigorous"; the incompatibility of lechery and drunkenness (247); the chastity, attractiveness, and agility of his father (247–48); drinking as the last pleasure age steals from us since our "natural liveliness" resides in our gullet at the end of life; his stomach's inability to engage in "an artificial and unnatural appetite" (248); Plato's recommendations for older people's drinking; two philosophers who drank themselves to death; a consideration of the old question "whether the soul of the sage is such that it would yield to the power of wine"; human vanity blinds us to our human weakness; "Wisdom does not overcome our natural limitations" (249); extraordinary actions are subject to "sinister interpretation"; the condition of holy frenzy (250); "runaway courage" as madness, as a transport beyond judgment and reason; and finally, Plato's definition of prophecy (251).

At first glance, it seems that only by chance, accident, or caprice could Montaigne have gotten from where and how he began this essay to where and how he ended it. Taking only the first and last links of his chain of thought and sampling the occasional link from in between these ends, it is hard to see any kind of "coherent" thought at work, any kind of logic in operation. How, for example, are we supposed to reconcile the contradiction between his early condemnation of the baseness of drunkenness and his later call for his contemporaries to make their drinking habits more expansive and vigorous? What kind of coherence could there be that would link notions as diverse as the inequality of sins, the agility of Montaigne's father, and Plato's definition of prophecy under the heading "Of Drunkenness"? If, however, we closely examine any individual middle link, we will see that it does, indeed, flow out of the one before it and into the one after it, that the text does, indeed, cohere. If we examine any three consecutive links in Montaigne's thought chain, we see that, according to chrono-logic, the text is perfectly logical and hardly accidental in arrangement.

Take, for instance, the sequence of thoughts that lead up to the most drastic turn in the essay. Montaigne's consideration of two philosophers who drank themselves to death comes in response to his preceding discussion of Plato's recommendation that older people drink heavily. In turn, his consideration of these unfortunate philosophers causes him to reconsider "the old question" of whether the sage's soul would yield to the power of wine. From here on, the essay has nothing ostensibly to do with drinking, progressing rather through questions of the human soul, its weaknesses, limitations, and madness. But it is crucial to note that had Montaigne not moved through each and every chrono-logical step in order up to this point, he would never have arrived here. It is not chance or caprice that arranges the subparts of this essay, but rather the simple facts that we can usually have only one idea in our head at a time and still function, that thoughts lead inevitably from and to other thoughts over time, and that time flows in only one direction. Indeed, according to the rigid requirements of chrono-logic, "Of Drunkenness" is arranged in the only possible way it could be.

Montaigne's use of chrono-logic has made several critics mistakenly remark that his essays portray a "more natural" form of thought than do other texts. While it is true that Montaigne does not condense, substitute, reorder, or delete his thoughts to make them fit the static model of a preexistent form, and while it is true that Montaigne follows chrono-logic in producing his essays, allowing his thought to associate over time more freely than is permitted in classical, formal logic and to retain their original chrono-logical order, it is *not* true that this form of thought is any more "natural" or any closer to "actual" thought than any other form. Thought is not "naturally" associative any more than it is "naturally" formally logical; it is not "naturally" intuitive any more than it is "naturally" explicitly programmed. Thought patterns are not innate structures, not biological imperatives, not human universals, but rather learned ways of using language. We learn (or fail to learn) to think associatively or intuitively in the same manner as we learn (or fail to learn) to think formally logically and explicitly. Working within the intellectual tradition of Western civilization, we yearn to set these contrasting patterns up as a dichotomy and privilege one over the other, natural over unnatural, actual over ungenuine. We would like to reduce the complexities of thought to an either/or situation: either we are thinking naturally (associatively and intuitively) or we are thinking unnaturally (formally logically and explicitly). What really happens, I believe, is that at any particular instant in a given series of thoughts, we are situated at some point on a continuum between these extremes. Rather than an either/or, our thinking is always and inevitably both/and. At any given point in our thinking we are using some complex combination of associative and formally logical thinking strategies in a synergistic simultaneity.

Therefore, while I agree that the essay allows for (and, indeed, relies on) a greater use of associative and intuitive thinking than some other prose forms, I cannot agree with those who say that it embodies more "natural" thought processes or more closely represents "actual" thought patterns. For example, while I agree with Chapman's premise that Montaigne's essays have an "exploratory" nature, the author seemingly "searching for his direction as he goes," through digressions, false starts, circumlocutions ("The Essay" 92) and "twists and turns of thought" ("The Essay" 95), I take exception to his conclusion that Montaigne's essays are thus much closer to actual thought than the carefully organized prose forms Montaigne rejected, that they reveal characteristics we associate with normal thought patterns, that they manifest not stream of consciousness nor complete chaos ("The Essay" 100), but the rambling development "typical of actual thought which moves by association and intuition rather than strict logical order" ("The Essay" 101). While Chapman sets this up as an either/or situation, either normal or abnormal thought patterns, either intuitive or logical order, I prefer the third possibility offered by chrono-logic, that of a both/and kind of thought, a strict but different logic of association over time as that which guides the development of Montaigne's essays. I must likewise disagree with Graham Good, who also sees the Montaignean essay as the practice of writing which most closely approximates the natural form of thought. The Montaignean essay, he says, is a practice that "reflects the process of thinking rather than reporting and ordering its results" since it follows "the forms of thinking rather than supplying its own ready-made ones." Good incorrectly posits the essay as the embodiment of some kind of primordial, uncontaminated, pre-rhetorical thinking process which spontaneously and continuously generates original forms, a thinking and forming more "natural" than that embodied in traditional rhetorical forms. He contends that "the essay should yield and adapt to the flow of thought" (42), as if there were only one kind of thought, one kind of cognitive flow "naturally" at work from which we have deviated. Similarly, Good says that the spirit of Montaigne's essay writing is "one of writing things down as they occur or emerge" without using any kind of "set 'frame' or filter for discourse" and that Montaigne's goal is "an unrepressed thinking-writing . . . rather than the application of a preconceived method or structure" (31). While Good believes that the essay manifests an "unrepressed thinking-writing" that does not impose a rhetorical design upon thought, I would argue that "writing things down as they occur or emerge" is itself a "set 'frame' or filter for discourse," an imposition of a rhetorical design I call chrono-logic, a design that significantly represses other kinds of equally "natural" thinking-writing.

Although he does not describe it as such, Montaigne recognizes that chrono-logic is not an unrepressed, unfiltered way of thinking-writing, but rather one that imposes new and sometimes difficult obligations on both the writer and the reader. As he says in "Of Vanity,"

> This stuffing is a little out of my subject. I go out of my way, but rather by license than carelessness. My ideas follow one another, but sometimes it is from a distance, and look at each other, but with a side-long glance. . . . It is the inattentive reader who loses my subject, not I. Some word about it will always be found off in a corner, which will not fail to be sufficient, though it takes little room. (761)

While adhering to the rules of chrono-logic grants him more freedom in development than other traditional rhetorical forms, grants him the license to go out of his way, it does not allow him complete and utter freedom to wildly or haphazardly associate ideas, nor does it allow him to forgo his responsibilities to his reader. He must stay attentive to his subject and not lose it, he says, continually offering the attentive reader some "sufficient word" that allows her to see how his ideas follow one another, even when they do so at a distance and with a "side-long" glance.

Montaigne's use of chrono-logic to order his essays is an outgrowth of his epistemological skepticism. For him, as we know, the world was a place where even stability was a languid motion and so the best one could hope for was to represent not being, but passing. The perpetually progressive and open-ended nature of chrono-logic seems well suited to this task, its fundamental tentativeness and inconclusiveness well matched to the search for truth in a universe in perpetual flux. Montaigne's epistemological skepticism cannot be overemphasized: he admonishes us to "consider through what clouds and how gropingly we are led to the knowledge of most of the things that are right in our hands" ("It Is Folly to Measure the True and False by Our Own Capacity" 132); he believes that his conceptions and judgments "move only by groping, staggering, stumbling, and blundering" ("Of the Education of Children" 107); he distrusts his thoughts "hardly any less for being second or third than for being first, or being present than for being past" ("Of Vanity" 736); he contends that "If my mind could gain a firm footing, I would not make essays, I would make decisions; but it is always in apprenticeship and on trial" ("Of Repentance" 611); and, he says, "I put forward formless and unresolved notions, as do those who publish doubtful questions to debate in the schools, not to establish the truth, but to seek it" ("Of Prayers" 229). As Newkirk says, for Montaigne, the adventure of groping and staggering toward some understanding, the process of his wondering, "was more important than the truthfulness of that which was found—because any truth was provisional, sure to be undone or revised by subsequent inquiries." For Montaigne, he says, knowledge, too, is not a mirror of some certain and immutable external reality, but rather "is provisional, subject to change, and always dependent on the 'posture' of the knower." The essay thus represents a crucial textual form for Montaigne, Newkirk says, one "open enough to allow for the exploration of a reality which was fundamentally unstable" (12). In short, Montaigne's epistemological skepticism required a textual form based on the "posture" or position of the writer/knower, which must necessarily and perpetually change over time as he or she explores and confronts an unstable reality, which must necessarily and perpetually change over time in search of truth and knowledge, which must necessarily and perpetually change over time. His usage of chrono-logic to structure his texts ably met this complex need.

With an understanding of Montaigne's belief in the tentativeness, uncertainty, instability, and inconclusiveness of human understanding—and his subsequent need for a textual form based on chrono-logic—in mind, we are better able to appreciate why

Hardison calls the Montaignean essay "the literary response to a world that has become problematic" (20), better able to appreciate what he calls "Montaigne's official motto" and "the basic question of the *Essais*," which is "Que sçais-je?" or "What do I know?" (19), and better able to appreciate why, as Alexander Smith relates, Montaigne inscribed in large letters over the central rafter in his library, "I DO NOT UNDERSTAND; I PAUSE; I EXAMINE" (40).

## THE EARLY ENGLISH ESSAY

As might be expected, when other writers began trying their hand at Montaigne's new genre, the shadow of its creator loomed large, heavily influencing their efforts. In this section, I will show how the early English essay closely follows Montaigne's lead in terms of its epistemological skepticism and use of anti-Ciceronian chrono-logic.

Just as in Montaigne's case, the essay embodied the early English essayists' epistemological skepticism, their appreciation of the tentativeness, uncertainty, instability, and inconclusiveness of human understanding. MacDonald has assembled a number of primary sources that reveal this strain in their thinking about the form. He begins with dictionary definitions, noting that John Baret's *An Alvearie or Quadruple Dictionary* (1580) defines "essay" as "*To assay*: to prove . . . a groaping or feeling of the way with ones hande" (qtd. on 3), while Nathaniel Bailey's *Universal Etymological English Dictionary* (1720) was the first English lexicon to define the word as applied to a form of literature: "Essay: an attempt, proof, tryal; also a short Discourse upon a subject" (qtd. on 4). We can thus see, MacDonald says, that "the original idea of 'trial' seems never to be absent from the minds of the earlier essayists" (6). Synthesizing other frequently expressed sentiments, MacDonald concludes that the early English essayists felt that "the subject-matter [was] rather crudely handled" or "undigested" in their works (7), that "the word essay, applied to whatever subject, or whatever kind of treatment of that subject, always implied a 'modest attempt' on the part of the author" (9), that their treatment of their subjects was "imperfect and incomplete" (15), and that they "always considered their efforts as a mere breaking of new ground" (16).

The early English essayists' conception of the essay as an epistemologically skeptical form, an incomplete and modest attempt at the truth and knowledge, is summed up nicely by Sir William Cornwallis in "Of Essais and Bookes," wherein he writes that there are many ancient and contemporary writings that he does not hold

> to bee rightly tearmed Essayes; for though they be short, yet they are strong and able to endure the sharpest tryall. But mine are Essayes, who am but a newly bound Prentise to the inquisition of knowledge and vse these papers as a Painter's boy a board, that is trying to bring his hand and his fancie acquainted. It is a maner of writing wel befitting vndigested motions, or a head not knowing its strength like a circumspect runner trying for a starte, or prouidence that tastes before she buyses. . . . If they prooue nothing but wordes, yet they breake not promise with the world, for they say, "But an Essay," like a Scriuenour trying his Pen before he ingrosseth his worke. (190)

In their skepticism, early English essayists, like Montaigne, rejected in one movement both the doctrine of truth/knowledge they received from tradition and the rhetoric in which that doctrine was embodied. These early essayists, as Hall says, utilized "Montaigne's subversive rhetoric" ("Emergence" 81) to display in their texts "the subversion of received opinion and even of accepted rational processes of thought, or at least of the deductive process which depends on established authority for its major premises and axioms" ("Emergence" 80). The early essayists' disdain for the traditional rhetoric they received is palpably apparent in Cornwallis's "Of Essais and Bookes":

> For wordes are but cloths; matters substance. Rethoricke's Cookery is the vomit of a Pedant, which to make saleable he imitated the Dyer, whose Fat working ill, hee makes amendes by giuing those ill colours new names; so this venting his inifinitie of words with calling it eloquence and fortifying eloquence with methodicall diuisions. (200)

In their rejection of traditional Ciceronian rhetoric, the early English essayists, like Montaigne, turned to the usage of chrono-logic to order their texts. And as in Montaigne's case, critics

examining the early English essay have mistakenly linked and confused the use of chrono-logic with what they see as an authorial
attempt to represent "actual" thought in its "natural" form. Just as
in my previous disagreement with Chapman's and Good's positions
that Montaigne's essays embody "actual" thought in its "natural"
form, here, too, I must disagree with Hall, for instance, who says
that the early English essayists sought "to portray in language the
actual process of the mind seeking truth" ("Emergence" 79). Hall
suggests two things here: first, there is some singular, prototypical,
and pristine thought process we follow in the search for truth that
Ciceronian rhetoric deviates from and masks (and to which
anti-Ciceronian rhetoric returns and faithfully represents); second,
that classical, formally logical reasoning is somehow not an "actual" process of a mind seeking truth. As I argued earlier in this chapter, both of these positions are untenable: we think in ways we have
been taught to think; classical, formally logical thought processes
are thus as "natural" and "actual" as any other. In like manner, I
must disagree with Pebworth, who contends that early English
essayists "attempted to picture the mind in its natural wanderings,
unfettered by textbook laws of exposition" (22), their texts thus
lacking proportion, methodical order, and internal consistency but
offering us instead the "intimacy and immediacy" of these writers'
"free association" (23). Here, Pebworth assumes a great many
things: that thought processes are "naturally" directionless, that
these essayists were working under no rhetorical constraints whatsoever, that these essays had no proportion, order, or consistency
whatsoever, and that the associative thought employed by these
writers was "free" or completely unrestrained. In contrast, I would
argue that thought processes are not "naturally" directionless, but
rather proceed inevitably forward through time, not wandering, but
lining up one after the other after the other; that these essayists,
though deviating from "textbook laws," still worked with fetters on,
composing under the different but no less rigorous rhetorical constraints of chrono-logic; that these essays embodied the different
but no less real proportion, order, and consistency required by their
chrono-logic base; and that the associative thought these essayists
used was not "free" or completely unconstrained, but rather carefully reined in. Like Montaigne, the early English essayists went out of
their way by license (by the right granted those who adhere to a

specific set of rules), not carelessness; did not lose their subject (even though the inattentive reader might think they did); and always provided a "sufficient word" to show the reader how their ideas followed one another (even when at a distance and with a sidelong glance).

Hall's and Pebworth's inaccuracies are easy to forgive, though, when we consider that the early English essayists themselves, like Montaigne, portrayed the ordering principle of their texts as one of accidental, chance, unmethodical, or "free" sequencing. As Cornwallis says of his essays, "Nor if they stray, doe I seeke to amend them; for I professe not method, neither will I chaine my selfe to the head of my Chapter" (202). In his extreme departure from the explicit and obvious structurings of the classical argument form that had held sway for two thousand years, Cornwallis, like Montaigne, surely must have felt that he was unchained in writing his essays and followed no method in their composition, a misconception that generations of readers and critics have perpetuated. Nonetheless, Cornwallis's essays are, indeed, chained and methodical in their composition. They are, like Montaigne's, crafted according to the rigorous demands of chrono-logic.

Let us consider, for example, Cornwallis's "Of Humilitie." Here is the sequence of the most obvious thoughts in this essay as they appear in the text's single paragraph: the difficulty in attaining and keeping virtue; the insidiousness of vice; having senses, we are subject to vice; virtue's invisibility; the difficulty of translating virtue out of words and into actions, since language must be interpreted by the senses; the worst vices are those that try to look like virtues; humility as the one virtue we can easily reach; humility teaches self-knowledge (105) and the mending of imperfections; humility as the most important virtue since an overweening opinion spoils all other virtues and since it truly understands our states and mixes with our defects to direct our minds to heaven; though different in our natures, we all dislike pride in another; we hide and cherish pride in ourselves; beauty without humility is loathed and the victim of envy; humility is as helpful as pride is dangerous; pride is never safe; pride multiplies enemies while humility enfeebles them; humility is the cause of preservation (106) since it allows us to know what we are no matter where we are and makes the mind constant and free; debased states unable to stand upon themselves have no refuge other than humility, which is the testimony of a mind that obeys but is not dejected or base (107).

While the development of this text is obviously not chained to the classical, formally logical reasoning of the traditional rhetoric he rejects, neither is it without any chains at all or completely devoid of method. It is not a simple either/or situation, although Cornwallis conceives of it as one. Rather, this text's development is differently chained, based on another method (one we are unaccustomed to looking for and thus often dismiss as unmethodical). That this text's development is chained to a method is demonstrated simply by examining what it does *not* allow to be included: classical, formally logical reasoning and the traditional subparts of the *dispositio* form. Thus, we see that there is a rhetorical design impressed on this discourse that represses some kinds of thinking/writing in favor of other kinds, a design I call chrono-logic, the rigorous but different logic of association over time.

The arrangement of the text suggests that as each idea presents itself to Cornwallis, so he presents it to the reader. As each thought inevitably leads into another, so he leads the reader through the text—first this, then this, then this, then this. If we examine any given link on the chain of ideas presented in this essay, we can easily see how it associatively flows out of the one before it and into the one following it. For instance, Cornwallis's essay lines up three separate and distinct ideas near the beginning of his essay: the insidiousness of vice; having senses, we are subject to vice; virtue's invisibility. He first tells us about the insidiousness of vice, how it "dogs us and . . . comes creeping, and by degrees gets into our bosomes." This first thought flows into the next as he says we cannot shut vice out, "for our gates will not be bard. Our senses keepe open houses." He continues to develop this thought for a while, noting how even if we lost four of our five senses, the remaining one would still "trouble vs as ill as all." This middle thought in this set of three flows into the third when Cornwallis says, "So hauing senses, we are subject to vice; hauing none, without feeling. The reason of Vertue's difficultie is her inuisibleness; it must bee touched or tasted or heard that they make much of" (105). Again, this associative flow of ideas is no more "natural," no closer to "actual" thought than any other rhetorical design. Nor is it free association. Cornwallis never randomly associates, never tangentially departs from his topic, never loses his subject—humility—but sticks close to it throughout the development of this text, maintaining a consistent focus on his topic despite the essay's associative arrangement. Working within the constraints imposed by chrono-logic (we can only have one thought in our heads at a time, one thought leads to another, and time flows only in one direction), Cornwallis has fashioned an essay that is well developed, well ordered, consistent, and methodical, though in ways we are unaccustomed to experiencing.

## THE FORMAL/INFORMAL SPLIT

Montaigne's powerful influence over the thinking about and practice of the English essay soon waned, however. The fundamental epistemological skepticism and use of rigorous anti-Ciceronian chrono-logic that marks the Montaignean and early English essays faded as the essay mutated into two new forms. Perhaps, as Lopate suggests, Montaigne's radical development of the form, taking the essay "to its outer limits right away," was simply too daunting a model to follow, and thus, afterward "came an inevitable specialization" which included the split between formal and informal essays (47). It is a common conception that the essay split into two distinct modes after Montaigne, one "informal, personal, intimate, relaxed, conversational, and often humorous," and the other "dogmatic, impersonal, systematic, and expository" (Richman x). According to C. Hugh Holman and William Harmon, the informal mode evolved through the periodical essays of Richard Steele, Joseph Addison, and Samuel Johnson in the eighteenth century, then through the personal essays of Charles Lamb, William Hazlitt, Leigh Hunt, Thomas De Quincey and the like in the nineteenth century, and then into the personal essays of writers like G. K. Chesterton, A. C. Benson, and George Orwell in our own century, while the formal mode developed into longer, argumentative, expository, or critical treatises like Milton's *Areopagitica* and Locke's *Essay Concerning Human Understanding* in the seventeenth century and the long, critical essays of writers like T. B. Macauley, Sir Walter Scott, Thomas Carlyle, George Eliot, and Matthew Arnold in the nineteenth century (187–89). During the three centuries of its development between Montaigne and Cornwallis and the twentieth century, however, the essay's evolution in both of these modalities caused it to lose the profound epistemological skepticism, transgressive anti-scholasticism, and use of radically anti-Ciceronian chrono-logic that marked its genesis. In the next chapter, however, I will show how these essential qualities of the form have resurfaced in the theories of the essay put forward by numerous twentieth-century critics.

---

# Chapter 3

# Twentieth-Century Theories of the Essay

## *OR*

## Back to the Future, Part Two

In this chapter we move from a consideration of the origins and originators of the essay to an examination of twentieth-century theories and theorists of the form. My goal here is not to scrupulously explicate each of the theories I will examine, but rather to accentuate the aspects of each that correspond closely to the thinking and practice of the earliest essayists as discussed in the last chapter. We will first see how the the essay's fundamental qualities of deep epistemological skepticism, anti-scholasticism, and anti-Ciceronian chrono-logic play prominent roles in the theories of Lukács, Adorno, Huxley, Holdheim, and Good. Then, using the work of Bakhtin, we will elaborate our rehabilitative theory of the essay to include a consideration of the form as the embodiment of centrifugal, dialogic, "novelistic," and carnivalesque textual tendencies.

## GEORG LUKÁCS

Perhaps the most obvious part of Georg Lukács's theory of the essay (which he presents in "On the Nature and Form of the Essay," his prefatory essay to *Soul and Form*), is its emphasis on the form's epistemological skepticism. Working from his conviction that "It is simply not true that there exists an objective, external criterion of life and truth" (11), Lukács sees the essay as a deconstructive form that resists the false immediacy and premature synthesis offered by conventionally accepted knowledge. He contends that the essay "tears the mask off everything that is only apparently positive and immediate, [and] reveals it as petty longing and cheap fulfillment . . . calmly and proudly [setting] its fragmentariness against the petty completeness of scientific exactitude" (17). In his conception, the essay's deep skepticism is directed not only outwardly at others' thinking, but also inwardly. As Kauffman notes, the essay, for Lukács,

> comes closest to fulfilling its essential nature . . . when it moves within a certain skepticism about its own presuppositions. Whatever conclusions it reaches must therefore be highly tentative in kind—temporary syntheses entertained by a mind ever ready to dissolve them so as to avoid reifying its own products and reflections. ("Theory" 89)

His emphasis on the essay's skepticism requires Lukács to similarly stress the essay's exploratory, modest, and inconclusive nature. He distinguishes the essay from other kinds of useful writings which "do not deserve to be described as essays because they can never give us anything more than information, facts, and 'relationships'" (2). The essay, for him as for its originators, must be an uncertain exploration of received opinion that searches for truth rather than trying to establish it. Lukács writes that

> It is true that the essay strives for truth: but just as Saul went out to look for his father's she-asses and found a kingdom, so the essayist who is really capable of looking for the truth will find at the end of his road the goal he was looking for: life. . . . It is highly questionable whether man should want the precise thing he sets out to attain, whether he has the right to walk towards his goal along straight and simple paths. (12)

In addition to this exploratory quality, Lukács also shares with the earliest essayists their sense of modesty about the project of essaying. The essayist, he says, "dismisses his own proud hopes which sometimes lead him to believe that he has come close to the ultimate," because, after all, he has, at best, "no more to offer than explanations of . . . his own ideas" (9). Furthermore, Lukács, like the earliest essayists, sees the essay as inherently inconclusive and open-ended. The essay, Lukács says, falls short of "the icy, final perfection of philosophy" (1). In this sense of inconclusiveness, he says,

> The life of Socrates is the typical life for the essay form. . . . For a tragic life is crowned only by its end, only the end gives it meaning, sense and form to the whole, and it is precisely the end which is always arbitrary and ironic here, in every dialogue and in Socrates's whole life. A question is thrown up and extended so far in depth that it becomes the question of all questions, but after that everything remains open. (14)

As a result of its profound epistemological skepticism, the meaning of the essay (like the meaning of Socrates's life), can, for Lukács, "only be expressed by a process, such as dialogue," only be expressed as "a *quest*" (Kauffman "Theory" 60). Thus, his own essays were themselves fragmentary and incomplete, "posing questions rather than finding solutions" (Kauffman "Theory" 86–7).

Lukács's melding of the meaning and form of Socrates's life with the meaning and form of the essay brings us to the second close parallel between his theory and the practice of Montaigne and the early English essayists: the embracing of an anti-Ciceronian chrono-logic as the basis of the form. In Lukács's conception, we see that the shape or organization of the essay—just like the shape of lived experience or the organization of the event of being alive—is a thing based on the logic of time. The essay, Lukács says, "has its models" in life:

> It is part of the nature of the essay that it does not create new things from an empty nothingness but only orders those which were once alive. And because it orders them anew and does not form something new out of formlessness, it is bound to them and must always speak "the truth" about them, must find expression for their essential nature. (10)

If it is bound to once-living things, if it is to "truthfully" order them and so express their "essential nature," then the essay must be based on a living chrono-logic. According to Lukács, "the truth of the essay . . . is the struggle for truth, for the incarnation of a life." In this, he says, essays are like portraits, because they give us "the life of a human being . . . forcing us to feel that his life was exactly as shown" (11). If the essay is to truthfully incarnate a life and force us to feel it has been exactly depicted as lived, if the essay is to be, as Lukács claims it is, "a coming-alive in real experience" (18), then it must follow the rigorous demands of the logic of time. The notion of the essay as a chrono-logic-based depiction of a life in progress helps us understand what Kauffman calls the "cognitive function of aesthetic form in Lukács's theory of the essay" ("Theory" 48). In Lukács's theory, he says, the essay's form is "able to evoke in the reader a response that corresponds in a cognitive sense to the writer's own *Weltanschauung*" or worldview ("Theory" 50) because the essay's aesthetic form is determined by the writer's cognitive experience ("Theory" 23). In other words, in writing an essay, the chrono-logic basis of the writer's thought processes are represented in the chrono-logic organization of the text. In its attempt to thus embody a life, to evoke in the reader a cognitive experience that corresponds to that of the writer, the essay seeks to represent the experience of "intellectuality," Lukács says, to portray "conceptuality as sensed experience, as immediate reality, as spontaneous principle of existence; the world-view in its undisguised purity as an event of the soul, as the motive force of life" (7). The experiential nature of living and thinking, its temporal event-ness, finds expression in the essay's form, according to Lukács, because in the essay, "Form *is* reality" (8). The form of the essay determines reality, Lukács contends, because it "defines the limits of the immaterial," because it "sets limits round a substance which otherwise would dissolve like air in the All" (7). In other words, if not for the essay's chrono-logic basis, the immaterial substance of thought might find no limitations to constrain it and so irrevocably dissipate. Chrono-logic, however, is all the basis one needs to limit thought, determine the experience of life, and order the essay, for as Lukács says, the essayist "needs form only as lived experience and he needs only its life, only the living soul-reality it contains. . . . [L]ife itself can be lived and given form through such a scheme of lived experience" (8). In sum, for Lukács, the form or scheme of the essay is that of a lived experience, an event that occurs in time and over time, and its chrono-logic basis offers us the means to "a conceptual re-ordering of life" (1).

Much like epistemological skepticism and anti-Ciceronian chrono-logic, anti-scholasticism is also embraced by both Lukács and the earliest essayists. Like Montaigne three hundred years earlier, Lukács is deeply disturbed by the fragmentation of experience he perceives around him, the division of life into mutually exclusive disciplines. The fragmentation of modern discourse poses a vexing problem for anyone considering questions such as "what is life, what is man, what is destiny?" he says, since "Any gesture with which such a man might wish to express something of his experience would falsify that experience, unless it ironically emphasized its own inadequacy and thus canceled itself out" (7). The root of that falsification and fragmentation of experience, the most basic disciplinary distinction that disturbs Lukács, is the split between science and art and the loss of unity and value that came with it. Science, he writes,

> affects us by its contents, art by its forms; science offers us facts and the relationships between facts, but art offers us souls and destinies. Here the ways part; here there is no replacement and no transition. In primitive, as yet undifferentiated epochs, science and art (and religion and ethics and politics) are integrated, they form a single whole; but as soon as science has become separate and independent, everything that has led up to it loses its value. (3)

Lukács, however, believes that the essay is a form that can combat the fragmentation of experience, dissolve the science/art distinction, and so recover this lost unity and value, because it "has not yet, today, traveled the road to independence which its sister, poetry, covered long ago—the road of development from a primitive, undifferentiated unity with science, ethics, and art" (13). In this manner, he says, the essay embodies "a longing . . . an original and deep-rooted attitude toward the whole of life, a final, irreducible category of possibilities of experience," an irreducible category which needs "to be given form which will redeem and release its most essential and now indivisible substance into eternal value. That is what the essay does" (17). The essay longs to recover and celebrate the undifferentiated unity and value of life. Thus, Lukács contends, the essay "encompasses a whole world in order to raise it to eternity, in all its uniqueness" and constitutes "an autonomous and integral giving-of-form to an autonomous and complete life" (18). This recovery of undifferentiated unity and value of life is the essayist's "moment of destiny," he says, "the moment when all feelings and experiences on the near or the far side of form receive form, are melted down and condensed into form. It is the mystical moment of union between the inner and outer, between soul and form" (8).

In its attempts to recover an undifferentiated unity of life, to encompass a whole world and give form to a complete life, the essay necessarily employs a mixture of multiple discourses. The essay, in Lukács's view, is a paradoxical linguistic hybrid of science and art. What essayists create, he says,

> must be science, even when their vision of life has transcended the sphere of science. Sometimes its free flight is constrained by the unassailable facts of dry matter; sometimes it loses all scientific value because it is, after all, a vision, because it precedes facts and therefore handles them freely and arbitrarily. (13)

As it tries to meld science and art and so encompass a whole world, the essay must embody the one/many paradox, the problem of creating a unity in multiplicity. The "universal problem of style," Lukács says, is "to achieve an equilibrium in a welter of disparate things, richness and articulation in a mass of uniform matter." In the essay, he continues, "the problem of equilibrium is posed in this way: the world and the beyond, image and transparency, idea and emanation lie in the two cups of a scale which is to remain balanced." We must beware the impulse to avoid this difficult balancing, to reduce the complexity of the world when we write essays. The more we lose the linguistic hybridization essential to the essay, Lukács says, "the more linear the images become, the smaller the number of planes into which everything is compressed, the paler and more matte the radiance of the colours, the simpler the richness and multiplicity of the world" (6). We must instead maintain that paradoxical and difficult discursive multiplicity if the essay is to truthfully incarnate a life, to fully and exactly render it. As Lukács notes, while each essay "creates a different world," to do so it "has to create from within itself all the preconditions for the effectiveness and validity of its vision" (11). The precondition for an essay's validity in encompassing a world is its inclusion of the multiplicity of discourses at work in that world. In short, in Lukács's theory the essay is an anti-scholastic text, one that in fighting the fragmentation of experience and discourse becomes problematic because "it sees and connects too many things," because "it is too intellectual and multiform to acquire form out of its own self" (15).

## T. W. ADORNO

Very much like Lukács, T. W. Adorno, in "The Essay as Form," situates the essay in a framework of epistemological skepticism, anti-scholasticism, and anti-Ciceronian chrono-logic.

In Adorno's account, the essay is a powerful weapon in the skeptical struggle against systematic thinking of all kinds. "Through its inner nature," he says, "it negates anything systematic and satisfies itself all the better the more it excludes the systematic" (165). According to Adorno, the essay operates as a challenge to the reductive scientific nominalism and positivism that dominate modern Western thought, attempting to demystify and unmask the fiction of objectivity. The essay, he says, "wants to blow open . . . the fact that the network of . . . objectivity is a purely subjective rigging" and destroy the notion prevalent since Plato that ideas exist eternally and immutably (170). The essay thus functions in stark opposition to "Positivism's irresponsibly bungled language," which "fancies itself to be responsibly objective and adequate to the matter at hand" (153). It exists as a critique of "method," of scientific procedure and its philosophic grounding in empiricism: "Doubt about the unconditional priority of method was raised, in the actual process of thought, almost exclusively by the essay," Adorno says, through its characteristic "refraining from any reduction to a principle" and accentuation of the fragmentary and the partial over that of the total (157). Thus, he argues,

> The essay does not obey the rules of the game of organized science and theory . . . does not strive for closed, deductive or inductive, construction. It revolts above all against the doctrine—deeply rooted since Plato—that the changing and ephemeral is unworthy of philosophy; against that ancient injustice toward the transitory. . . . The essay shys [*sic*] away from the violence of dogma, from the notion that the result of abstraction, the temporally invariable concept indifferent to the individual phenomenon grasped by it, deserves ontological dignity. (158)

In contrast to the reductive empirical positivism of science, Adorno says, the essay does not desire "to seek and filter the eternal out of the transitory; it wants, rather, to make the transitory eternal" (159). It exists as a critique of "the conception of truth as something 'ready-made,' a hierarchy of concepts" (166). In the essay, he says, "thought gets rid of the traditional idea of truth" because "the essay seeks truth contents as being historical in themselves." In this way, the essay "abandons the main road to the origins . . . denies any primeval givens" (159), and "refuses to glorify concern for the primal as something more primal than concern for the mediated" (167). In short, Adorno contends that the essay "is obeying an epistemological motive" in that "the need arises in the essay as form to annul the theoretically outmoded claims of totality and continuity, and to do so in the concrete procedure of the intellect" (164).

As with Lukács, Adorno's emphasis on the essay's epistemological skepticism leads to his discussing its exploratory and inconclusive natures. As a form, the essay abrogates and defies the ideals of absolute, indisputable certainty, he notes, and thus always remains susceptible to error, paying "for its affinity with open intellectual experience by the lack of security, a lack which the norm of established thought fears like death." Rather than seeking truth in certainty, he contends, "The essay becomes true in its progress, which drives it beyond itself" (161). Adorno also agrees with Lukács's assessment of the essay's inherent inconclusiveness. He states simply that "the essay comes to no final conclusions and makes explicit its inability to do so" (165). The essay, he writes, "stops where it feels itself complete—not where nothing is left to say," and its concepts do not "arrive at any final principle" (152). And in one of his characteristically paradoxical statements, Adorno says that the essay's "totality . . . is that of non-totality" (165). Furthermore, the essay's inconclusiveness and non-totality derive, in part, from the fact that in the essay,

> the claim of any particular truth is taken literally to the point where there is evidence of its untruth. The risked, anticipatory, and incompletely redeemed aspect of every essayistic detail draws in other details as negation; the untruth in which the essay knowingly entangles itself is the element of its truth. (166)

In sum, when it comes to the essay, Adorno believes that "Self-relativization is immanent in its form" (164), since "its tendency is always toward the liquidation of opinion, even that from which it takes its own impulse" (166).

One final aspect of the essay's epistemological skepticism in Adorno's theory is its function as a deconstructive, politically transgressive form for thinking and writing. As Bob Hullot-Kentor says, Adorno presents the essay as "the singularly adequate form of social criticism" (145), a form whose "critical force depends on its autonomy" and which "will harden itself against what it fears will mythically engulf it" (150). The essay "is the critique of ideology," Adorno states flatly (166): it "perceives that the longing for strict definitions has long offered, through fixating manipulations of the meanings of concepts, to eliminate the irritating and dangerous elements that live within concepts" (160); it "shakes off the illusion of a simple, basically logical world that so perfectly suits the defense of the status quo" (163). In the end, Adorno maintains, "the law of the innermost form of the essay is heresy. By transgressing the orthodoxy of thought, something becomes visible in the object which it is orthodoxy's secret purpose to keep invisible" (171).

In addition to stressing the skeptical nature of the essay, Adorno also argues that it has a staunch anti-scholastic function. He decries the departmental specialization of modern Western culture, arguing that "these divisions simply attest institutionally to the renunciation of the whole truth" and that the "ideals of purity and cleanliness" that this division/specialization clothes itself in "bear the marks of a repressive order" (156). The essay, he says, counters this repressive compartmentalization: it "absorbs concepts and experiences" and "swallows up theories that are close by" (166); it "does not permit its domain to be prescribed" (152); and it "insists that a matter be considered, from the very first, in its whole complexity" (162). According to Adorno, the essay recognizes and represents that thought cannot be usefully separated into distinct strands. It acknowledges that thought has aspects that "interweave as in a carpet" and that "the fruitfulness of the thought depends on the density of this texture" (160). In this way, Hullot-Kentor notes, Adorno's view of the essay "replaces a compositional form whose model is a repetitive and fateful nature with a compositional form whose idea of nature is one of plenitude" (149–50).

Finally, the essay manifests an anti-Ciceronian chrono-logic in Adorno's formulation. The aim of the essay, he says, "is the new as something genuinely new, as something not translatable back into the staleness of already existing forms" (169). From a chrono-logical perspective, the form of each essay must necessarily be something fresh, something genuinely new, something that cannot already exist, but rather must be freshly created each time the writer proceeds through time. The essay "erects no scaffolding, no edifice," Adorno maintains. He argues instead that "Through their own movement the elements [of the essay] crystallize into a configuration" (161). In other words, rather than following some preexistent blueprint in structuring its form, the essay utilizes the always present-tense and progressive structuring of chrono-logic, allowing the essay's sub-parts' own movements through time to determine their ordering. "The essay's openness," he asserts, "is not vaguely one of feeling and mood, but obtains its contour from its content" (165) as the essayist "transforms himself into an arena of intellectual experience, without simplifying it" (161). The essayist does not simplify cognition, does not remove it from its sometimes messy chrono-logic progression, but rather lets the essay receive its form from its content, from the sequence of thoughts as they develop. One reason that this progression can be messy, Adorno notes, is that the development of thought over time is sometimes marked by discontinuity rather than continuity. Discontinuity is a fundamental quality of the essay, Adorno says, because "It thinks in fragments just as reality is fragmented and gains its unity only by moving through the fissures, rather than by smoothing them over." The essay thinks in separated bits, achieving unity only by acknowledging and moving through the gaps between those bits rather than masking them. The unity the essay does achieve comes through its chrono-logic ordering of its discontinuous fragments. As Adorno contends, the essay's structure "results not programatically but as a characteristic of the form's groping intention" (164), of its exploratory ordering of thought-bits over time. Through a "groping" reminiscent of Montaigne, association, ambiguity, equivocation, and neglect of all logical synthesis "are fused in the essay with its truth-content," the essay attempting to establish "internal cross-connections" by means of associative, paratactic transitions rather than by means of rigid, formally logical ones. The form of the essay, Adorno says, thus verges "on the logic of music, the stringent and yet aconceptual art of transition" (169). However, he underscores, the essay

> is not unlogical; rather it obeys logical criteria in so far as the totality of its sentences must fit together coherently. . . . It is just that the essay develops thoughts differently from discursive logic. The essay neither makes deductions from a principle nor does it draw conclusions from coherent individual observations. It co-ordinates elements, rather than subordinating them; and only the essence of its content, not the manner of its presentation, is commensurable with logical criteria. (169–70)

The essay, then, is not unlogical, but rather *differently* logical, not incoherent, but rather *differently* coherent. It develops its thoughts not according to the traditional criteria of classical, formal, subordinating logic, but rather according to the different but equally rigorous criteria of chrono-logic, the coordinating association of thoughts over time. Thus, the essay is not an easy or frivolous form to compose. Its nature, Adorno says, requires the essayist to take "the matter of presentation more seriously than do those procedures that separate out method from material and are indifferent to the way they present their objectified contents" (161). In conclusion, understanding that, in Adorno's theory, the essay is a form distinctly and decidedly opposed to all accepted philosophical and rhetorical norms (is a form based on deep skepticism, anti-scholasticism, and an alternative logic) helps us to resolve his paradoxical pronouncement that the essay "proceeds, so to speak, methodically unmethodically" (161).

# ALDOUS HUXLEY

In the preface to his *Collected Essays*, Aldous Huxley reveals that he, too, views the essay in our now familiar terms: as an epistemologically skeptical text that counters the scholastic compartmentalization of knowledge and utilizes anti-Ciceronian chrono-logic.

In Huxley's theory, the skepticism of the essay mocks the discourse of the "professional sages" and their "language of highest abstraction and widest generality." This discourse is, he notes, "a language that, for all its gnomic solemnity is apt, in a tight corner, to reveal itself as ludicrously inappropriate to the facts of life as it is really and tragically lived" (viii). According to Huxley, the essay counters this deficiency by employing a discourse that attempts to get *all* of life as it is really lived, *all* areas of knowledge, into a single text. To introduce this idea, Huxley quotes D. H. Lawrence. Since "in the novel are *all* things given full play," Lawrence asserts, by being a novelist, he is, therefore, "superior to the saint, the scientist, the philosopher, and the poet, who are all great masters of different bits of man alive, but never get the whole hog" (qtd. on v). Huxley responds that "What is true of the novel is only a little less true of the essay. For, like the novel, the essay is a literary device for saying almost everything about almost anything." The essay, he says, is a textual form whose

> extreme variability can be studied most effectively within a three-poled frame of reference. There is the pole of the personal and the autobiographical; there is the pole of the objective, the factual, and the concrete-particular; and there is the pole of the abstract-universal. Most essayists are at home and at their best in the neighborhood of only one of the essay's three poles, or at most only in the neighborhood of two of them. (v)

The essay thus counters the scholastic compartmentalization of knowledge, the "most richly satisfying essays" being

> those which make the best not of one, not of two, but of all three worlds in which it is possible for the essay to exist. Freely, effortlessly, thought and feeling move in these consummate works of art, hither and thither between the essay's

> three poles—from the personal to the universal, from the abstract to the concrete, from the objective datum to the inner experience. (vii)

The essayist's task, then, according to Huxley, is to do his best to make "his cottage upright say as much as the great orchestra of the novel . . . to 'give all things full play,'" to weave together as many varied voices, textures, and discourses as possible. Thus, in his own essays, Huxley says, "I have tried to make the best of all the essay's three worlds, have tried to say everything at once in as near an approach to contrapuntal simultaneity as the nature of literary art will allow" (ix).

Besides discussing the now familiar notions of the essay's skepticism and anti-scholasticism, Huxley also addresses the essay's anti-Ciceronianism. And while he does not explicitly refer to it as such, it seems clear that he, too, conceives of the essay as having a chrono-logic basis. The essay has always defied rhetorical norms, Huxley says, but after a few years of practice, Montaigne's

> patchwork grotesques had turned into living organisms, into multiform hybrids like those beautiful monsters of the old mythologies, the mermaids, the man-headed bull with wings, the centaurs . . . [those] impossibilities compounded of incompatibles, but compounded from within, by a process akin to growth, so that the human trunk seems to spring quite naturally from between the horse's shoulders . . . as easily and inevitably as a musical theme modulates from one key to another. Free association artistically controlled—this is the paradoxical secret of Montaigne's best essays. One damned thing after another—but in a sequence that in some almost miraculous way develops a central theme and relates it to the rest of human experience. (vii)

I believe that the internal "process akin to growth" that Huxley refers to here, a process that allows for the compounding of incompatibles, is that of chrono-logic-based textual development, the associative development of thoughts over time. As we have seen, a chrono-logic textual basis permits one discontinuous fragment "to spring quite naturally" from another, allows one thought to flow into another "as easily and inevitably" as music changes keys (or, we might say, as easily and inevitably as one moment flows into the next), and piles up a sequence of "one damned thing after another." I take exception, however, with Huxley's assertion that there is something "almost miraculous" about this kind of textual development. There is nothing superhuman, nothing mystical about Montaigne's essays, because the time-logic on which they are based is intimately bound to all of human experience. So unaccustomed are we to seeing texts develop a central theme according to chrono-logic, however, so habituated in reading and writing textual forms based on a different, atemporal logic, that chrono-logic seems an impossibility. It is easy, then, to see why Huxley is admiringly baffled by the essay's distinctive development pattern. Chrono-logic, or as Huxley calls it, "free association artistically controlled," is the "paradoxical secret" at the base of Montaigne's best essays.

## W. WOLFGANG HOLDHEIM
## AND GRAHAM GOOD

The theories of W. Wolfgang Holdheim and Graham Good echo the themes we have seen in the theories of Lukács, Adorno, and Huxley and the practice of Montaigne and Cornwallis. Both see the essay as an epistemologically skeptical form—one in which subject and object mutually and provisionally define each other—and stress its anti-scholasticism and basis in chrono-logic.

The essay, Holdheim says, has "a strong tradition" of "epistemological agnosticism" (26) and "is in its very essence the form of the problematical" (21). For Holdheim, the "substance of the essay" is an "ongoing though ever-unfinished unification of the discrete" elements of experience, an ongoing process which helps prevent our relapsing "into the illusion of timeless unity, total objectivity, taxonomic totality, or systematic coherence." Rather than treating objectivism and subjectivism as "absolute alternatives" or "mirror images of each other," the essay, he contends, has the "privileged task" of activating these poles "into a dialectic, a spiraling movement of mutual approximation," a movement which accounts for its "peculiar form." The essay, Holdheim says, thus "executes a to-and-fro movement between subject and object" (28), a movement that creates, tests, and advances our understanding (29).

Good similarly considers the essay to be a skeptical textual form in which subject and object momentarily define each other. According to Good, in the essay, "neither the self nor the world is fixed, but reciprocally shape or reshape each other within the experimental or experiential field of each essay" (12). The essay, he writes,

> is a reflection of and on the changing self in the changing world, not the pure, abstract Cartesian construction of the self or Newtonian construction of the world, but a construction of, and a response to, this time and place in the world, by this self. The indeterminacy of both self and world attains a temporary determination in the essay. (23)

Good argues that the essential instant of an essay is the "moment of reciprocal identification" in the text when "self and object reciprocally clarify and define each other" (8), the moment when "the self finds a pattern in the world and the world finds a pattern in the self," the moment when "Self and object are configured in a mutually illuminating way" (22). However, Good emphasizes, "this illumination is temporary." Thus, the essay can only offer "knowledge of the moment, not more" and its wisdom cannot be abstracted from the moment (8). Self and object organize each other in the essayistic text, Good says,

> but only in a temporary way. Nothing can be built on this configuration, no rules or methods deduced from it. Self and object define each other, but momentarily. The self will go on to other definitions through other objects; the objects (whatever places, works of art, or issues) will find other definitions in other selves. The essay makes a claim to truth, but not permanent truth. Its truths are particular, of the here and now. Other times and places are not its affair. (4)

In addition to seeing the essay as a skeptical text in which subject and object provisionally define each other, Holdheim and Good also underscore the form's anti-scholastic transgression of disciplinary and discursive boundaries. "We have too many systems," Holdheim argues. Thus, he says, we need and employ the essay since it serves as "a counterpractice that may function as a counterstatement: one that opposes . . . dogmatic reductions and . . .

reified theory" (30). Good likewise contends that the essay militates against dogmatic, reductive, reified theory and the compartmentalization of knowledge. The essay, he writes, is a form that "opposes doctrines and disciplines, the organizing structures of academic knowledge." Doctrines and disciplines are "inimical to the spirit of the essay" (5), he maintains, since they "seek unity" where the essay "cultivates diversity" (6). By invoking the "essayistic principle of all-inclusiveness" (42) and attempting to represent "the unsorted 'wholeness' of experience" through its "mixture of elements" (8), the essay represents "a kind of hybrid of art and science" for Good, a text that offers "aesthetic knowledge" (14–15) and can therefore potentially (or at least partially) overcome the modern split that posits science and art as mutually exclusive entities (177; 185).

Finally, both Good and Holdheim point out the essay's basis in anti-Ciceronian chrono-logic. Good notes that while academia organizes discourse into disciplines and always gives priority to theory and system, "to the structures of learning," the essay privileges "personally and provisionally structured" knowledge, "the lived individual experience" as a counterweight (182–83). The essay, Good says, "lets its discourse take the shape of experience" (7). Thus, thought in this form "tends to be presented *as experienced*, not as afterthought; as it responds to objects and events on the spot, not as it is later arranged and systematized" (8). In like manner, Holdheim argues that essays counter the academic impulse to present "knowledge as a closed and often deceptively finished system" because they "enact cognition in progress, knowledge as the process of getting to know" (11). The essay, he says, embodies "the enactment of the way in which understanding in human studies . . . evolves" through a "flow of ideas and preoccupations." In the essay, he says,

> Themes and concepts appear, develop, overlap, go underground, they reemerge, and are progressively sharpened and expanded; they gradually assemble into a shifting configuration that still remains open to further displacement and evolution. . . . [S]ystematic exposition would constitute not only a tiresome duplication but a downright falsification of the process—an arbitrary closure imposed upon its temporal open-endedness. . . .

> [R]epetition . . . is a primary category of time. Not, of course, exact and literal recurrence, but *accretive repetition*, the elucidatory reemergence of problems and discoveries in varied contexts and nuances. The essayistic project is temporal . . . in nature. (31–2)

Knowledge created in the essay, Holdheim concludes, "reflects our universal condition as finite beings that live in time, that endure only in and through change" (29).

## MIKHAIL BAKHTIN

We could continue in this vein, explicating the epistemological skepticism, anti-scholasticism, and anti-Ciceronian chrono-logic present in other twentieth-century theorists' conceptions of the essay. It would be easy to illuminate these aspects in the work of J. C. Guy Cherica, Max Bense, and Robert Musil, for instance. But to do so, I think, is unnecessary; it would be overkill. The essay is the essay is the essay, it seems. Lukács, Adorno, Huxley, Holdheim, and Good are not some carefully selected and slanted sample of theorists who were chosen because they fit my theses. Rather, they were simply the first five twentieth-century theorists of the essay I examined closely. Despite the widely divergent contexts in which these five people worked and from which their theories of the essay evolved, despite the remarkable differences between their collective milieu and that of Montaigne and Cornwallis three centuries before, all of these writers and critics nonetheless consistently portray the essay in the same ways. Thus, I think it safe to conclude that our view of the essay as an epistemologically skeptical text that transgresses disciplinary and discursive boundaries and develops according to the strictures of chrono-logic follows in a long historical tradition of similar views and enjoys wide support.

However, there is more that can and should be said about the theoretical natures of the essay. The work of Russian linguist and literary critic Mikhail Bakhtin offers us a powerfully explanatory framework within which we can position the essay. Bakhtin's concepts can be used to elaborate the theoretical basis for the rehabilitation of the essay we have been discussing so far. The application of his theories to the essay allows us to build upon our established notions of the form as an epistemologically skeptical, anti-scholastic, and anti-Ciceronian text to achieve an enhanced conception of the essay as a centrifugal, "novelistic," dialogic, and carnivalesque form. While Bakhtin's major works, "Discourse in the Novel" (DIN), *Problems of Dostoevsky's Poetics* (PDP), and *Rabelais and His World* (RHW), develop his ideas of centrifugal, "novelistic," dialogic, and carnivalesque writing in service of his theories of the novel, these ideas can be applied productively to the essay as well. As Bakhtin himself contends, dialogical relationships "are an almost universal phenomenon which permeates all human speech and all relationships and manifestations of human life and, in general, everything that has meaning and significance." They are present "in all the manifestations of conscious and intelligent human life," he says, since "dialog begins at the same point where consciousness begins" (PDP 34). Bakhtin similarly asserts that although Dostoevsky created "a wholly new type of artistic thought" in polyphony, "a new artistic model of the world" that found expression in his novels, the importance of this type of thought "extends beyond the bounds of the novelistic genre, affecting certain basic principles of European aesthetics as well" (PDP vii). He likewise considers the creation of polyphonic textuality

> an enormous step forward not only in the development of novelistic prose . . . but in general in the development of the *artistic thinking* of mankind . . . [because] this special *polyphonic mode of artistic thinking*, which extends beyond the bound of the novelistic genre . . . opens up aspects of man—above all the *thinking human consciousness and the dialogical sphere of . . . that consciousness's existence* . . . [which] are inaccessible to the monological artistic approach. (PDP 228)

Bakhtin's neologisms have been left undefined up to this point because they are best understood in the light of their opposing terms. Bakhtin's literary theories argue that a text exists in a field of opposing tendencies which can be visualized as the poles of various continua: centripetal versus centrifugal forces, monologic versus dialogic thought, "poetic" versus "novelistic" discourse, and the official feast versus the carnival. In order to help explicate these opposing terms and more efficiently place the essay within this framework, I will discuss the thesis/support form and the essay as similarly opposing terms, as the embodiments of the first and second halves of each of the above pairs, respectively:

| | | |
|---|---|---|
| centripetal forces | ←——→ | centrifugal forces |
| monologic thought | ←——→ | dialogic thought |
| "poetic" discourse | ←——→ | "novelistic" discourse |
| official feast | ←——→ | carnival |
| thesis/support form | ←——→ | the essay |

To begin with, Bakhtin posits two general forces at work in the development of any language, which he calls the *centripetal and centrifugal forces*. The centripetal forces have a "vital connection with the processes of sociopolitical and cultural centralization" (DIN 271) and thus strive "*to unify and centralize the verbal-ideological world*," to create a unitary language. This unitary language is always "opposed to the realities of heteroglossia" (the plurality and variety of discourses at work at any given time and place), seeking to impose specific limits upon it (DIN 270). The thesis/support form, as it is typically and repeatedly taught through much of a student's primary and secondary education, serves such a centripetal function. It seeks to centralize and unify students' ideological values and thinking: it requires their adherence to a traditionally accepted kind of logic, to the metaphor of a text as a battleground with positions to be attacked and defended, and to the notion of the infallible author, for instance. The thesis/support form also strives to impose strict limits upon the various discourses students bring to class—their regional, racial, ethnic, and socioeconomic jargons, for example—and so to create an acceptably unitary academic discourse. In contrast to the centripetal tendency, Bakhtin says, there are also centrifugal forces at work in a language at any given moment in its evolution, stratifying it into heteroglossia, "into languages that are socio-ideological: languages of social groups, 'professional' and 'generic' languages, languages of generations and so forth" (DIN 272). The essay is a textual form embodying this centrifugal tendency: in its anti-scholasticism, it acknowledges, and indeed celebrates, the realities of heteroglossia, incorporating a diversity of differentiated discourses. The form's embracing of het-eroglossia has been apparent since its inception, since Montaigne's inclusion of both "high" and "low" discourse in his essays, his use of the languages of both the court and the street.

Bakhtin associates these general centripetal and centrifugal tendencies with two general generic categories, which he calls the *"poetic in the narrow sense"* and the *"novelistic,"* respectively. We should note that the division between these categories is *not* based on a simple opposition of poetry and prose, but rather upon these categories' contrasting historical/ideological and epistemological functions. Historically, Bakhtin contends,

> when major divisions of the poetic genres were developing under the influence of the unifying, centralizing, centripetal forces of verbal-ideological life, the novel—and those artistic-prose genres that gravitate toward it—was being histori-cally shaped by the current of decentralizing, centrifugal forces. (DIN 272–73)

The thesis/support form is essentially a "poetic in the narrow sense" genre, while the essay is one of those "artistic-prose genres" that gravitate toward the novel. Genres that are "poetic in the narrow sense" operate within a positivistic kind of epistemology and rhetoric it seems. According to Bakhtin, in these genres artistic con-sciousness "fully realizes itself within its own language," expressing itself directly, immediately, and unconditionally, each form, word, and expression possessing an "unmediated power to assign mean-ing" and thus to purely and directly express the author's intentions (DIN 285). Moreover, he says,

> The language in a poetic work realizes itself as something about which there can be no doubt, something that cannot be disput-ed, something all-encompassing. Everything that the poet sees, understands and thinks, he does through the eyes of a given lan-guage, in its inner forms, and there is nothing that might require, for its expression, the help of any other or alien lan-guage. The language of the poetic genre is a unitary and singular Ptolemaic world outside of which nothing else exists and noth-ing else is needed. . . . The world of poetry, no matter how many contradictions and insoluble conflicts the poet develops within

it, is always illumined by one unitary and indisputable discourse. Contradictions, conflicts and doubts remain in the object, in thoughts, in living experiences—in short, in the subject matter—but they do not enter into the language itself. In poetry, even discourse about doubts must be cast in a discourse that cannot be doubted. (DIN 286)

In this sense, the thesis/support form is clearly a "poetic" genre. In evaluating our students' papers, we typically assume that the thesis/support forms before us embody a direct expression of their writers' intentions, their pure and unmediated meaning. For instance, we assume that an unclear or incoherent paper is an expression of the writer's unclear or incoherent intention or meaning. We usually take points off for writers/papers that do not present themselves as indisputable and all-encompassing (that waffle or overly qualify themselves), that imply that a unitary, Ptolemaic language is not sufficient (that deviate from academic discourse), and that include contradictions, doubts, and conflicts.

Bakhtin uses "poetic" discourse as an explanatory foil for his notion of "novelistic" discourse, a discourse also embodied in the essay. He defines the novel "as a diversity of social speech types (sometimes even diversity of languages) and a diversity of individual voices, artistically organized" (DIN 262), the whole of the novel being constructed, he says, "out of heteroglot, multi-voiced, multi-styled and often multi-languaged elements" (DIN 265). The "indispensable prerequisite" for the novel, according to Bakhtin, is the

internal stratification of any single national language into social dialects, characteristic group behavior, professional jargons, generic languages, languages of generations and age groups, tendentious languages, languages of authorities, of various circles and passing fashions, languages that serve the specific sociopolitical purposes of the day, even of the hour (each day has its own slogan, its own vocabulary, its own emphases). . . . The novel orchestrates all its themes, the totality of the world of objects and ideas depicted and expressed in it, by means of the social diversity of speech types and by the differing individual voices that flourish under such conditions. (DIN 262–63)

The essay, in this sense, is clearly a novelistic genre, since it transgresses disciplinary and discursive boundaries to marshal multiple voices, styles, and languages and thus better re-create the totality of the world it seeks to represent. Recall Huxley, for instance, who argues that the best essays are those that are able to incorporate the totality of experience, to exist in all three "worlds" co-instantaneously, to present personal/subjective, scientific/objective, and universal/abstract discourses in a simultaneous counterpoint.

A third pair of Bakhtinian terms that illuminate the contrast between the thesis/support and essay forms—and that thus help to elaborate our rehabilitative theory of the essay—is that of *monologism and dialogism*, two poles on an ideological/epistemological continuum. According to Bakhtin, monologism begins with an assumption of the unity of existence which it transforms into "the principle of the unity of the *consciousness*." From a monologic perspective, then, "Everything that is true finds a place for itself within the bounds of a single consciousness," and thus "a single consciousness and a single mouth are completely sufficient for total fullness of cognition" (PDP 65). Bakhtin contends that modern European rationalism, "with its cult of unified and exclusive reason," cemented the monological principle and produced our cultural faith "in the self-sufficiency of a single consciousness in all spheres of ideological life." Our faith in the sufficiency of monologic determines the outer and inner shape of our discourse, he says (PDP 66), since it requires a unified point of view to "weld together the most formal elements of style as well as the most abstract philosophical conclusion" (PDP 67). Since the entire mass of one's discourse and ideology must be "subordinated to a single accent and express a single and unified point of view," only those thoughts or "ideas which fall into the groove of the author's point of view can retain their significance without destroying the single-accented unity of the work," Bakhtin says. Thus, in monologism, foreign ideas can only be assimilated or polemically refuted in light of the author's unified viewpoint (PDP 68). Furthermore, there can be "only a single form of cognitive interaction between consciousnesses: he who knows and possesses the truth instructs him who errs and is ignorant of it, i.e., the interaction of teacher and pupil" (PDP 66).

The thesis/support form, we can now see, is a monological text. To be effective it must be formally and substantively unified, expressing a single point of view and single consciousness in a single accent, style, or voice. In the thesis/support form, foreign ideas (or cited sources) appear only so that they may be assimilated into or refuted by the writer's steadfast viewpoint, and the writer is presented as a self-sufficient (if not omniscient) authority, independently capable of full cognition. Thus, the relationship between the writer and reader is one of teacher to student, of the truth-full pouring knowledge into the truth-empty.

Bakhtin praises Dostoevsky for his ability to transcend the reductiveness of monologism and recognize the dialogic natures of human thought and the idea. Bakhtin maintains that an "idea does not *live* in one person's *isolated* individual consciousness—if it remains there it degenerates and dies." Rather, he says, an idea takes shape, develops, finds expression, and generates new thoughts "only when it enters into genuine dialogical relationships with other, *foreign*, ideas," only when it comes into "living contact" with another person's consciousness and voice. "It is in the point of contact of these voice-consciousnesses that the idea is born and has its life," Bakhtin says (PDP 71–2). He commends Dostoevsky's understanding that an idea is an "interindividual and intersubjective" entity:

> The sphere of its existence is not the individual consciousness, but the dialogical intercourse *between* consciousnesses. The idea is a *living event* which is played out in the point where two or more consciousnesses meet dialogically. . . . [T]he idea wants to be heard, understood and "answered" by other voices from other positions. . . . [Dostoevsky sees] the idea as precisely such a living event played out between consciousness-voices. (PDP 72)

Thus, for Dostoevsky, Bakhtin says, the fundamental units of cognition are not individual thoughts, but rather the integrated positions of personality whose intersection enables thought to exist. According to Bakhtin, Dostoevsky considers subject-oriented meaning to be inseparable from these positions of personality (PDP 76) and sees even the "truth about the world" as "inseparable from the truth of the personality" (PDP 63). He therefore considers thought to be "a concrete event of organized human orientations and voices, not merely [a] unified system based on the subject matter" and likewise considers the combining of thoughts to be the combining of integrated positions of personality. Bakhtin notes that Dostoevsky develops even his most scholarly articles by dialogically "juxtaposing deeply individualized integral voices," by organizing voices and coupling philosophical orientations (PDP 76). In his scholarly articles, Bakhtin says, Dostoevsky "juxtaposes orientations and among them builds his own orientation," all of his material unfolding before him "as a series of human orientations," his path leading "not from idea to idea, but from orientation to orientation" (PDP 78). In short, Dostoevsky's dialogism recognizes no "single *impersonal* truth, as is the case in the monological world," and his works include "no detached, impersonal verities." Instead, in dialogism, there is only the intersection and interaction of "integral, indivisible idea-voices or viewpoint-voices" (PDP 78–9). Indeed, existence itself is contingent upon a dialog of voices, according to Bakhtin:

> To be means to communicate dialogically. When the dialog is finished, all is finished. Therefore the dialog, in essence, cannot and must not come to an end. . . . One voice alone concludes nothing and decides nothing. Two voices is the minimum for life, the minimum for existence. (PDP 213)

The essay, I believe, is a dialogic textual form. Thoughts and ideas in the essay are concrete, living events—experiential, chrono-logic-based episodes developing over time—played out in the points of contact and intersection of various voices and consciousnesses—in the anti-scholastic interaction of divergent disciplinary knowledges and discourses. Truth of the world is inseparable from the truth of the personality in the essay—the subject and object mutually, provisionally, and temporarily defining each other within the bounds of the text. The fundamental unit of cognition in the essay is not the individual thought, but rather an integrated position of personality—Montaigne, for instance, presenting himself to us not "as a grammarian or a poet or a jurist," but as an "entire being, Michel de Montaigne." The essay operates by organizing and juxtaposing dissimilar human voices and philosophical orientations, among which the author builds his or her own orientation—Montaigne offering us, as Spellmeyer put it earlier, "a 'coming-together' of dissonant perspectives to restore the lived world." In the essay, each idea or thought wants to be answered by other voices from other positions. Thus, the essay is fundamentally inconclusive: the dialog cannot come to an end. Furthermore, in the essay, the path of the writer's thought unfolds before him not as a movement from idea to idea in a unified system based on the subject matter, but as a movement from human orientation to human orientation—a skeptical exploration moving from perspective to perspective, discipline to discipline, discourse to discourse, personal-subjective to scientific-objective to universal-abstract. Finally, in the essay, truth is not detached and impersonal, existing previous to and outside of human communication, but rather is produced through a dialogic intersection and interaction of viewpoint-voices, through the dialectic transactions among individuals working within a social epistemic rhetoric.

A last pair of Bakhtinian terms that helps elaborate the rehabilitative theory of the essay we have been sketching is that of *official feast and carnival*. In medieval culture, Bakhtin says, there were two opposing kinds of public ritual, the official feast and the carnival, each with its distinctive ideological-political function and discourse, an opposition I see mirrored in the distinction between the thesis/support and essay forms. According to Bakhtin, the official feasts "sanctioned the existing pattern of things and reinforced it." They "looked back at the past and used the past to consecrate the present." The official feast, he says,

> asserted that all was stable, unchanging, perennial: the existing hierarchy, the existing religious, political, and moral values, norms, and prohibitions. It was the triumph of a truth already established, the predominant truth that was put forward as eternal and indisputable. (RHW 9)

Moreover, he notes, an official feast "was a consecration of inequality." Each person's respective rank "was especially evident during official feasts" since "everyone was expected to appear in the full regalia of his calling, rank, and merits and to take the place corresponding to his position" (RHW 10).

The thesis/support form clearly operates as a Bakhtinian "official ritual." In its positivistic epistemology and rhetoric, it asserts that truth is stable, unchanging, already established, and indisputable—that truth is certain, singular, objective, prior to language, and thus knowable from a singular and immobile point of view. The thesis/support form looks back at the past in order to consecrate the present (it uses research, cites sources, and marshals past examples and testimony only to sanctify the writer's present position and thesis). It functions to sanction and reinforce existing hierarchical sociopolitical patterns of values and prohibitions (as we have seen, according to Fort, it embodies the proper attitudes toward authority, mystifies the nature of that authority, and so makes students blindly revere and replicate the existing hierarchical power structures in society). The thesis/support form also consecrates inequality, expecting each participant to take the position corresponding to his or her rank in the existing power structure. Those who possess the truth, who are truth-full and thus powerful (the omniscient writer and the sources she cites), are enthroned at the top of the textual hierarchy, while those who are truth-empty and thus powerless (the readers) are placed at the bottom, passively awaiting the knowledge that will be poured into them from above.

Carnival stands in opposition to the official feast, Bakhtin says, because rather than consecrating and reinforcing official culture, it shows the "entire official ideology and ritual . . . in their comic aspect" (RHW 13). Its fundamental and ritual laughter temporarily functions to free its participants "from all religious and ecclesiastic dogmatism, from all mysticism and piety." Carnivalesque laughter thus functions to revive and renew the world (RHW 7), to allow people to "escape from the usual official way of life" (RHW 8) and enter into a "utopian realm of community, freedom, equality, and abundance" (RHW 9). In contrast to the official feast, he says,

> carnival celebrated temporary liberation from the prevailing truth and from the established order; it marked the suspension of all hierarchical rank, privileges, norms, and prohibitions. Carnival was the true feast of time, the feast of becoming, change, and renewal. It was hostile to all that was immortalized and completed. (RHW 10)

The carnival experience was "opposed to all that was ready-made and completed, to all pretense at immutability," Bakhtin says. Thus, it "sought a dynamic expression; it demanded ever-changing, playful, undefined forms . . . filled with this pathos of change and renewal, with the sense of the gay relativity of prevailing truths and authorities" (RHW 11). Carnival's temporary suspension of rank allowed for a special kind of contact and discourse among people. During carnival

> a special form of free and familiar contact reigned among people who were usually divided by the barriers of caste, property, profession, and age . . . a special type of communication impossible in everyday life . . . frank and free . . . [liberated] from norms of etiquette and decency imposed at other times. (RHW 10)

The laughter at the basis of carnival "is universal in scope," Bakhtin says, "directed at all and everyone, including the carnival's participants." Carnival sees the entire world "in its gay relativity" (RHW 11). Its laughter is thus "also directed at those who laugh" since "They, too, are incomplete" (RHW 12). In sum, it embodies "the ever-growing, inexhaustible, ever-laughing principle which uncrowns and renews" (RHW 24). Thus, Bakhtin says, the function of carnivalesque writing is

> to consecrate inventive freedom, to permit the combination of a variety of different elements and their rapprochement, to liberate from the prevailing point of view of the world, from conventions and established truths, from clichés, from all that is humdrum and universally accepted. This carnival spirit offers the chance to have a new outlook on the world, to realize the relative nature of all that exists, and enter a completely new order of things. (RHW 34)

The essay is clearly a carnivalesque form of writing. It functions to counter the entirety of official ideology, ritual, and dogmatism, to offer us temporary liberation from the prevailing truth and established order, from the ready-made, completed, and immutable. The essay originated, as Holdheim told us earlier, as Montaigne's *Abbau* of tradition, as an antigenre designed to deconstruct the intellectual and philosophical baggage he inherited from the past. It is filled with the sense of the relativity of prevailing truths, and, indeed, of all that exists, its laughter directed even at those who laugh, since they, too, are incomplete (as we know, Montaigne's deep epistemological skepticism is directed inwardly as well as outwardly, directed toward himself as much as toward anything and anyone else). The essay consecrates inventive freedom in its anti-scholasticism and anti-Ciceronianism: it permits a special kind of free and frank discourse among people usually divided by sociopolitical or disciplinary barriers, a combination and rapprochement of a variety of elements, a discourse liberated from the prevailing conventions, from the norms of etiquette usually in force. The essay is a true feast of time, celebrating becoming and change, seeking dynamic expression in ever changing and undefined forms; it is a substantive and formal expression of chrono-logic, of a cognitive and discursive becoming over time. The essay offers us a new outlook on the world, a new order of things: the differently logical perspective of chrono-logic with which to order experience.

We thus come to the end of our consideration of the theoretical natures of the essay. Earlier, we acknowledged Winterowd's challenge that "if the essay is to serve as the kind of writing through which students realize their full potential as liberally educated beings, they, and we, need an expanded conception of what the essay is and what it can do" (146). Having elaborated a rehabilitative theory of the essay as an epistemologically skeptical form that transgresses disciplinary and discursive boundaries and develops according to the requirements of chrono-logic, one that embodies centrifugal, dialogic, "novelistic," and carnivalesque textual tendencies, we have met that challenge on an abstract level. The extent to which our abstract construction actually meshes with concrete, "real world" phenomena, the extent to which our theory actually accounts for the practice of professional essayists, is an entirely different enterprise, of course, and the matter to which we now turn our attention.

Chapter 4

# The Practice of Some Contemporary Essayists

## *O R*

## Living in the Real World

Working in the realm of abstract theory is engrossing and entertaining. The construction of elaborate models, with minute parts that mesh perfectly, is an intellectually stimulating and fascinating exercise. The problem comes, of course, when we attempt to move out from the safe and insulated land of abstraction, when we try to bridge the gulf and dwell amid the uncontrollable, problematic complexities of the real world. When we try to apply our intricate and sometimes delicate theoretical constructions to material phenomena, we often find that the facts are obstinately contrary, refusing to submit to our beautifully erected schemes. The test of a theoretical model, then, is its explanatory power, its ability to account for and help us understand the nature of the concrete phenomena we are studying, its ability to mesh with the real world. In this chapter, I will examine the work of seven contemporary essayists—Aldous Huxley, Joan Didion, Charles Simic, Alice Walker, Scott Russell Sanders, Gretel Ehrlich, and Joseph Epstein—in order to demonstrate the validity of the model of the essay I have been developing over the last two chapters.

Since we are familiar with Huxley's theory of the essay, having examined it in the last chapter, let us begin here by looking at his practice as an essayist, taking "Music at Night" as our example. First of all, this text demonstrates the essay's anti-scholastic integration of multiple perspectives and discourses. In Huxley's terms, "Music at Night" moves easily among the personal/autobiographical, the objective/factual (or concrete/particular), and the abstract/universal poles, the essay effortlessly connecting his thoughts about having Shakespeare rammed down his throat as a schoolboy (177), the smells of wet earth and lime trees (176), and the "certain blessedness lying at the heart of things" (177). It likewise counters the compartmentalization of knowledge by incorporating numerous areas of inquiry into a single, four-page text: education (177), philosophy, psychology, literary criticism (178), art criticism, aesthetics (179), theology, epistemology, and music criticism (180) are all invoked. The essay similarly orchestrates numerous voices or discourses, from the poetic—"the warm living body of the night" (176)—to the syllogistically logical—"Now, it is a matter of observation that painters and musicians are *not* monsters. Therefore . . . The conclusion follows, inescapably" (178). Next, the essay's basis in chrono-logic (or "free association artistically controlled") is obvious from the outset and accentuated by Huxley's use of present tense verbs: "Moonless, this June night is all the more alive with stars," he begins. For the rest of the first paragraph, Huxley apparently piles up his sense-sparked thoughts one after the other as they come to him. His use of chrono-logic is obvious, for instance, in the associative, flowing quality of the progressive qualifications he places on his description of the silence he hears: "There is silence; but a silence that breathes with the soft breathing of the sea and, in the thin shrill noise of a cricket, insistently, incessantly harps on the fact of its own deep perfection" (176). Longer sequences of the essay's thoughts are also clearly based on chrono-logic, associatively flowing from one into another into another. We glide, for instance, from the meditation on "the warm living body of the night" that opens the essay (176) to a consideration of the music playing ("now in a fine interweaving of melodies, now in pulsing and almost solid clots of harmonious sound it pours itself"), to a pondering of the "mysterious blessedness" in things we can only accidentally and fleetingly be aware of, then back to the music as "One after another the voices take up the theme propounded by the orchestra," then suddenly to the music's stopping and the "stupid insect-like insistence" of the phonograph needle's steel point rasping, and then into his reminiscence of being an "inky urchin" forced to laboriously translate Shakespeare into his own words, an association perhaps sparked by a memory of the "stupid insect-like insistence" of the rasping steel point of his pen as a student (177). Furthermore, the skepticism of Huxley's essay is apparent in his attack on the "professional sages," in his assertion that "The limits of criticism are very quickly reached" (179). His essay mocks those who write the analytic programs for concerts, the pamphlets "that will tell you exactly" what the music means—"much too exactly; that is the trouble" (178)—because, he concludes, "We cannot isolate the truth contained in a piece of music" (180).

While Huxley's essay demonstrates ties to all the threads we have woven into our model, the work of Joan Didion likewise provides fine examples of the essay in action, but examples that emphasize one particular thread over the others. Didion's work accentuates how the essay enacts the evolution of an author's understanding over time, how the essay embodies an author's skeptical groping toward an uncertain truth. We could look, for instance, at "On Morality" or "At the Dam" (meditations on the nature of morality and the meaning of the Hoover Dam, respectively) to see excellent specimens, but let us examine her well-known "On Keeping a Notebook" instead. The essay begins with a fragment from one of her notebooks. "Since the note is in my notebook," Didion says, "it presumably has some meaning to me." Although she studies it "for a long while," she yet has "only the most general notion" of its meaning at the outset (131). Her reconstruction of this fragment's meaning, however, only begins her exploration, only starts her quest for knowledge. It prompts her to ask a number of questions that the remainder of the essay attempts to answer:

> Why did I write it down? In order to remember, of course, but exactly what was it I wanted to remember? How much of it actually happened? Did any of it? Why do I keep a notebook at all? It is easy to deceive oneself on all those scores. (132)

In Didion's observation/admission that it is easy to deceive oneself about numerous things, we see the characteristic inwardly directed skepticism of essayists, an authorial self-critique that Didion later reiterates, saying, "I sometimes delude myself about why I keep a notebook" (135). This authorial self-skepticism helps determine the modest and uncertain nature of the essay's search for insight, which is evident in Didion's tentative consideration of the compulsion to write things down: "I suppose that it begins or does not begin in the cradle" (132). She guesses at the truth; she speculates; she supposes—she does not declare. Moreover, Didion repeatedly and explicitly indicates that "On Keeping a Notebook" is a tentative, open-ended, chrono-logical act of cognition in progress. For instance, at one point, as she reflects on what she has just said in the previous paragraph, she apparently comes to a realization: "So the point of my keeping a notebook has never been, nor is it now, to have an accurate factual record of what I have been doing or thinking" (133). Soon after, Didion achieves another provisional insight: "*How it felt to me*: that is getting closer to the truth about a notebook" (134–35). Later, she again seems to present her thought as she experienced it, showing us where and when she achieves an understanding:

> "*He was born the night the Titanic went down.*" That seems a nice enough line, and I even recall who said it, but is it not really a better line in life than it could ever be in fiction?
>
> But of course that is exactly it: not that I should ever use the line, but that I should remember the woman who said it and the afternoon I heard it. (138)

In short, Didion's essay represents the skeptical movements of her mind as they happen over time. Take the following passage, for instance:

> I would like to believe that my dread then was for the human condition, but of course it was for me, because I wanted a baby and did not then have one and because I wanted to own a house that cost $1,000 a month to rent and because I had a hangover.
>
> It all comes back. (139)

In this way, Didion allows us to see knowledge as the process of getting to know. She also underscores the tentative and provisional nature of truth and knowledge by repeatedly liquidating her opinion even as she tries it out through qualifications, equivocations, ambiguous rejoinders, and self-contradictions. At one point she says, "I imagine, in other words, that the notebook is about other people. But, of course, it is not" (135). Later, she asks, "Does not the relevance of these notes seem marginal at best?" and answers, "Well, perhaps not entirely marginal" (137). Elsewhere, pondering the nature of the notebook, she suggests (but then waffles) that

> we are talking about something private, about bits of the mind's string too short to use, an indiscriminate and erratic assemblage with meaning only for its maker.
>
> And sometimes even the maker has difficulty with the meaning. (136–37)

And finally, Didion hedges and circles around, refusing to make any definitive assertion about the purpose of her notebook, asking questions instead, and then even backing away from those questions lest we think she has come to rest on any solid ground:

> It is a long way from that world to Mrs. Lou Fox's world, where we all live now, and is it not just as well to remember that? Might not Mrs. Minnie S. Brooks help me remember what I am? Might not Mrs. Lou Fox help me remember what I am not?
>
> But sometimes the point is harder to discern. (137–38)

That the essay enacts the way understanding evolves over time, enacts the way the writer's skeptical mind searches for provisional insights but refrains from reaching toward any totalizing conclusions, is nowhere more evident than at the end of "On Keeping a Notebook," where Didion writes

> It is a good idea, *then*, to keep in touch, and I *suppose* that keeping in touch is what notebooks are all about. *And* we are all on our own when it comes to keeping those lines open to ourselves: your notebook will never help me, nor mine you. (140, italics mine)

In addition to helping us appreciate how Didion's essay enacts the evolution of her understanding over time, the theoretical model of the essay we have been elaborating also helps us understand the most difficult and striking characteristic of Charles Simic's "Reading Philosophy at Night": its rampant anti-scholasticism, its flagrant and nonstop transgression of disciplinary and discursive boundaries and hybridization of multiple discourses. Simic's essay begins with aphorisms from Nietzsche and Magritte, then shifts into a striking bit of poetic hyperbole ("I could have been sitting on the edge of a cliff with my back to the abyss trying to look normal"), then shifts again into a conversationally toned autobiographical tableau about reading in "the sparsely furnished room above the Italian grocery" (307). Next, without warning, it dives into arrestingly stark description ("It was six o'clock in the morning. It was winter. It was dark and very cold.") to begin the story of his first epiphany. After that comes a series of vaguely worded glimpses into some of his dreamvisions (308) followed by some self-conscious metacognitive jargon: "All my experiences make a kind of untaught ontology which precedes all my readings. What I am trying to conceptualize with the help of the philosopher is that which I have already intuited." Simic then presents a passage from Descartes, part of an Eastern European folk song (309), an autobiographical instant (about "lying in a ditch and looking at some pebbles while German bombers were flying over our heads"), some quotes from Wittgenstein, and several dauntingly abstract assertions ("Competing phenomenologies are impoverishments, splendid poverties"). The dialogic interaction of different discourses becomes explicit and obvious in the next section, where philosophy, mysticism, and poetry intersect and clash in a contrapuntal simultaneity:

> There are people who tell you, for example, that you can speak of a pencil's dimension, location, appearance, state of motion or rest but not of its intelligence and love of music. The moment I hear that the poet in me rebels and I want to write a poem about an intelligent pencil in love with music. In other words, what they regard as nonsense, I suspect to be full of unknown imaginative possibilities. (310)

Next, after first importing a third party anecdote about Wittgenstein and a colleague, Simic relates how a philosophical argument with a friend "about silence being the language of consciousness" degenerated into profane "bickering" ("It got to the point where we were calling each other 'you dumb shit'") before he launches into a story from his childhood in Yugoslavia about his class trip to the town War Museum (311). We are then privy to

Simic's internal polylogue, the diverse variety of voices that were active in his consciousness one evening. The essay's basis in anti-Ciceronian chrono-logic becomes manifest in this section as Simic presents his thought as sometimes discontinuous cognitive/discursive fragments ordered by the linearity of time, as an unsimplified and sometimes messy string of personally structured elements that are coordinated rather than subordinated. He evidently presents his thoughts as they were experienced on the spot rather than being later systematized and rearranged.

> And here's what went through my head just the other night as I lay awake in the dark:
> The story had nothing to do with what you were talking about.
> The story had everything to do with what you were talking about.
> I can think of a hundred objections.
> Only idiots want something neat, something categorical . . . and I never talk unless I know!
> Aha! You're mixing poetry and philosophy. Bertrand Russell wouldn't give you the time of day.
> "Everything looks very busy to me," says Jasper Johns, and that's the problem. I remember a strange cat, exceedingly emaciated, that scratched on my door the day I was scratching my head over Hegel's phenomenology.
> Who said, "Whatever can be thought must be fictitious?"
> You got me there! Error is my first love. I'm shouting her name from the rooftops.
> Still and all! And nevertheless! And above all! Let's not forget "above all."
> "The Only Human Way to Catch a Metaphysical Mouse" is the name of the book I work on between three and four in the morning.
> Here's what Nietzsche said to the ceiling: "The rank of the philosopher is determined by the rank of his laughter." But he couldn't really laugh. No matter how hard he tried he couldn't laugh.
> I know because I'm a connoisseur of chaos. All the good-looking oxymorons come to visit me in bed. . . . (313)

The polylogue, though meandering, never degenerates into random associations or stream of consciousness; the subject, philosophy, is never lost. After this section, Simic incorporates, in order: some snippets from Wallace Stevens's poetry ("'where shines the light that lets be the things that are'"); more metacognitive abstraction ("Understanding depends upon the relation of what I am to what I have been. . . . Consciousness waking up conscience—waking up history"); a series of frustrated interjections about the messiness of history ("Chaos! Bedlam! Hopeless tangle!"); some memorable poetic similes about the character of poetry ("Poetry as imperturbable [Buster] Keaton alone with the woman he loves on an ocean liner set adrift on the stormy sea") (313); and a metacognitive allusion to Cervantes ("And always the dialectic: I have Don Quixote and his windmills in my head and Sancho Panza and his mule in my heart"). As we approach the end of the essay, the radical skepticism of the essayist becomes clear in Simic's groping efforts toward understanding:

> That's a figure of speech—one figure among many other figures of speech. Who could live without them? Do they tell the truth? Do they conceal it? I don't know. That's why I keep going back to philosophy.
>
> It is morning. It is night. The book is open. The text is difficult, the text is momentarily opaque. My mind is wandering. My mind is struggling to grasp the elusive . . . the always hinting . . . What do you call it?
>
> *It, it*, I keep calling it. An infinity of *it* without a single antecedent—like a hum in my ear.

And, as the essay ends, we again witness the form's enactment of cognition in progress as Simic reaches the kind of present-tense, inconclusive "conclusion" that marks the stopping point of many essays:

> Just then, about to give up, I find the following on a page of Heidegger. . . . And it all comes together: poetry, philosophy, history. I see—in the sense of being able to picture and feel the human weight of another's solitude. So many of them. Seated with a book. Day breaking. Thought becoming image. Image becoming thought. (314)

In sum, "Reading Philosophy at Night" is an excellent example of how the essay juxtaposes and intersects diverse viewpoints and discourses in an attempt to combine numerous areas of knowledge and thus both address whole problems of human existence and offer the reader the unsorted wholeness of the writer's experience. As the essay unfolds, we observe Simic's movement among dissimilar orientations and his attempts to build his own orientation among these.

While Simic takes great advantage of one aspect of the essay among others, primarily offering us a virtuoso performance in the orchestration of heteroglossia, Alice Walker carefully and quietly plays upon other, more subtle facets of the form. Our model of the essay helps us account for Simic's verve as well as for Walker's grave modesty, her skeptical, exploratory attempts at understanding, her essays, such as "Father," that present knowledge as a very serious process of getting to know. Walker begins "Father" by explicitly signaling that she is about to embark on an urgent journey to discover something of her father: "Since I share so many of my father's characteristics, physical and otherwise, coming to terms with what he has meant to my life is crucial to a full acceptance and love of myself" (9). And early in the essay she reiterates that she is engaged in the present-tense struggle for new insights, saying, "I'd like to tell [my father] how hard I am working to understand" (10). Throughout the essay we find indicators of the uncertain nature of this journey of discovery, with key phrases repeated to underscore the speculative and tentative qualities of her exploration—*wonder, feel/felt, perhaps, probably, suppose, think/thought, seemed, yet:*

> I wonder sometimes if the appearance, in 1968, of my first book . . . surprised him. It is frustrating that, because he is now dead, I will never know. (9)

> In my heart, I have never wanted to be at odds with my father, but I have felt, over the years, especially when I was younger, that he gave me no choice. Perhaps if I could have relaxed and been content to be his favorite, there would have been a chance for closeness. . . . If he ever read the poem, I wonder what he thought. We never discussed my work, though I thought he tended to become more like some of my worst characters the older he got. (11)

Did he actually beat me on voting day? Probably not. I suppose the illegal abortion caused me to understand what living under other people's politics can force us to do. (11–12)

I confessed. I broke the jar, I said. I think he hugged me. He probably didn't, but I still feel as if he did, so embraced did I feel by the happy relief I noted on his face and by the fact that he didn't punish me at all, but seemed, instead, pleased with me. I think it was at that moment that I resolved to take my chances with the truth. (12)

Years later, when I knew him, he seemed fearful of both education and politics and disappointed and resentful as well. . . . Education merely seemed to make his children more critical of him. (13)

[M]y older sister, Mamie, was favorite among the first [set of children]. In her case the favoritism seemed outwardly caused by her very light color, and of course she was remarkably intelligent as well. In my case, my father seemed partial to me because of my "smartness" and forthrightness, but more obviously because of my hair, which was longest and "best" in the family.
   And yet, my father taught me two things that have been important to me. (14–15)

I didn't listen to my father because I assumed he meant that in the eyes of a *man*, in his eyes, a woman's hair is her glory . . . and that is probably what he did mean. (15)

[T]here is power (would an ancient translation of glory *be* power?) in uncut hair itself. The power (and glory) perhaps of the untamed, the undomesticated; in short, the wild. (15–16)

"Father" also operates according to chrono-logic, showing us Walker in the process of thinking through issues surrounding her father, in a sometimes untidy process of cognitive "becoming" over time. "Why do certain things stick in the mind?" she asks, pondering a pair of events from when she was three or four years old. Two paragraphs later, she works through a sequence of five successive realizations, the progressive transitions signaled by the repeated use of "and" and a final "actually":

> It was the unfairness of the beating that keeps it fresh in
> my mind. (And this was thirty-seven years ago!) And my disap-
> pointment at the deterioration of my father's ethics. And yet,
> since I am never happy in my heart when estranged from my
> father, any more than I would be happy shut off from sunlight,
> in writing this particular poem I tried to see my father's behav-
> ior in a context larger than our personal relationship.
>    Actually, my father was two fathers.
>    To the first four of his children he was one kind of father,
> to the second set of four he was another kind. (12–13)

The essay's basis in chrono-logic is especially evident near the end
of the text when Walker makes several explicit references to how
her thinking about her father has changed and is changing over
time. "Only recently have I come to believe he was right in wanting
me to keep my hair," she says. Soon afterward, she adds, "But now I
begin to sense something else, that there is power . . . in uncut hair
itself" (15). And in the final sentence of the essay, Walker reaches
her explicitly chrono-logically based, somewhat ambiguous, and
highly qualified "conclusion" about her father, having left the
known and found a new vision of the truth:

> And thinking of you now, merging the two fathers that you
> were, remembering how tightly I hugged you as a small child
> returning home after two long months at a favorite aunt's, and
> with what apparent joy you lifted me beside your cheek; know-
> ing now, at forty, what it takes out of body and spirit to go and
> how much more to stay, and having learned, too, by now, some
> of the painful confusions in behavior caused by ignorance and
> pain, I love you no less for what you were. (17)

While our model of the essay provides us with useful avenues
into the modest, tentative, and untidy ambiguities of Walker's practice, it also helps us accommodate and appreciate both Scott Russell
Sanders's decisive and unequivocal critical statements on the form
and his more elusive and slippery practice as an essayist.
Understanding our model's emphasis on the essay as the
chrono-logical enactment of how the writer's understanding develops over time, we are better prepared to accept Sanders's con-
tentions that "the essay is the closest thing we have, on paper, to a

record of the individual mind at work and play," that the essay offers the reader "the spectacle of a single consciousness making sense of a part of the chaos" of experience ("Singular" 660). Now familiar with the notion of the essay as a journey of discovery that leaves old orders behind, we can both easily accept his assertion that the essay works by "following the zigzag motions of the inquisitive mind" ("Singular" 661) and better appreciate his extended simile for essay writing:

> The writing of an essay is like finding one's way through a forest without being quite sure what game you are chasing, what landmark you are seeking. You sniff down one path until some heady smell tugs you in a new direction, and then off you go, dodging and circling, lured on by the songs of unfamiliar birds, puzzled by the tracks of strange beasts, leaping from stone to stone across rivers, barking up one tree after another. ("Singular" 662)

Furthermore, being well acquainted with the idea of the essay as an uncertain exploration in search of new knowledge, we can readily understand why Sanders says that "essays . . . are experiments in making sense of things" (*Paradise* xiii).

Just as it helps us deal with Sanders's straightforward and unvarnished critical assessments of the form, our model of the essay similarly allows us to unravel his more complex and subtle practice as an essayist. Let us take his "The Men We Carry in Our Minds" as our example. This piece begins with an anti-scholastic juxtaposition of opposing perspectives, with the intersection and counterpoint of dissimilar voices:

> "This must be a hard time for women," I say to my friend Anneke. "They have so many paths to choose from, and so many voices calling them."
> "I think it's a lot harder for men," she replies. . . . "[T]he men I know are eaten up with guilt." (111)

The interaction of these incongruous points of view spurs Sanders into searching for new insights. Twice we see the dialogic infusion of Anneke's contrasting voice immediately prod him into taking mental journeys of discovery. Anneke says

"Men are the ones who've been discredited, who have to search their souls."

I search my soul. I discover guilty feelings aplenty—toward the poor, the Vietnamese, Native Americans, the whales, an endless list of debts—a guilt in each case that is as bright and unambiguous as a neon sign. But toward women I feel something more confused, a snarl of shame, envy, wary tenderness, and amazement. This muddle troubles me. To hide my unease I say, "You're right, it's tough being a man these days."

"Don't laugh." Anneke frowns at me, mournful-eyed, through the sassafras steam. "I wouldn't be a man for anything. It's much easier being the victim. All the victim has to do is break free. The persecutor has to live with his past."

How deep is that past? I find myself wondering after Anneke has left. How much of an inheritance do I have to throw off? Is it just the beliefs I breathed in as a child? Do I have to scour memory back through father and grandfather? Through St. Paul? Beyond Stonehenge and into the twilit caves? (112)

This string of questions highlights the groping and inconclusive nature of the essay, the way in which essayists characteristically ask questions they do not have the answers to rather than making declarative statements. Sanders uses another long string of questions in this essay, the piling up of interrogatives enacting the progressive movement of his skeptical mind. In discussing his disorientation upon entering college, he writes that

for the first time I met women who told me that men were guilty of having kept all the joys and privileges of the earth for themselves. I was baffled. What privileges? What joys? I thought about the maimed, dismal lives of most of the men back home. What had they stolen from their wives and daughters? The right to go five days a week, twelve months a year, for thirty or forty years to a steel mill or a coal mine? The right to drop bombs and die in war? The right to feel every leak in the roof, every gap in the fence, every cough in the engine, as a wound they must mend? The right to feel, when the lay-off comes or the plant shuts down, not only afraid but ashamed? (115)

In this essay, Sanders underscores the tentative and equivocal nature of the form in much the same way that Walker does in "Father," through the repeated usage of the words *seem/seemed* and *think/thought:*

> Warriors and toilers: those seemed, in my boyhood vision, to be the chief destinies for men. . . . [T]he men on television—the politicians, the astronauts, the generals, the savvy lawyers, the philosophical doctors, the bosses who gave orders to both soldiers and laborers—seemed as remote and unreal to me as the figures in tapestries. (114)

> Before college, the only people I had ever known who were interested in art or music or literature, the only ones who read books, the only ones who ever seemed to enjoy a sense of ease and grace were the mothers and daughters. . . . By comparison with the narrow, iron-clad days of fathers, there was an expansiveness, I thought, in the days of mothers. (115)

> But if I had been asked, as a boy, to choose between tending a baby and tending a machine, I think I would have chosen the baby. (Having now tended both, I know I would choose the baby.)
> So I was baffled when the women at college accused me and my sex of having cornered the world's pleasures. I think something like my bafflement has been felt by other boys (and by girls as well) who grew up in dirt-poor farm country, in mining country, in black ghettos, in the shadow of factories, in Third World nations. (116)

In addition to thus stressing the tentative nature of the essay, Sanders also includes an extended example of the inwardly directed skepticism characteristic of essayists in general, pursuing the kind of self-critique that undoes his old suppositions. In discussing his highly positive boyhood perspective on the "expansiveness" of the lives of mothers, Sanders writes that

> They went to see neighbors, to shop in town, to run errands at school, at the library, at church. No doubt, had I looked harder at their lives, I would have envied them less. It was not my fate to become a woman, so it was easier for me to see the graces. . . .

> I didn't see, then, what a prison a house could be, since houses seemed to me brighter, handsomer places than any factory. I did not realize—because such things were never spoken of—how often women suffered from men's bullying. (115–16)

Sanders's "experiment in making sense of things" ends much the way it began. The last two paragraphs of his essay embody a clash of contrasting viewpoints or orientations, an inconclusive dialogic collision between his perspective and that of the women he met in college that attempts to more fully and deeply address the whole of the problem of the men we carry in our minds, that attempts some kind of hybridization or unification of visions, but that yet must remain unresolved:

> When the women I met at college thought about the joys and privileges of men, they did not carry in their minds the sort of men I had known in my childhood. They thought of their fathers, who were bankers, physicians, architects, stockbrokers, the big wheels of the big cities. . . . These fathers made decisions that mattered. They ran the world.
>
> The daughters of such men wanted to share in this power, this glory. So did I. They yearned for a say over their future, for jobs worthy of their abilities, for the right to live in peace, unmolested, whole. Yes, I thought, yes yes. The difference between me and these daughters was that they saw me, because of my sex, as destined from birth to become like their fathers, and therefore as an enemy to their desires. But I knew better. I wasn't an enemy, in fact or in feeling. I was an ally. If I had known, then, how to tell them so, would they have believed me? Would they now? (116–17)

Sanders concludes with questions, a most fitting way to end an essay, since it accentuates the essential incompleteness of the essay, its open-endedness.

While our model makes Sanders's use of the characteristic methods of development in the essay seem familiar and simple, it can also aid in our perception and comprehension of the novel, uncommon, and/or puzzling techniques we sometimes encounter in the work of professional essayists such as Gretel Ehrlich. Our model helps us understand how and why "The Source of a River,"

"Island," and "The Smooth Skull of Winter" (her challenging meditations on a hiking trip, her relationship with a particular piece of
land, and the nature of winter, respectively) work, for instance. But
let us look closely at "Looking for a Lost Dog," in which a physical
search for a lost pet induces and parallels Ehrlich's mental explorations, an essay in which Ehrlich employs a new and subtle technique I call "echoing" along with the other, more familiar methods
of development we have been discussing. Let us begin, however,
with the familiar. "Looking for a Lost Dog" fuses a number of discourses, weaves together a number of areas of knowledge, the heteroglossia presenting the reader with unsorted wholeness of the
writer's experience. Ehrlich glides easily from quotations from
Thoreau to homey anecdotes about the lost dog to metacognitive
musings on human narcissism and perception to the philosophy of
a Hungarian friend to a discussion of Navajo diviners to poetic
descriptions of nature ("the sky hangs over like a frown") to an
Eskimo explanation of weather to the confession of what she longs
for in life. "Looking for a Lost Dog" is also clearly structured according to chrono-logic, which is indicated in a variety of obvious and
subtle ways. One obvious signal is that the essay uses mostly present tense verbs. The present tense verbs emphasize the progressive
nature of cognition—enact the linear order in which Ehrlich's
thoughts are developing over time—and underscore the notion of
the essay as a discursive "becoming" over time:

> I'm walking and looking and listening for him, though there is
> no trail, no clue, no direction to the search. Whimsically, I head
> north toward the falls. . . . A raven creaks overhead, flies to the
> left, glides toward a panel of white water splashing over a ledge,
> and comes out cawing. (4)

> I walk and walk. Past the falls, through a pass, toward a larger,
> rowdier creek. The sky goes black. In the distance, the snow on
> Owl Creek Mountain glares. . . . A string of cottonwoods whose
> tender leaves are the color of limes pulls me downstream. I
> come to the meadow with the abandoned apple orchard. (5)

> I see a dog track, or is it a coyote's? I get down on my hands
> and knees to sniff out a scent. What am I doing? I entertain pre-
> posterous expectations of myself. (6)

> To my left a towering cottonwood is lunatic with bird song.
> Under it, I'm a listening post while its great, gray trunk—like a
> baton—heaves its green symphony into the air. (7)

Another patent way Ehrlich indicates the essay's basis in chrono-logic is through explicit references to the present moment. Her repeated uses of the words *now* and *today* seem to allow her to present her thoughts as they occurred to her on the spot and help to highlight the inescapable linearity of time:

> Today I'm filled with longings. . . . Now I'm following a game trail
> up a sidehill. . . . Now I sniff the ground and smell only dirt. . . .
> Those days, like today, I walk with a purpose but no destination.
> . . . Today it is enough to make a shadow. (6–7)

Ehrlich's most obvious indication of the essay's use of chrono-logic, however, is the highly self-conscious transition she uses to bridge the fourth and fifth paragraphs of the essay. Realizing that the temporally grounded, linear associations she has been making over the last two paragraphs (about human narcissism and her Hungarian friend's philosophy) may have wandered too far afield, she returns to her ostensible subject by saying, "But back to the dog" (4). This phrase simply but powerfully suggests that as each thought presents itself to Ehrlich, so she presents it to us, that although the chrono-logical sequence of her thoughts is sometimes messy and discontinuous, the text represents her cognition in its progress.

But Ehrlich also uses a novel and more subtle way of signaling the essay's chrono-logical basis. Through her use of what I call "echoing," her slight alteration and unobtrusive repetition of phrases and ideas from one section of the text in later sections, Ehrlich shows us that her essay is based not on random or free association, but rather on the strict logic of association over time, that she does not lose the subject, but rather always provides a "sufficient word" to keep our eye on it through her exploratory wanderings. In the first half of the essay, for instance, Ehrlich repeatedly echoes upon the notion of hearing. It begins in an anecdote about the lost dog, then resounds in her consideration of human narcissism, and then reverberates again in her discussion of her Hungarian friend's philosophy:

> While moving cows once, the dog fell in a hole and disap-
> peared. We heard him whining but couldn't see where he had
> gone. I crouched down, put my ear to the ground, and crawled
> toward the whines.
>
> It's no wonder human beings are so narcissistic. The ways
> our ears are constructed, we can hear only what is right next to
> us or else the internal monologue inside. I've taken to cupping
> my hands behind my ears—mulelike—and pricking them all the
> way forward or back to hear what's happened or what's ahead.
>
> "Life is polyphonic," a Hungarian friend in her eighties
> said. She was a child prodigy from Budapest who had soloed on
> the violin in Paris and Berlin by the time she was twelve.
> "Childishly, I once thought hearing had mostly to do with
> music. Now that I'm too old to play the fiddle, I know it has to
> do with the great suspiration of life everywhere."
>
> But back to the dog. I'm walking and looking and listen-
> ing for him. (3–4)

The echoes on hearing continue a little later in the essay, through
her discussion of Navajo diviners and after, Ehrlich always pointing
us back to the subject of the lost dog through what otherwise might
be construed as tangential ramblings:

> When I asked one such diviner what it was like when she was in
> a trance, she said, "Lots of noise, but noise that's hard to hear."
>
> Near the falls the ground flattens out into a high-altitude
> valley before the mountain rises vertically. The falls roar, but
> they are overgrown with spruce, pine, and willow, and the clos-
> er I get, the harder it is to see them. Perhaps that is how it will
> be in my search for the dog. (4–5)

The echo on hearing is voiced one last time, helping to chrono-logically integrate Ehrlich's digression on her longings with the rest of
the essay. She says, "Passions of all sorts struggle soundlessly, or else,
like the falls, they are all noise but can't be seen" (6). Ehrlich also
uses an echo on "sauntering" to provide another chrono-logical "sufficient word" to help the text cohere. This echo begins in Ehrlich's
musing on the nature of human perception, rings again in a quotation from Thoreau, and yet again in a description of animal tracks:

As with viewing the falls, we can lose sight of what is too close, and the struggle between impulse and reason, passion and logic, occurs as we saunter from distant to close-up views.

The feet move; the mind wanders. In his essay on walking, Thoreau said, "The saunterer, in the good sense, is no more vagrant than the meandering river, which is all the while sedulously seeking the shortest course to the sea."

It's a mosaic of tracks—elk and deer, rabbit and bird. If city dwellers could imprint cement as they walked, it would look this way: tracks overlap, go backward and forward like peregrine saunterings of the mind. (6)

Finally, Ehrlich finishes "Looking for a Lost Dog" in a manner that is quite appropriate, considering the open-ended, nontotalizing nature of the essay. Not only is the ending inconclusive—she does not find the dog, nor even come to a mental or physical resting place—but rather ambiguous as well: "I walk and walk, from the falls, over Grouse Hill, to the dry wash. Today it is enough to make a shadow" (7).

Our model's ability to explain the techniques used by professional essayists, to make us comfortable with the complex developments of their texts and help us to penetrate the intricacies of the more adventurous and dense texts, can best be seen, however, through an examination of the work of Joseph Epstein. Epstein, I think, is one of the best and most consistent essayists working today, and we might look at his "A Few Kind Words for Envy," "Tea and Antipathy," or "What's So Funny?" (explorations of the natures of envy, hate, and humor, respectively) as superior examples of the form. But let us take his "What Is Vulgar?" as our example to critique, in which Epstein essays the concept of vulgarity. That this text embodies an uncertain exploration, that it enacts a quest or search for new knowledge is apparent in its title, a question Epstein explicitly reiterates three times in the text (126—twice, 131), but implicitly returns to throughout the course of the writing. This text, moreover, is a prime example of the heteroglossia one can find in an essay. Epstein transgresses disciplinary and discursive boundaries, weaving together a multitude of voices, juxtaposing a wide variety of discourses and viewpoints in an attempt to offer us as full a picture as possible of the many complex qualities—the whole human problem—of vulgarity. In this piece, the reader hears

Epstein's words about vulgarity, of course, but also hears the voices of his Uncle Jake (128), some unnamed writers and editors, a coat salesman (130), *The Oxford English Dictionary*, William Hazlitt (131), French art historian Albert Dasnoy, Max Beerbohm (132), Matthew Arnold, Lionel Trilling, Cyril Connolly (133), a woman from a moving company, an unnamed friend (134), Barbara Walters (136), the Aspen Institute for Humanistic Studies, John Keats (137), "an old *Punch* cartoon" (138), a young woman in an "old joke," a Chicago politician, a Harvard philosophy professor (139), Vladimir Nabokov (140), and Oscar Wilde (141). Epstein also displays the characteristic inwardly-directed skepticism of the essayist through his use of the kinds of tentative diction with which we are now familiar: *seems, might have, appears, I (don't) think, I assume, I suppose, so far as I know, probably, I am not sure, perhaps, I suspect:*

> [I]t somehow seems wrong to call anyone vulgar who is good-hearted. But more to the point, I don't think that if you had accused him of being vulgar, he would have known what the devil you were talking about. . . . "Wulgar," he might have responded . . . "so vat's dis wulgar?" (127–28)

> There is, similarly, over the attached garage, a sun deck whose only access appears to be through a bathroom window. The house seems to have been built on the aesthetic formula of functionlessness follows formlessness. (128)

> [T]he family that lives in this house no doubt loves it; most probably they feel that they have a real showplace. Their house, I assume, gives them a large measure of happiness. Yet why does my calling their home vulgar also give me such a measure of happiness? I suppose it is because vulgarity can be so amusing—other people's vulgarity, that is. (129)

> So far as I know I have been called vulgar three times. (129)

> I am not sure I have a clear picture of vulgar thumbs, but if it is all the same, I would just as soon not have them. (130)

> Such seems to me roughly the social history of the word vulgar. (132)

> Perhaps the only safe thing to be said about charm is that if you think you have it, you can be fairly certain that you don't. (134)

Furthermore, Epstein's essay is undoubtedly based in chrono-logic, the author offering us numerous explicit references indicating that the text tracks the present-tense and progressive structuring of his thinking, the sometimes messy, linearly sequential process of his getting-to-know:

> You want vulgar, I am inclined to exclaim, I'll show you vulgar: the house I have just described is vulgar, patently, palpably, pluperfectly vulgar. . . . Yet as I described that house, I noted two contradictory feelings in myself: how pleasant it is to point out someone else's vulgarity, and yet the fear that calling someone else vulgar may itself be slightly vulgar. (129)

> Vulgarity, it begins to appear, is often in the eye of the beholder. What is more, it comes in so many forms. It is so multiple and so complex—so multiplex. There are vulgarities of taste, of manner, of mind, of spirit. There are whole vulgar ages—the Gilded Age in the United States, for one, at least to hear Mark Twain and Henry Adams tell it. (Is our own age another?) To compound the complication there is even likable vulgarity. (133)

> It would be helpful in drawing a definitional bead on the word vulgar if one could determine its antonym. But I am not sure that it has an antonym. Refined? I think not. Sophisticated? Not really. Elegant? Nope. Charming? Close, but I can think of charming vulgarians. . . . If vulgarity cannot be defined by its antonym, from the rear so to say, examples may be more to the point. I once heard a man describe a woman thus. . . . (134)

> Coming at things from a different angle, I imagine myself in session with a psychologist, playing the word association game. "Vulgar," he says, "quick, name ten items you associate with the word vulgar." "Okay," I say, "here goes:
>
> 1. Publicity
>
> 2. The Oscar Awards . . . ."

> This would not, I suspect, be everyone's list. Looking it over, I see that, of the ten items, several are linked with one another. But let me inquire into what made me choose the items I did. (135–36)

Reviewing my list and attempting to account for the reasons why I have chosen the items on it, I feel I have a firmer sense of what I think vulgar. Exhibitionism, obviousness, pretentiousness, self-congratulation, self-importance, hypocrisy, overconfidence—these seem to me qualities at the heart of vulgarity in our day. (138)

Finally, like many of the other writers we have examined, Epstein, too, ends his essay inconclusively, speculating, equivocating: "*Vulgar! Vulgar! Vulgar!* The word might save us all" (141).

In this chapter we have moved from the safe and insulated land of abstraction to live and work in the real world. We have repeatedly held up the theoretical construction we have been developing over the last two chapters to the light of concrete phenomena, held up our model of the essay to the work of seven real writers. Our model seems to meet the test: it apparently has the power to help explain and help us understand the practice of a variety of contemporary essayists. But the realm of professional writers and literature is still a comparatively insulated and safe place to play. What remains to be done, of course, is to take our model and make the final move into one of the most uncontrollable and problematic of realities, the writing classroom. In the next chapter, we make that move, addressing how the essay can dwell in the world of student writers and student writing.

# Chapter 5

# The Essay in the Composition Classroom

## *OR*

## Adventures in Writing

Running uphill. Swimming against the tide. Teaching and writing the essay in the composition classroom. All these activities involve going against the flow, battling against powerful, "natural," inescapable forces. And all three offer us the promise of our eventually earning attractive rewards for engaging in the struggle: new, more powerful vantage points; fluidity and freedom of movement; stronger, more active, more flexible positions from which to work. Teaching and writing the essay in the composition class is a challenging endeavor, but one that my students and I have found is well worth the difficulties involved. It requires both teacher and students to rethink almost everything they know about writing in academia. This required rethinking is both the most important outcome and the greatest difficulty of teaching the essay in the composition class. Teaching the essay rather than the thesis/support form requires both the teacher and students to leave the safety of known roles and ways of thinking and to occupy new, perhaps uncomfortable positions. As my student Mickey asked me once, "You're trying to undermine everything I've ever been taught, aren't you? Am I supposed to just forget everything I've learned about writing?" To which I had to reply, "Well, yes. For now." Teaching the essay forces both teacher and student into true adventures in teaching and learning, into risk-filled encounters with the unknown whose outcomes are also unknown. In this chapter I report on the explorations my students and I have made into teaching and learning to write the essay in our composition classes. I will discuss the methods I use to prepare my students to write this distinctive form, explain the prewriting processes I have created and suggest they follow, examine three resulting student essays, and report on students' responses to the presence of the essay in their composition classroom.

## PREPARING TO WRITE

The essay is in many ways antithetical to the thesis/support form that our students are thoroughly steeped in, both in terms of the written product and the writing processes needed to compose that product. Thus, it was worthwhile to spend a significant amount of time preparing my students to write essays through careful presentation and explanation of the assignment, through preparatory activities designed to lead students gradually into the unusual kinds of thinking and writing processes they would need to employ, and through the study of a model essay.

The assignment sheet I handed out to students strove repeatedly to underscore the distinctive natures of the essay, its radical departures from the kind of writing that has almost always been required of them in school. It was designed to introduce them to the many ways they would need to be different thinkers and writers in order to compose successful essays. Moreover, the assignment sheet attempted to show students that many "quotable" authorities have notions about the form that are quite similar to mine. In this way, I hoped quickly to demonstrate to students that my ideas about and assignment of the essay could not be dismissed as simply the idiosyncratic whims of this one particular (and especially off-the-wall) English professor, but instead enjoyed substantial critical support. The full references for those people cited in the assignment can be found in Appendix B.

# Writing Assignment—The Essay

What is an essay? It is probably unlike anything you have written before in school. The word *essay* comes from the French verb *essai*, "to try, to attempt," which, in turn, is based on the Latin verb *exagium*, "to weigh," or figuratively, "to weigh alternatives." The essay is tentative, incomplete, inconclusive. It does *not* try to prove a point. It does *not* try to persuade the reader to adopt a certain point of view. An exact definition of the essay has eluded writers and critics since the birth of the form over 400 years ago, but here is what some of them have said:

The essay's "purpose is not to convey information, although it may do that as well, but rather to tell the story of the author's thinking and experience."

—Chris Anderson, "Literary Nonfiction and Composition"

The "form of the essay . . . acknowledges uncertainty and ambiguity. . . . [T]he essay is by definition an attempt. . . . It doesn't pretend that everything is clear and worked out."

—Chris Anderson, "Hearsay Evidence and Second-Class Citizenship"

The "essay is the closest thing we have, on paper, to a record of the individual mind at work and play . . . [is] the spectacle of a single consciousness making sense of a part of the chaos" of experience. The essay works by "following the zigzag motions of the inquisitive mind. . . . The writing of an essay is like finding one's way through a forest without being quite sure what game you are chasing, what landmark you are seeking." An "essay is a weighing out, an inquiry into the value, meaning, and true nature of experience; it is a private experiment carried out in public."

—Scott Russell Sanders, "The Singular First Person"

Essays "are experiments in making sense of things."

—Scott Russell Sanders, *The Paradise of Bombs*

"[E]ssays do not march smartly forward. . . . The itinerancy of the writing, its own being in motion, generates and arranges thoughts, and they take form from their own movement, not their mass." Essayists "think less *about* writing than *through* it: they watch it unfold and grasp its meaning as it emerges."

—William Howarth

The essay does not seek "to fix, to define, to delimit, so that clarity and precision are perfect within a certain scope," nor does it press "toward assent, conformity, submission, so that force of expression and argument are translated into belief and action." Rather, the essay "tries to open, to stimulate, to inject multiple overtones so that insight is expanded and pleasure is aroused. This opening, stimulating, multiplying vision is useful *because* it is opening, stimulating, multiplying, not because it is practical."

—Howard Brashers

The essayist writes "not so much with the hope of gaining adherence as of stimulating and disturbing thought."

—Walter Beale

The "genuine essayist . . . is the writer who thinks his way through the essay—and so comes out where perhaps he did not wish to. . . . He uses the essay as an open form—as a way of thinking things out for himself, as a way of discovering *what* he thinks. . . . [A]n essay is not meant to be the 'whole truth,' the sociological truth, the abstract and neutral truth . . . [It is instead] an expression of the self thinking. . . . In an essay, it is not the thought that counts but the experience we get of the writer's thought; not the self, but the self thinking."

—Alfred Kazin

Essays are "not reports of objective truth but explorations of [the writer's] own attitudes and thoughts. . . . That struggle, that *essaying* to clarify the writer's views, should really be included in the definition of an essay."

—Douglas Hunt

An "essay is the shape of an 'inner life' in the act of *reaching* a decision." The "essay give[s] shape to the process preceding conviction."

—Thomas Harrison

"The essay makes visible the patterns of an individual's thoughts. It allows us to see the process of contemplation that results in understanding that in turn leads to action."

—Pamela Klass Mittlefehldt

In an essay, we do not see "writing as a demonstration of understanding—after a writer has worked through his or her uncertainty," but rather see "writing as a means of achieving understanding, an achievement that demands the willingness to surrender instrumental control."

—Kurt Spellmeyer

An essay "neither . . . advances an argument . . . nor is . . . informative in the sense of reducing the reader's uncertainty about a topic or of supplying fresh data."

—W. Ross Winterowd

The essay's "extreme indefiniteness is partly inherent in the nature of the thing: etymologically, the word *essay* indicates something tentative, so there is a justification for the conception of incompleteness and want of system."

—Hugh Walker

When writing an essay, we "should start without any fixed idea of where we are going to spend the night, or when we propose to come back; the journey is everything."

—Virginia Woolf

"The essayist is not sure of what he is going to find, which accounts for the digressive form of his work. . . . [T]he essay is also a well-rounded piece of composition . . . in which the artist's point of view is constantly shifting while the object of perception remains what it is. . . . [T]he essayist is sure of the result, namely an expansion of his scope of vision, which he seeks to communicate. . . . [T]he goal of the essayist is not truth in its finality, but wisdom as the sought-after prize of the search for truth. . . . [T]he discourser expresses himself at fits and starts, following the meanderings of his own thought in its attempt to describe a mercurial subject. . . . [T]he extremely digressive form of the essay . . . follows its winding course as the various themes run into each other almost imperceptibly. . . . Each peripheral theme is an outgrowth of an idea previously expressed rather than an additional point introduced for the purpose of maintaining the argumentative discussion on its determined course. . . . [T]he essay itself is the image of structured thought in motion. . . . [T]he essay ceases to be an essay when it can be predicted."

—J. C. Guy Cherica

"Rarely does the . . . essay set out hiking boots afoot and compass in hand; instead it meanders. . . . Instead of driving hard to prove a point, the essay saunters, letting the writer follow the vagaries of his own willful curiosity. Instead of reaching conclusions, the essay ruminates and wonders. Rather than being right or informative, it is thoughtful."

—Samuel F. Pickering Jr.

"The hero of the essay is the author in the act of thinking things out, feeling and finding a way; it is the mind in the marvels and miseries of its makings, in the *work* of the imagination, the search for form. . . . [T]he essay interests itself in the narration of ideas—in their *unfolding*—and the conflict between philosophies or other points of view becomes a drama in its hands. . . . The essayist speaks one mind truly, but that is far from speaking the truth. . . . The essay . . . turns round and round upon its topic, exposing this aspect and that; proposing possibilities, reciting opinions, disposing of prejudice and even of the simple truth itself—as too undeveloped, not yet of an interesting age."

—William H. Gass

"The essayist plays cat-and-mouse with his subject, circling it, toying with it, only dispatching it after the life has gone out of it. . . . All essays share the characteristic of indirection. Rather than a straightforward recitation of the available facts, the essayist usually takes a more roundabout approach. . . . The rambling structure of . . . [an essay] is really a form in its own right. . . . [The essayist] does not pour his substance into a hollow form but carves out a form that is inseparable from the object he produces. . . . The essay is never the final word on a subject . . . [because it] recognizes the fallibility of human understanding, the mutability of human affairs. . . . [E]ssays advertise themselves to be fluid works-in-progress."

—David W. Chapman

The essay "is a literary trial balloon, an informal stringing together of ideas to see what happens . . . and it has no standard method."

—O. B. Hardison Jr.

"To essay is to experiment, to try out, to test—even one's own cognitive powers and limits. The word connotes a tentative, groping method of experience, with all its attendant risks and pleasures. . . . Entering the road laid down by tradition, the essayist is not content to pursue faithfully the prescribed itinerary. Instinctively, he (or she) swerves to explore the surrounding terrain, to track a stray detail or anomaly, even at the risk of wrong turns, dead ends, and charges of trespassing. From the standpoint of more 'responsible' travelers, the resulting path will look skewed and arbitrary."

—R. Lane Kauffman

The "essay exploits the uncertainty of the writer's situation, transforming uncertainty into a fundamental quality of the essay form. . . . [T]he essay records the track of an individual mind exploring and resolving a problem. . . . [T]he essay must be open to a multiplicity of voices in order to become a means of understanding."

—Thomas E. Recchio

Working in the essay form "allows you to ramble in a way that reflects the mind at work. . . . [I]n an essay, the track of a person's thoughts struggling to achieve some understanding of a problem *is* the plot, is the adventure. The essayist must be willing to contradict himself . . . to digress, and even to end up in an opposite place from where he started. . . . The essay offers the chance to wrestle with one's own intellectual confusion."

—Phillip Lopate

There is nothing "resembling a standard essay: no set style, no set length, no set subject matter. . . . A certain modesty of intention resides in the essay. It is a modesty inherent in the French verb that gives the form its name—*essayer:* to try, to attempt, to taste, to try on, to assay. However many words the essayist may avail himself of, he instinctively knows, or ought to know, that the last word cannot be his."

—Joseph Epstein

The Essay *is* the act of thinking through writing. . . . The essay not merely allows for but actually celebrates—indeed is characterized by—surprise, interpretation, meandering, and slow discovery." We should note "the open-endedness, skepticism, and critical spirit that characterizes the essay form: it resists easy definition (of itself, its subject matter, its 'conclusions,') avoids coming to rest in some positive truth or absolute knowledge, remains wary of systems and systematizing, and not only acknowledges but also embraces and even celebrates . . . uncertainty and ambiguity." The essay is the act of "narrating a journey toward some understanding of a textual, personal, or political problem."

—G. Douglas Atkins

"Every essay is the only one of its kind. There are no rules for making beginnings, or middles, or endings; it is a harder, more original discipline than that. . . . Setting out to write an essay, you have no predetermined course to follow, no generic mold to fill or rules of composition to draw on." The essay "takes its characteristic outings, has a look around, rambles on in its multiplicity of voices about this and that . . . [and] stays closer to the largely tentative movements by which we make our individual ways through time. . . . [T]he route is not planned beforehand. . . . The route is mapped in the going. And except for a general familiarity with the terrain to be walked, there's no anticipating what will come your way; you set out to see what is out there to be seen." The essay is "not exhaustive or systematic, never more than an attempt, a go at something that might be tried again on another occasion, in quite a different way. Every essay is, thus, necessarily incomplete. . . . [I]t obeys no compulsion to tie up what may look like loose ends, [and] tolerates a fair amount of inconclusiveness and indeterminacy."

—Lydia Fakundiny

———————

     The students and I read through this assignment sheet carefully, aloud, and then engage in a thorough discussion of what we have read. This discussion usually centers on the various images for the essay invoked by these authors: journeying, walking, meandering, hunting, and so on. [Please see the Afterword for an in-depth examination of images of the essay and their import.] I have found that foregrounding these images at the outset offers students a facile place to begin reconstructing their notions of the essay and essaying. Nonetheless, in the course of this initial discussion, it is usually apparent that many students are not only dumbfounded by the unusual nature of the essay, but frightened by the prospect of composing in this alien form. I try to directly address and alleviate this confusion and fear during the next class period by having the students engage in what I called the "Mellow" activity, which utilizes Langston Hughes's poem "Mellow" to introduce students to the concept of chrono-logic as an alternative structure for cognition and composition. This exercise takes up an entire class period and allows the students some unhurried, ungraded, rudimentary practice in the thinking and writing behaviors fundamental to essaying; it offers them a nonthreatening entrée into the foreign ways of thinking and writing that an essay requires for its construction. What follows is a reconstructed transcript of how I presented the "Mellow" activity in one class and how two of my students, Cari and Bret, responded.

*Heilker:*   Take out a clean piece of paper and draw a line down the center of the paper from top to bottom. For the first half of this exercise we'll write only in the left-hand column. We'll use the right-hand column later. I'm going to read you a poem. What do you think it will be about? If you are not sure, then guess, speculate. Take your time and jot down your answer or answers at the top of the left-hand column. When you are through, draw a line under your answer all the way across the paper from the left margin to the right one.

*Cari:*     Romance

*Bret:*     Life, relationships, love

*Heilker:*   The title of the poem is "Mellow" [writes title on chalkboard]. Now that you know the title of this poem is "Mellow," *now* what do you think it will be about? Again, if you aren't sure, then guess or speculate, jotting down your answer or answers in the left-hand column under your first response. As before, when you are done with this response, draw a line under it from one side of the paper to the other.

*Cari:*     A relaxing scene in spring

*Bret:*     Yellow, tranquility, calm

*Heilker:*   Now I'll read you the first two lines of the poem. They are: "Into the laps / of black celebrities" [writes lines on chalkboard]. Now that you know that the title of the poem is "Mellow" and the first two lines are "Into the laps / of black celebrities," *now* what do you think it is about? Once more, write down your answer in the left-hand column under your first two responses and draw a line under it when you are done.

*Cari:*     How celebrities spend their time relaxing with their pets

*Bret:*     Jazz

*Heilker:*   Okay, the next two lines of the poem are "white girls fall / like pale plums from a tree" [writes lines on chalkboard]. You probably know the drill by now. Now that you know the third and fourth lines, *now* what do you think the poem is about? Write down your answer in the left-hand column and draw a line under it. We'll do this two more times.

*Cari:*      Black celebrities and white fans lusting after them

*Bret:*      Dancers

*Heilker:*   The fifth and sixth lines of the poem are "beyond a high tension wall / wired for killing" [writes lines on chalkboard]. Now that you know the next two lines of the poem, *now* what do you think it is about?

*Cari:*      White wives who come visit black husbands in jail

*Bret:*      Prison camp in Germany WWII

*Heilker:*   The last two lines of the poem are "which makes it / more thrilling" [writes lines on chalkboard]. Now that you know the last two lines and thus the entire text of the poem—

> Mellow
> Into the laps
> of black celebrities
> white girls fall
> like pale plums from a tree
> beyond a high tension wall
> wired for killing
> which makes it
> more thrilling

—*now* what do you think it is about? Write your answer in the left column.

*Cari:*      White wives who are proud their black husbands are in jail—a matter of anti-racism and attention

*Bret:*      Rape

*Heilker:*   That completes the first part of the exercise. Good work! Now we'll be working in the right-hand column, in the boxes that correspond to your responses in the left-hand column.

Okay, when I said I was going to read you a poem, *why* did you put down what you put down at the top of the left-hand column? When all you knew was that it was going to be a poem, why did you think it would be about "X," that is, whatever you wrote down? If you're not sure why you said what you said in the left column, then guess or speculate why you did. Put your answer or answers in the box at the top of the right-hand column.

Cari:      *Romance.* I wanted it to be that way.

Bret:      *Life, relationships, love.* Because that is what poems are usually about. What I perceive "poems" as.

Heilker:    Now, when I told you the title of the poem was "Mellow," why did you put down what you put down in the left-hand column? Why did you think it would be about "X"? Jot down your answer or answers in the top box available in the right-hand column.

Cari:      *A relaxing scene in spring.* I wanted it to be that way and the title reminded me of a relaxing day in spring.

Bret:      *Yellow, tranquility, calm.* I relate these words to mellow, almost synonymously. It seems the poem would go with this theme.

Heilker:    You probably have guessed where this is going by now. When I read you the first two lines of the poem, "Into the laps / of black celebrities," why did you write what you wrote in the left column? Why did you think it would be about "X"? Again, put your responses in the corresponding box in the right column.

Cari:      *How celebrities spend their time relaxing with their pets.* I thought pets was a safe idea about which they were writing.

Bret:      *Jazz.* When I think of black celebrities, I think of Jazz.

Heilker:    Now, when I read you the next two lines, "white girls fall / like pale plums from a tree," why did you write what you wrote in the left-hand column. Why did you think it would be about "X"? Put your answer in the corresponding box.

Cari:      *Black celebrities and their white fans lusting after them.* I thought it had to do with transracial relationships—exploiting them.

Bret:      *Dancers.* I picture girls falling as dancers, almost ballerinas flowing on stage.

Heilker:    When I then read you the fifth and sixth lines of the poem, "beyond a high tension wall / wired for killing," why did you write what you wrote in the left column? Why did you think it was about "X"?

Cari:      *White wives who come visit their black husbands in jail.* The word "wall" made me think of jail.

Bret:      *Prison camp in Germany WWII.* High tension wall—wired for killing reminds me of Jewish prisoner camps in Germany.

Heilker:   When I next read you the last two lines of the poem, "which makes it / more thrilling," why did you put what you put in the left column? Why did you think it was about "X"?

Cari:      *White wives who are proud their black husbands are in jail—a matter of anti-racism and attention.* I thought it was a sick ending if it was about what I thought it was about. Only sick people would be proud their husband was in jail—and used that for attention.

Bret:      *Rape.* Thrilling . . . for trapping women, makes it more challenging, almost too exciting, almost dangerous, rape.

Heilker:   Okay, having gone through this process and looking over everything we have, the full text of the poem and all your responses in both the left and right columns, at the bottom of the page, in two or three complete sentences, write down what you *now* think the poem *means.* Take your time.

Cari:      I hope this poem doesn't mean what I think it does. I think the title is supposed to be ironic in that it's just the opposite of what the poem says—I guess I still stick with what I think.

Bret:      I believe that the poem is about the killing of women in the German concentration camps. It is explained here as a game that is played behind the walls of high tension.

Heilker:   Again, really good work! And congratulations! You've just essayed this poem. You've just done all the essential things you need to do in order to write an essay. The two columns and couple of sentences you have before you tell the story of your thinking about this poem. They provide a record of your mind at work as it attempted to make sense of information I gave you. They offer you a map of the zigzag-ging motions of your mind as you journeyed from uncertainty to some kind of understanding about the poem. They narrate the explo-ration of your thinking, your unfolding struggle to clarify what you thought. The left-hand column details *how* your thinking about the poem evolved over time, while the right-hand column attempts to explain *why* it evolved that way. And the couple of sentences at the bottom of the page are the kind of temporary, tentative, inconclusive understanding you typically come to at the end of an essay. Give yourself a pat on the back.

For those of you who are interested, this poem was written by Langston Hughes in the 1930s, a black poet associated with a movement called the Harlem Renaissance. Now, how and why does *that* change your thinking about his poem?

For homework, I would like you to rework these two columns and couple of sentences of notes into a few coherent paragraphs that clearly and coherently tell the story of how and why your thinking about this poem changed over time. In other words, for homework I would like you to quickly draft your first essay.

---

## Cari's Homework

At the beginning of the exercise I thought the poem would be what I wanted it to be. Romance was on my mind at the time and I wanted to hear a poem on it. After seeing the title "Mellow," I thought of what I thought mellow would be to me. Trees, water, sun, relaxing atmosphere, and silence are all things that remind me of mellow.

Then, when I saw the first two lines, my mind ran away with me, but I tried to find a "safe" idea. Celebrities and pets seemed to be a very "tame" answer and I hoped it would be that way. After the next couple of lines, I thought it had to do with transracial relations. I remembered that this class is about controversial topics, so then I thought this poem was about controversial, transracial relations. The next thought I had was that the walls with wire to kill were walls around a jail and white women were coming to see black men.

In the last lines of the poem, I was trying to fit what the lines said into my thoughts on what the poem was going to be about. The only thing I could come up with was that the white women were proud (in a sickening way) that their black husbands were in jail to get attention. This is a terrible thought to me but I couldn't think of anything else. But I did know the title was supposed to be ironic.

---

## Bret's Homework

In the exercise in class today my opinion of the "idea" changed dramatically. *Poem*—Life, relationships, love. Because that is what I usually relate poems to in general. *Mellow*—I relate this to yellow, calm, tranquility, because they are synonymous in my view and would go well with a poem. When I think of black celebrities, I think of Jazz. When I think of white girls falling, I think of dancers.

Here is where I was misled in my own interpretation of the poem. "High tension wall . . . wired for killing." All I could think about was the Jewish prisoner camps in Germany. "Which makes it more thrilling." Women . . . Dark, black, well . . . for some reason my thoughts were provoked to rape. The trapping of women, which makes it all the more thrilling, rape? Well, to say the least, I was confused, had no idea what the poem was *really* about. I had only my interpretations.

I learned what the poem was really about when I learned about the author. I was put back on track. Jazz, white women. The author was a black writer in the Jazz age. That enabled me to read the poem through his eyes and interpret it the way he felt it should have been interpreted.

It is difficult to interpret someone else's thoughts if you don't know where the thoughts are coming from.

————————

In the same way that students find the concept of chrono-logic challenging and their initial attempts at producing a chrono-logically structured text disconcerting, they likewise have difficulty dealing with the essay's anti-scholastic hybridization of multiple discourses. For example, the idea of their using "I" in their essays, using their own voices, incorporating their own undisguised personal feelings and opinions in their academic writing, strikes many of them as heretical, an impossibility. The best way through this resistance, I have found, is to present my students with a widely used metaphor for the essay: I suggest that they conceive of the essay as a "conversation" the writer has with her sources and herself.

As preparation for their attempts at textual dialogue, I have students practice by having "conversations" with a series of quotations over three or four class meetings. These exercises are designed to give students the opportunity to come to see themselves and their discourses (their unmasked feelings, opinions, and voices) not as somehow unworthy of mention, not as somehow below and subservient to the voices of the authorities in their sources (nor above them as their capricious and imperious masters), but rather as equals. These "conversations" with quotations allow students to both practice using their own voices in an academic setting and to practice engaging with a variety of other voices on a level plane.

Before their first "conversation" with a quotation, I ask students to brainstorm as a group on the question, "What happens in a conversation? What do you do in a conversation?" One class responded as follows:

| | |
|---|---|
| listen | question |
| debate | get to know the other person |
| comment | yell/scream |
| put in your ideas | complain |
| agree | gossip |
| disagree | plan |
| doubt | curse |
| wonder | bully |
| compromise | tell stories |
| cry | flirt/seduce |
| flatter | challenge |
| argue | threaten |
| convince | ridicule |
| exchange information | guess |
| laugh | analyze |
| greet | tell jokes |
| get new ideas | |

Next, as a preface to each of their "conversations" with a quotation, I ask students to imagine that they are sitting in the cafeteria one day, just eating their lunch, and their good friend, the quoted speaker, comes in, sits down across the table from them, and says, "You know, I've been thinking." I ask them to imagine that they reply, "Oh really? What about?" and that their friend responds to this question with the quotation. Their job, after listening to the quotation, is to continue the conversation. The exercise works well. Students seem to enjoy engaging their voices with those of quotable authorities. Some examples:

**"In politics, if you want someone to make a speech, ask a man. If you want something done, ask a woman."** —*Margaret Thatcher*

"Margaret, Margaret, dear. As true as this may be, it is a no-no. This is one of those things you can whisper to a confidant or friend but never say publicly. It reveals an obviously sexist view of things. As a political leader, you have to show an example. It's like telling a bigoted joke—as innocent or truthful as it may sound, it widens the gap."

—Diana

"Excuse me?! I think you're crazy. I'm offended, not only for women but for people of both sexes. Stereotypes really piss me off. Personally, I don't think these activities exclude either sex. A woman can make a speech while a man can definitely get things done. You seem resentful of the tendency of people to pay attention to and follow a man. You seem to hold a high, powerful position that you have made much use of. It's unfortunate that someone of your stature is propagating these stereotypes."

—Barrett

"Are you comfortable with your position of leadership? Do you have animosity toward men in general? What makes you think men always talk and never get things done? I don't understand where you base your feelings of women getting things done."

—Jason H.

"Margaret, I think your aggressive personality and willingness to speak out have gotten you a long way. I applaud your obvious feminist stand and I can tell that what you said is mostly only a humorous and exaggerated observation. But I hope that's all it is. I would expect a person with your authority to be able to look past stereotypes. Although women have been degraded throughout time and perhaps men deserve their share, I don't think this is the way. Women should show their worthiness to be equal or superior by their actions, not by cheap comments."

—Janell

**"To understand means one must first come to doubt the certainty of one's own self and world."** —*James Baumlin*

"What do you mean? How can you ask me to doubt the only things that I know are true? Such as my self and my thoughts? "But are they true?" I can hear you asking. "Is anything certain?" No, I don't think so. *You can only live in today, reflect on yesterday, and hope for tomorrow.* (Hey! I like that. I wonder if someone else said that or if I made it up.) But to doubt myself—how is that going to make me understand!? Someone explain that to me. I've heard this sort of thing before, but I still don't know what people mean when they say it or what they want to hear or what I'm supposed to learn and figure out."

—Sarah

"Well, yes, I guess. I never thought about it that way before. Some things, though, we will never understand. What exactly do you mean when you say 'to doubt the certainty of one's own self and world'? I didn't think it was healthy to doubt yourself. Of course, I am always doubting myself. Do I personally understand things because I doubt myself? Not always. There are very few times when I actually understand what is going on in my life."

—Laura

"So you're saying be open-minded. Don't assume you know everything. Well, I agree. First, nothing's ever black and white. Second, people learn more by listening than talking. What are you, Jim? A talker or a listener? From what you said, I assume a listener. But if you're like most teachers, you're just a talker. Not just any talker, but one that talks at people. I agree with you. But, more importantly, what *are* you?"

—Kim

"I like that. I'm with you. I feel like that's what's happening to me now. I wonder about who I am sometimes. I guess I used to do it more than I do now. Now, I'm learning a lot about myself, my values and such, and I like who I am. I'm also wondering about the world around me. I'm only a sophomore, but I know in a couple of years I'll have to get out and tackle the world. It's scary. I don't yet understand everything, and maybe I never will. But I'm learning."

—Delicia

"Well, I don't think that doubting your own certainty is the only way to understand. Anyway, what are we trying to understand here? Understanding of ourselves? Of someone else's viewpoint? What? If we are dealing with something other than ourselves, then we don't have to doubt ourselves! We simply have to see the other viewpoint and the facts—to learn something we didn't know to begin with. That's how we understand. But as a general statement—I follow what you say—but I just don't think it's always the best thing to doubt yourself—even though if we do we can think of other possibilities than our own."

—Angela

---

**"Any system of education is a political way of maintaining or modifying the appropriation of discourses along with the knowledges and powers they carry."** —*Michel Foucault*

"Making such a blanket statement such as that goes to show how ignorant you are in the matter of education. And I hope after saying something like that you can at least provide something a little less stupid and radical to support it."

—Andrew

"That is so true! Because today the rich have the better schools, better education, better resources. They have the power because they went to the 'right' school. The poor of this country don't get a chance because no money is put into their schools. Think about it—we at TCU have to pay outrageous amounts for books, articles, supplements, supplies, models, etc. . . . just to get a *D* in a course."

—Cari

"That is so untrue! Have you personally experienced *every* education system? I didn't think so. Education systems, depending on what type, help expand people's knowledge, not control them. Anyone is allowed to say anything they want. There's no one or nothing that can control you or your power except you."

—Allison

"Don't get me wrong. I respect your views on education, but education to me means the best possible transfer of what we call knowledge. And though much knowledge is proven fact and is accepted by all, I think much knowledge is simply the popular beliefs and ideologies of those before us and taken as truth because it is no longer challenged."

—Chris

"That may be true, but you can't say *any* system of education is a political way of controlling who is allowed to say what and how they think. Some educational systems may do exactly the opposite. I think you need to reevaluate things before you generalize so much."

—Dana

———

Having gone through these introductory exercises, my students are usually less nervous about writing essays than they were at the outset. Their anxiety levels are still typically pretty high, however, because, as they tend to put it, they "still don't know what one of these things is supposed to look like." Here, then, is where I provide a model for them to study.

Let me pause a minute to articulate a better context for the model essay that follows. Most composition programs require students to satisfy a two-course sequence. The second course is usually the "research and argumentation" component of the sequence. It is here—in the first half of this second course—that I teach (and advocate teaching) the essay. One of my primary objectives when teaching this kind of course is to facilitate and promote my students' use of library resources and other forms of research in the construction of socially active, rhetorical civic discourse. Thus, it is my practice in this kind of course to ask students to write only on particular topics, to write only about contemporary controversial issues of their choice. Since professional essays addressing contemporary controversial issues tend to be too daunting and sophisticated to be of good use for this purpose—since my students need a model that is accessible and inviting, a model written by someone they could actually emulate, not some "impossibly" talented professional writer—I took the plunge a few years back and wrote an essay myself in response to my own assignment (an enlightening exercise I heartily recommend for every writing instructor). The resulting text not only provides students with a happily imperfect model to critique and learn from, but also demonstrated to me just how difficult it can be to leave the safety and familiarity of the thesis/support form when doing academic writing. By writing an essay myself, I gained a far better understanding of what, exactly, I was asking them to do by having them compose essays. Here, then, is my essay.

# Fetal Tissue and the Face in the Sonogram

Life was a lot simpler for me before Aileen and I got pregnant, before I saw our five-month-old baby's face on a sonogram. It was just easier to take a stand on issues. Now, I don't know—I don't know about a lot of things. My views are unsettled, complicated, difficult. Life is just a lot more complex. Take, for instance, the issue of fetal tissue transplants. Before I saw our baby's face, I don't think I would have gone beyond my initial notion that science and medicine and their development are usually for the good, that if we can use tissues from dead fetuses to reduce the suffering of people with Parkinson's disease (like my aunt Mary), or diabetes (like Aileen's sister Kris), or Alzheimer's (like her uncle Honey), then we should do it, regardless of the cost. But now, having seen a fetus, our fetus, face to face, I'm not so sure. Science and medicine keep outrunning my ethical and moral ability to keep up with them, I guess.

According to Stephen Post, fetal cells are special: they spread and grow quickly when transplanted, and there is little chance that the host body will reject them. Thus, they hold out the promise of curing many devastating diseases, even AIDS ("Gift" 1119). What a great development that would be. We need to do fetal tissue research to find out if this is true, I think. But, if it is true, what would be the price? Post says many people believe that fetal tissue transplants will encourage people to have abortions in order to supply the needed tissues, that doctors should not improve the condition of one person at the expense of another, and that by using fetal tissue transplants, doctors are condoning and encouraging fetal murder.

On the other hand, he says, people have argued that although doctors use transplants from young adult murder victims to save other people's lives, it does not mean that they condone or encourage *these* murders ("Gift" 1120). I feel that if the body, fetal or adult, is already dead, then why shouldn't we make use of it to help the living? In this respect, fetal tissue transplants seem no different than adult tissue transplants. Proponents of fetal tissue research also point out that the National Institutes of Health has strict guidelines to prevent abuses of fetal tissue transplantation. Mothers must first consent to an abortion before they can consent to offer the fetal remains for research and they cannot specify who will receive the fetal tissues (Post "Gift" 1119–20). In all honesty, however, I have very little faith that government regulations are going to stop the inevitable abuses of this procedure from occurring. No matter how tight you make the laws, people will do anything, *anything*, to reduce the suffering of a loved one or to take advantage of a way to make big bucks.

As an English teacher, I am especially interested in the language surrounding the contributions of fetal remains to research. This language frightens me, big time. If you change a person's language, you change the way he or she thinks. According to Post, words like *harvesting* a *donation* or *gift* are typically used to describe the giving of fetal remains to research ("Gift" 1120). These new names can radically alter the way we think about that thing in the womb. And the way we think can radically alter our actions.

I need to work hard to keep the issues of abortion and fetal tissue research separated in my mind. Although people seem to lump them together, and although the controversies overlap, they are not the same thing. Even if Roe v. Wade is thrown out and there are no more legal elective abortions in this country, there will still be miscarriages, stillbirths, and tubal pregnancies, and thus there will still be fetal tissue with which scientists and doctors will want to do research. Nevertheless, these two issues keep sliding together. I am greatly disturbed by the possibility of women choosing to or being forced to become fetal tissue "factories," becoming pregnant just to abort the fetus and sell its remains. Kim Lawton writes that in a very strange partnership, both pro-lifers and feminists agree that if abortion is the accepted method of obtaining fetal tissue, then there is the possibility of women being abused, of their being manipulated into having abortions and later being coerced into more harmful procedures to "harvest" more beneficial fetal tissues (52). In a scene like something from a science fiction movie, I see an apocalyptic vision of women systematically abused into becoming "breeders" and "spare parts factories." But, I quickly realize, this is an alarmist fantasy. It is an emotional appeal used by those against fetal tissue research, designed to make me not think, but feel strongly—and it works very well.

I have other strong feelings about this. I know from my own experience that decisions about abortions are incredibly difficult. So when I hear that 92% of women having abortions would agree to allow researchers to use their fetal remains because "it would allow some good to come out of it" (Lawton 52), I remember. I remember all the pain that is involved in that monumental decision. The idea that some good might come out of all that tragedy, I think, would be very comforting for those who have no choice but to go through it, the way someone I used to love and I did. That baby's life, however short, might not have been for nothing, but for something important.

I guess I won't be able to keep the issues of abortion and fetal tissue transplants separate after all. If abortion wasn't legal and fetal tissues were thus not readily available, scientists probably would not have begun doing this kind of research. And as long, and only as long, as abortion is legal and fetal tissue is readily available, scientists can continue such research. Fetal tissue only from miscarriages and stillbirths alone would not supply their needs. Or would it? I guess a severely cut back supply would necessarily severely cut back research. So, there is the possibility that researchers could start getting involved with the pro-choice movement in order to keep their supply line intact, that the big business of medical research might start pumping megabucks into the movement in order to keep their raw materials coming in steady flow. But, again, I'm speculating. This is another alarmist fantasy at this point.

Rather than looking into the science fiction fantasy future, I should look back into real-world historical reality. Peggy Orenstein says that fetal tissue research is not new. It has been going on for decades. In fact, fetal tissue research was crucial in discovering vaccines for both polio and small pox (298). Would we rather that we didn't have vaccines for these horrendous diseases? But as she notes, it is only in the last five years that doctors have been transplanting fetal tissue. Orenstein remarks that one doctor believes it would now be unethical *not* to try to alleviate the suffering of patients through the use of fetal tissue transplants (298). She likewise quotes John Robertson, professor at the UT Austin School of Law, who says, "If aborting in cases of rape and incest or genetic defect is acceptable, to abort to save someone's life should be acceptable as well" (300).

But will fetal tissue research lead, as some claim, to the sacrifice of living fetuses in the name of research, to abortion clinics selling fetal remains to the highest bidder (Orenstein 300)? As I said before, the notion of some good coming out of an abortion may be a comforting notion to those who have no choice but to go through with it. Maybe too comforting. Maybe even attractive. Maybe the notion that some good might come out of it will tip the scales for those people who are yet undecided about whether abortion is the way they must go and will encourage them that it is the way they *should* go. From my own experience, I would have to say that I don't think altruistic notions of benefiting humankind in general through the donation of fetal remains will often enter into the decision of whether to have an abortion. The deciding factors are far more personal, emotional, spiritual. Questions about whether you will be helping the progress of science or about how this action will affect people you do not know somewhere, sometime down the line—well, they really just don't enter into the picture. Trust me. The decision is a lot closer to home and heart and bone than that.

In the end, as Post notes, we simply do not know what the impact of fetal tissue transplants will be on the incidence of elective abortion. We can speculate: that it will give boyfriends, husbands, and families more leverage in encouraging women to have abortions, that they could then better justify it since it might help those who are suffering from devastating diseases; that it will lead to a cultural idealism in which donating fetal tissue is as noble a gesture as donating blood or your own organs; that it might make abortion seem less tragic since it could possibly save someone else's life ("Progress" 15). We just don't know. It could, for all we now know, do just the opposite and reduce the number of elective abortions. If, for instance, a couple knows that researchers might buy the remains of their fetus and perform experiments on it, that knowledge might cause them to reconsider the "desecration of their unborn," the thought of doubly "sinning" against their unborn becoming to much for them to bear. We just don't know at this point and it is fruitless and misleading to argue about it. The only way to find out for sure is to proceed with fetal tissue research and study whether it does or does not increase the rate of elective abortions. Otherwise we will never know for certain one way or the other.

One thing we *can* be sure of, though, is that if widespread uses for fetal tissue are found, then the medical-industrial complex in this country will do its very best to take advantage of this profit-making opportunity. If widespread uses for fetal tissue are found, then stable and increased supplies of it would be needed to meet that demand. To what extent might we go? I shudder to think—I go off on another science fiction fantasy. It is not inconceivable that if enough uses for fetal tissue are found, then we might make it a moral, ethical, and patriotic duty for every couple to have at least one abortion and donate the fetal tissue to research.

Ultimately, it seems to me, the question of fetal tissue research and transplantation, like many other issues in the news these days, rests on the question of whether medicine *should* do everything it *can* do. Modern medicine can keep people's bodies alive for a long time after their brains have died; but should it? It can prolong people's lives long after they have ceased to be productive, useful, dignified, and happy; but should it? It can offer people who are suffering gravely the means to end that suffering through euthanasia; but should it? Medicine, through fetal tissue research and transplantation, may discover cures for many of the diseases that cripple many peoples' lives, like diabetes, Alzheimer's, Parkinson's, and maybe even those that threaten *everyone's* health, like cancer and AIDS; but should it?

## Works Cited

Lawton, Kim A. "Fetal-tissue Transplants Stir Controversy." *Christianity Today* 18 Mar. 1988: 52–53.

Orenstein, Peggy. "The Use of Aborted Fetal Tissue in Medical Research Is As Controversial As Abortion Itself." *Vogue* Oct. 1989: 298–308.

Post, Stephen. "Fetal Tissue: A 'Gift' for Transplanting?" *The Christian Century* 105 (1988): 1119–1120.

———. "Fetal Tissue Transplant: The Right to Question Progress." America 5 Jan. 1991: 14–16.

After telling my students that although I am biased, of course, I still think this is a pretty good essay, I have them read, critique, and annotate the model for homework. Their assignment is to "Read the essay carefully, and write down what you *notice* about it. How does it differ from 'normal' school writing? What about the style, the form, the tone of the essay surprises you? Concerns you? Appeals to you? Repels you?" During the next class period, I break the class into small groups to discuss what they have uncovered in the analyses they had engaged in for homework. I charge each group with reporting their collaborative response to the following question: "What does your group think are the three most important features of this essay?" At the end of the small groups' work, we put all their findings on the chalkboard. One class listed the following:

looks at both sides of the controversy

depth of content

writer is sometimes confused, changes his mind

explains why the writer thinks, feels, and believes what he does

uses a number of sources

informal

uses personal voice, slang

essay really flows

tells the story of the writer's thinking, how it developed over time

a mixture of facts and reflections, what others say and what you say

interesting

uses "I" a lot

uses questions a lot

includes many personal experiences, feelings, and opinions

clearly shows the writer's biases

leaves space for the reader to decide where they stand on the issue

writer contradicts himself

has a weird conclusion

writer takes detours

After exhausting each group's list, I have students copy down our master list from the chalkboard. "Judging from all that you have said here," I tell them, "You clearly know *what* makes for a good essay. Keep this list handy. These are the criteria by which I will evaluate your essays. Of course, knowing what makes for a good essay and knowing *how to put one together* are two different things. And, beginning next time, we will begin working on how to write one."

## PREWRITING

In trying to help students compose in what seems to them a slippery if not "formless" form, I suggest that they use two cognitive "scaffolds" to help them direct their prewriting processes. Both methods—the first building upon Peter Elbow's technique of freewriting, the second transcribing a kind of scripted dialogue between the writer and her sources—help the writer achieve a chrono-logical structure and a hybridization of multiple discourses in their texts.

My students are quite unaccustomed to looking for and appreciating the temporal nature of their thinking. The idea that their thoughts develop over time is foreign to them. They are very good at telling me where they end up in their thinking, very good at stating their conclusions, but they are typically almost completely unable to tell me how they got there. They cannot detail the processes by which they come to those positions. What they need, I have realized, is some way to slow down their thinking processes so they can have a better look at them, some way of taking "snapshots" of their thinking along the way. Later, they can use these "snapshots" to remind themselves of where they were at the beginning of their journeys toward understanding and of the various places they have gone through before arriving at their destinations. Building upon Peter Elbow's technique of freewriting, I suggest to my students that a quick freewrite after each time they engage with some source material can help them keep a detailed "travelogue" of the mental journey they go through while prewriting. This way they will be better able to tell the whole story of their thinking in their essays, rather than just the ends of those stories. I also have students do a second freewrite for each source they engage with, have them do a "subjective response" to each "objective snapshot" they take along the way. This enables them to inject and fuse together a variety of discourses and voices into their prewriting. In this way, they can consistently address the essay's chrono-logic and anti-scholasticism from the beginning of their composing processes.

In practice, my modification of freewriting works this way. I first ask the students to select a topic for their essays. To help them with their research and maintain unity with the rest of the course, the topic has to be a contemporary controversial issue, but they are free to choose which issue they want to address. The only advice I give them about topic selection is that they should choose an issue they are interested in but don't know all that much about at the outset. This way the essay can truly track their growth from ignorance to understanding over time. Moreover, this way will help them stay motivated: everything they find out in their research will be new and interesting information. After they have decided on their topics, I have the students do some initial, "baseline," directed freewriting in class. I ask them to freewrite for five minutes in response to the following prompt: "At this point, what do you know about your issue? How do you feel about it? What do you want to know about it?" One student, Kari, chose the issue of homelessness. Her first, "baseline" freewriting read as follows.

### Freewrite #1

Do communities have certain responsibilities to the homeless?? Some homeless people on the street are there because they're too lazy to find a job or don't have any motivation. Should we reward these lazy bums just because they are labeled "homeless?" But—there are some that don't have a choice, maybe they're just not fortunate enough to become lucky. How much responsibility does the community show for the homeless, if any? How do we know when to help the homeless and do we have a responsibility to help them? I always wonder if the community *does* have a responsibility. It seems like they would out of pity and sympathy because we all want to make this world a better place and we all have hearts. But there are some homeless who would take these responsibilities for granted and misuse them! Certain homeless people are just bothersome and invade private space, so why offer them any benefits if they're not offering anything towards the community. How do we know what the right thing to do is? Are we helping or hurting the homeless by what we do?

---

The students complete their "baseline" freewriting in class and are then given a homework assignment sheet that reads

---

A.   Using one of the databases or indexes we have learned about, find *one* source on your topic.

B.   Read the source carefully, then put it away where you cannot see it.

C.   Then, freewrite for five minutes on what you learned about your topic from that source. *Report* what the writer said. What do you remember *the writer* saying?

D.   Next, freewrite for five minutes on what *you* think and feel about what you learned. *Respond* to what the writer said. What do you *now* think and how do you *now* feel about your topic?

---

Kari's homework reads as follows.

---

### Freewrite #2

### Jon Loe—"Homeless rights, community wrongs"
*—U.S. News/World Report*

The community surrounding the homeless seems to be never taken into consideration. All programs related to the homeless forget to think about what the community has to weigh. These programs focus on "compassion" for the homeless, not the community. The community faces many obstacles sometimes such as having to walk over bodies to get to their doors. This brings us to the argument of whether or not the homeless have a right to sleep wherever they want. In spring the homeless migrate to the park and take up space. The park is not a park anymore because the homeless use it as their temporary homes. They sleep on benches, urinate in sand boxes, etc. It becomes a bad environment and people tend to keep away. The homeless deprive the public of a safe, peaceful place to enjoy. N.Y.C. is trying to stop destabilization in the parks. Police tear down shelters and shacks to aid in halting these bad environments of the homeless, but the homeless keep putting them back. It's an ongoing process that doesn't stop. The Parks Department is trying to keep the parks for recreation, not habitation. Shelters and homes are provided for the homeless but the homeless state that they are unsafe and full of problems.

*It seems like the homeless are taking away most of the community rights and privileges. I don't think that's fair. They shouldn't have the right to degrade the public environment just because they're homeless. It sounds like the community doesn't have a say so when it comes to helping the homeless. If these street people are going to disrupt social structure, then something should be done. If the shelters are unsafe then they should be made safe so the homeless can go there instead of the streets. I agree that the homeless need food and shelter, but they don't have the right to make the environment unstable for anyone else. If aims to stop this destabilization aren't working, then what can be done? I guess it's not an easy subject to alter, but somewhere along the line, something must be accomplished. We're giving the homeless too much freedom and in turn they're imposing on our rights with their bad habits. I do want the homeless to have a safe place to live, but that space shouldn't be the public environment! But then again, if they feel the shelters are unsafe, where are they to go? There has to be something that can help this problem.*

---

I require the students to repeat this procedure several more times, in the same manner each time. In order to faithfully record the temporally based evolution of their thought, it is important that students find, read, and freewrite in response to only one article at a time. In this way, Kari, for instance, left a cognitive "paper trail" behind her as she moved through her developing understanding, a "map" of where she began and how her position relative to her issue changed over time. This technique also allowed her to juxtapose a diversity of discourses—the various voices incorporated in her sources, her own "objective/cognitive" voice and "subjective/affective" voices, for instance—and to document how they came to dialogically intersect and interact. Kari's prewriting over the next couple of cycles is reproduced below.

---

## Freewrite #3

### Sam Roberts—"Padlock on Public Space"
#### —*The New York Times*

Jackson Square Park is padlocked at night by the community to keep homeless dwellers out at night. The community doesn't want this beautiful park's image and prestige ruined by these street dwellers. The homeless that do dwell in the parks drive away the people who live indoors. In the 1900s people were charged money to rent chairs in parks. In 1989 the city made park rules to halt the dwelling of the homeless. Most city parks now have a curfew and high security in an effort to keep the park a park. Director of the neighborhood space coalition sympathized with the homeless, but feels it's not a function of the Parks Department. The Housing and Social Services Department should deal with it. The President of the Parks Department says that fencing parks would create a "series of cages" but, if that's what it takes to keep the parks usable then that's the only solution.

*I'm all for keeping the park an enjoyable place, but gosh—padlocking a park that is surrounded by a fence seems a little extreme! A park shouldn't have to be imprisoned by fences to keep the "bad" people out. That takes away the whole image of the park being a safe, open place to roam. These enforcements may keep the homeless out of the parks, but they'll just end up somewhere else to sleep. Should those other places be fenced and locked too? If people keep putting fences around every place the homeless dwell, then this whole world will be a big "cage." Then, where are the homeless supposed to go? I feel sorry for these people. Of course, I don't want the street dwellers migrating to the parks and creating a bad environment—but I don't want to see parks looking like prisons at night. That's ridiculous! I'm sure something else can be done. If these homeless people feel like they have to sleep in parks, then the Social Services must not be living up to their responsibilities in aiding these unfortunate people. I truly wonder how these people can survive living the unstable life that they do. With all these restrictions, what are they to do now? I'm just so confused. I'm against them sleeping in the parks but where else are they supposed to sleep? They're homeless and don't have anywhere to go. I'm sure locking the parks is a big stab in the back and decreases their will to survive. Of course, the homeless are outcasts to the public, but enforcing these extreme regulations on parks must make them feel even more alienated. This enforcement is not just taking something away from the homeless, but it's also taking away the right of the public to be able to sit in a park when they please.*

---

### Freewrite #4

### M. D. Aeschliman—"No More Shacks"
*—National Review*

Out of "natural" obligation and Christian charity for the homeless, Habitat for Humanity has been established. This is a program that brings inexpensive housing to the less fortunate, where they can work on their own houses, putting in a "sweat equity" to basically earn their keep. This is a voluntary initiative to improve the life of our society. One day a month, Christian organizations and well-off families help low-income families improve their living conditions.

*We all want to make this world a better place and this program sounds like a great idea for the homeless. Instead of the homeless having to live in shacks and shelters and on the streets, they can live in a better environment. It's not like we're giving them these benefits, but they're working hard to earn their keep. Maybe now that this is offered it will increase the self-respect and motivation of the homeless. It is a start for something to look forward to in life. They can be more stable and take on more responsibilities and feel like a human being again. This is just such a good idea for a lot of the homeless who stay away from shelters because they're filled with bad habits and bad atmospheres. I think people that do have money to spare should feel obligated to contribute if this will keep the homeless off the streets. It's not going to hurt the wealthy, but it might make a definite improvement for the suffering homeless.*

Communities should contribute to this program if they have the chance because it will benefit both the homeless and themselves. If some of the homeless who sleep in their yards or their parks are invading their space, then they can't complain if they didn't make an effort to help the homeless. If they can't live in a decent place, then the only place to go for them is the street, yard, or park!

---

## Freewrite #5

### "Inhuman Rights"
*—The Nation*

The Reagan Administration indicated what it thinks about homelessness: it's a matter of choice. Reagan feels that helping the homeless is a local, not federal responsibility. Most human rights leaders in other countries have been saying a U.S. president shouldn't be wagging a disapproving finger since in his own country the right to a decent life should be as highly regarded as the right to vote or a voice in the press. The moral equation isn't balanced with the Bill of Rights on one side and the homeless on the other.

*Homelessness may be a matter of choice, but I would bet that 99% of the homeless don't choose to be in that position. So I think the government should take part in helping these poor people. I think Reagan was being a bit selfish in his view. The homeless aren't getting the right to a decent life because the government isn't taking responsibility to make this world a better place in which to live, for everyone! The government has the power to improve this sad problem, so why don't they put more into it? It's no skin off their backs.*

---

The second method of "scaffolding" I suggest to students to help guide their prewriting uses a different means but attempts to achieve the same ends: to help the writer slow down and capture the chrono-logical development of his or her thinking and help the writer achieve a counterpoint and hybridization of dissimilar voices. This method is an elaboration of the preparatory exercise described above that has students respond to quotations. While the preparatory exercise has students compose a single rejoinder in their "conversations" with the quoted speaker, this "scaffolding" technique requires them to engage in extended dialogues with each of their sources and to transcribe that "conversation" in the form of a script.

I implement this "scaffolding script" in the following manner. After having the students choose their essay topics one day in class, I ask them to find their first source on their topic for homework. I direct them to scan the source to determine that it is of good quality, but to *not* read it carefully. I ask them to photocopy this source and bring it to our next meeting. During our next class, I tell them to take out a clean sheet of paper and to put the name of the author of their source in the left-hand margin. I then have them begin carefully reading their sources. I ask them to stop when they come to the first bit of information that they think is shocking, surprising, intriguing, important, interesting, remarkable, or stimulating. When they have found that first important bit of information, I ask them to record that first intriguing snippet after the author's name on their papers, either by directly quoting or paraphrasing it. Next, after quickly reminding students of what they said they do in conversations (debate, compromise, scream, ridicule, question, complain, challenge, etc.), I have them put their own name in the left-hand margin and ask them to respond to this transcribed snippet as if it were the first utterance in a conversation. When they have finished responding, I then instruct the students to read their sources again until they find the next important, remarkable, or stimulating bit of information. They then transcribe this quoted or paraphrased snippet onto their papers in script form as the next rejoinder in their conversations with the author. They then respond to *this* snippet. This cycle continues until they have exhausted their first source, at which point they continue the conversation by introducing a new participant, by transcribing the voice of the author of their second source on their chosen issue. Again, they work chrono-logically through this source, and a third, and a fourth, and so on, until they finish researching their topic. In this manner, each student leaves behind a transcript of his or her conversation with a number of other voices, a script that documents how his or her thinking developed over time in dialogic interaction and integration with those other voices. For example, Kari's second essay was on transracial adoption. Below is an extract from the middle of her running conversation with her sources:

*McRoy:*   Our study showed no difference in self-esteem between transracial and inracial adopted children. As a matter of fact, the self-esteem of the adoptees was as high as that of individuals in the general population (525).

*Me:*   Finally! An answer to one of my nagging questions. Now I can feel good about my Aunt's decision to adopt little Willie. Why do I feel like a big sigh of relief is about to come out? But gosh, this is only one factor supporting transracial adoption. I think I need to stay openminded—but I can still be excited to know that Willie can acquire a positive self-esteem—hopefully as positive as mine!

*McRoy:*   However, black children with white families have more of a problem with racial identity. White parents need to nurture the child's black identity, make role models accessible to them and provide special attention to their black heritage in order to shape a positive racial identity (526).

*Me:*   Wow—that kind of scares me! One thing I don't want Willie to lose is his racial identity. I feel like that's imperative in creating the person he is—and will be. Now I think that maybe transracial adoption isn't such a good idea. Maybe Willie is better off with a black family. But I guess I shouldn't make such a judgment against transracial adoption now because racial identity is only *one* factor—but I feel it's an important one. At least I know for a fact that there's a problem of racial identity in this situation so I can urge my Aunt to make the necessary adjustments to shape a positive identity for little Willie. He's so young that if my Aunt starts nurturing his racial identity now, he'll be in good shape when he's old enough to understand his true identity. My Aunt is in for a big responsibility. She'll have to make some changes and maybe even sacrifices by moving to a neighborhood with integrated people and making opportunities accessible for Willie to interact with black role models and black children. She made the choice to adopt Willie, so she must make the effort to provide a positive racial identity for Willie. Big, big responsibility!! Don't you think?

*McRoy:*   Although most white families adopting black children can provide the love and support a child needs, not all of them can fulfill a black child's need to feel positive about their identity (526).

*Me:*　　I think that's safe to say, so people planning to adopt black children need to take many factors into consideration before making such an important decision. I guess love may not be enough in this situation—but you would think it would be. How would you know if a family can or cannot fulfill these needs? Do families planning on adopting black children get interviewed or counseled before the adoption occurs? Do agencies consider such factors affecting black children in white homes before finding parents for the children? I'd like to know. I think that agencies should have specific criteria in selecting parents for transracial adoptees—I truly think it's a necessity. I wonder if my Aunt was counseled before adopting her baby and if she met special criteria about providing for the special needs of Willie.

*Chimezie:* The Child Welfare League of America has said, "While we specifically affirm transracial adoptions as one means of achieving needed permanence for some children, it is preferable to place a child in a family of his own racial background" (296).

*Me:*　　Are you saying that black children adopted by black parents are prioritized over black children in white families? Black parents may be better for black children, but if they're not available for the children, then I think the white parents will be just as sufficient. To me, it seems like there aren't enough blacks willing to adopt. I feel if there were, then there wouldn't be so many white parents adopting black children. If these children don't have black parents available for them, should they be left in foster homes? No! I don't think the black community can provide the needed black adoptive parents and that raising a child in a white home is far better than raising him or her in a foster home! The need for a home is *the* issue, I think.

*Chimezie:* Black children adopted by black parents don't suffer humiliation and racism because of the similar characteristics among them. A black child under white adoptive parents will be likely to suffer hostility and racism because of the differences in their characteristics (298).

*Me:*　　Yes, this is all very true. So if there are available black parents to adopt them, black children will do just fine in these homes. But the key word is *if*. I know that little Willie will come across some problems in the future, but I think he'll realize that it's all worth it in the end. He has a loving mother now who is giving him a lovely home. At this point, I don't think there is anything more important.

*Chimezie:* A black child in a white home is reminded of negative exceptionality which leads to a feeling of imperfection and inferiority. For example, one black child in a white home tried to get his skin as "clean" as his white sisters by washing his hands continuously (299).

*Me:* I don't think that a black child would resort to such an extreme as washing his/her hands trying to get whiter if the parents had been responsible in shaping the child's identity. If the parents were responsible, the child wouldn't feel so imperfect and inferior. Racial identity is very important in how a child will perceive things. Without it, a child would be very confused.

*Chimezie:* We can't forget about the last factor against transracial adoption. A white neighborhood would be racist.

*Me:* Oh really?! How would you know? Maybe a white neighborhood would see a black child as unique and special and even treat that child better than other white children. Who can know? This could be a possibility. Besides, I believe that white parents adopting black children won't live in a neighborhood that's predominantly white. That's a bit stupid. If you really want your child to be discriminated against, then go for it—live in a totally white community and be unrealistic. I wonder if there are white families raising black children in solely white neighborhoods? If there are—I'd like to give them a piece of my mind!

*Howard:* The majority of blacks don't oppose transracial adoptions—and in fact most of them favor this under certain conditions. The black community feels that it is more important that black children receive love than be placed in foster care (188).

*Me:* I'm impressed. Now I know how black society feels about this. It's really reassuring that blacks have such a positive attitude about these adoptions. I would have thought they would be against it because of the possible loss of racial identity. I believe that love is the main need for black children also. All of a sudden I feel a great deal of comfort knowing that the majority of black society will understand that my cousin Willie is getting a lot of love—something we all agree on as being essential for a child. Learning this has really hit the spot for me!

## STUDENT ESSAYS

With their series of freewrites or transcribed "conversations" between their sources and themselves in hand, the students are ready to draft, workshop, and revise their essays. What follows are three student essays. They do not represent a carefully selected set of the very best writing done in response to this assignment, but rather simply a trio of the better papers I have seen. They are not exceptional in their excellence, but rather representative of the better work many students have produced.

---

## *Should You Kiss Your Aspartame Goodbye?*

### Julie

1    Grocery shopping today is a lot harder than it used to be. It used to be so simple; just walk in and grab what you need. But today shoppers are surrounded by choices as a result of the sugar-free craze. Seven years ago, when I was diagnosed with diabetes, only diabetics used aspartame, more commonly known as NutraSweet. It was the brand-new sugar substitute at that time. But today it is used widely by non-diabetics, not only as a sugar substitute, but as part of their normal, daily diet. Is this too much? Does the use of aspartame need to be limited? Should aspartame be taken off the market since it could pose health problems? I don't know. I was never told about any dangers of aspartame in my three Nutrition classes. To tell you the truth, I was told that "aspartame is a sugar substitute which is composed of two naturally occurring amino acids." Since amino acids are the building blocks of protein, they are found in many foods. So what's the big deal? It doesn't sound too life-threatening to me!

2    Research revealed in *Business Week* states that the euphoria over aspartame may be short-lived since charges that aspartame decomposes into toxic levels of methyl alcohol under certain conditions caused a major plummet in sales ("Bitter Dispute" 24). This really surprises me because just the other day my Nutrition teacher taught us that NutraSweet is just phenylalanine and aspartic acid (the two amino acids I mentioned earlier). So, of course, I assumed that it is just something my body needs anyway. Phenylalanine is even an essential amino acid (she taught us that too). That means we *must* eat it because we *need* it! I feel so cheated. I feel cheated because I don't understand why she didn't tell us it could be toxic. I not only feel let down by my Nutrition

teacher, but by the distributors of NutraSweet. They owe it to society to provide any information on the dangers of their product! As for my Nutrition teacher, she has a doctorate in Nutrition, so she must know more than she is telling us. How could she cheat me and the rest of the class like that? She even asked us how many of us had used NutraSweet. Most people in the class had and she made it sound like a good thing. That is just not fair!

3    The same article further states that "the Food and Drug Administration decided that methanol, at the low level produced by aspartame, does not pose a health hazard. The product also occurs in other products, including fruit juice" ("Bitter Dispute" 24). This really bothers me because they always say that. They say that about saccharin, but that doesn't take away from the fact that it still causes cancer! They should regard NutraSweet the same way they regard saccharin. They should put warning labels on products containing aspartame, or else people will automatically think it is fine. I have been using aspartame for over seven years. Seven years. What has it been doing to my body? If methanol is found in fruit juices, I guess that makes me feel a little better—or does it make me feel worse? That is just another product containing methanol which in large amounts will poison me! Great.

4    On the other hand, Searle (the makers of NutraSweet) pointed out that they tested the effect of doses up to 8000mg of aspartame per kg of body weight for two years. The FDA already determined that 99% of the population would only ingest 34mg per kg of body weight at the most ("Bitter Dispute" 25). This makes me feel much better. No one consumes that much aspartame—at least I don't. But that was only for two years! What about the long-term effects? And what about me? I've been using it for seven years. What about when I am thirty? It will have been eighteen years by then. How scary! Will they know by then? Will they know what it does? Or will I be a mentally retarded amoeba, and they'll say, "That's why we banned aspartame!"? I said that no one consumes that much aspartame, but I guess I meant that *I* don't consume that much. What about the people who *do* consume that much? Not only that, but how did the FDA come with 99 percent? They sure as heck didn't survey me! Did they just guess that number? They have no way of knowing how much is consumed per person. You can't tell by looking at the total amount that is sold because you can't tell how many people are actually *consuming* that amount. For example, my mom buys diet cola for our family, but only two of us, out of six, actually consume it!

5    I was reminded of the saying "You don't want to spoil a good thing" when I read in Lewis Stegink's article that Toxicology is a whole science based on the fact that all compounds are toxic at some dose. Salt, water, sugar, or a mother's love could be detrimental to a person's health (119). Anything, almost anything that looks good is going to be bad at some level. I think people freak

out too much when something new comes out. They need to chill out and real-ize that too much fruit is just as bad as too much alcohol. Maybe not in the same way, but you get my point. I think people need to realize that *all* things will, at some point, become toxic. I'm not saying to run out and try something that could be harmful right away (like drugs), but just relax about things that won't hurt you until you have ingested huge amounts of it.

6      Stegink also states that "Grossly high phenylalanine concentrations, such as those found in children with phenylketonurea (PKU) are associated with men-tal retardation" (119). This is true. I learned about PKU in Nutrition. These are children who can't break down phenylalanine, and as a result, build up large amounts of it and become severely retarded. But have they tested aspartame consumers for a high phenylalanine content? It didn't say that. If no one has become retarded yet as a result of aspartame—namely me—why should they—why should I—be worried? I think phenylalanine poses no problems unless, of course, you have PKU. Why should you be worried if you can break down phenylalanine? We take it everyday in other foods. And I don't think it would hurt anyone who is capable of breaking it down. It would be like eating a food with phenylalanine in it. Instead, you are eating it straight in NutraSweet.

7      Another study found that consumer complaints about aspartame included headaches, depression, menstrual disturbances, convulsions, confusion, dizzi-ness, visual blurring, and memory loss (Stern 214). The voice of Professor Heilker is pounding in my head asking what I think and *feel* about this. Well, I may be jumping the gun, but these same symptoms are often associated with caffeine, too! I think these complaints are stupid and paranoid. How do they know it's not something else? They are stupid because they offer no proof that the cause of these symptoms is NutraSweet. The cause could be caffeine. And I don't know how the average consumer could tell the difference. These com-plaints are paranoid, to me, because they are just responding in the typical rejection of a new product. People automatically assume that just because it is new, it's dangerous.

8      However, Stern reports, other research found that rats which were fed large amounts of aspartame (like the equivalent of three diet sodas) and then fed carbohydrates nearly quadrupled the amount of phenylalanine in their brains. And a neurotransmitter that normally accompanies a carbohydrate meal was blocked (214). Well, here's the answer to my question. The pheny-lalanine levels *quadrupled*! Wow! I bet that could cause mental retardation. And the neurotransmitter was blocked! It doesn't take a neuroscientist to realize that that is pretty bad. Now I realize that I am changing my whole outlook on this. This research shocks me! How come I didn't know? It's just not fair! I really get startled when I see something like that because, well, it could *kill* you! You can only quadruple something so many times before it becomes toxic!

9     Moreover, aspartame is commonly associated with allergic reactions. An article called "Low-Calorie Allergy" in *Science News* reported that aspartame can cause skin hives and swelling of the throat. Six out of forty-four people studied had an allergic reaction to it. One patient's throat swelled so bad that she was rushed to the hospital (410). I always thought that people who claimed to be allergic to NutraSweet were full of it. I thought they were part of the para-noids who won't try anything. I guess I was wrong. I really feel different as I uncover new information. I am beginning to change my mind about this. I guess those people who were complaining did have valid cases. I am starting to realize that this could be pretty dangerous. I guess I didn't realize this before because nothing physically happens to *me* when *I* use aspartame.

10     "Sweet Taste of Distress" is an article about a woman who was put on medication for severe depression. For many years she had been drinking iced tea with sugar. One day she decided to start using NutraSweet instead. Several weeks later she began going into unexplainable seizures and her depression symptoms changed into mania, insomnia, euphoria, disconnected speech, and hyperactivity. After she was hospitalized, the doctor realized the cause of the sudden changes had to be the aspartame, not the caffeine. She had already been consuming the caffeine. She switched back to sugar and returned to nor-mal (248). I guess this rebuts my statement earlier about caffeine being the real cause of these symptoms. I don't understand why I don't have any of these symptoms. After all, I consume so much NutraSweet everyday. Even when I deliberately stay away from aspartame, I feel the same. Why do some people experience symptoms while others don't? How come this article was published in *Science News* and not in other magazines more commonly read by the pub-lic? Are they trying to hide something from the average citizen? I am really beginning to wonder why the dangers of aspartame were never publicized like the dangers of saccharin. Saccharin even has warning labels on it. Why doesn't NutraSweet have labels on it? Did they just slip it by the Food and Drug Administration?

11     Aspartame breaks down into three substances. We know these are phenylalanine, aspartic acid, and methanol. Beatrice Hunter recognizes these and finds that each one poses a specific problem in our bodies. First of all, phenylalanine is dangerous for those with PKU. It could also interfere with fetal development (22). I already commented on my feelings about this. However, Hunter also says that aspartic acid is a neuroexcitor (excites the central nervous system). Merely a temporary rise in its level in the blood could "silently destroy" neurons (23). This really scares me. I find myself angry again because I have never heard information like this—along with most of the public, I bet. So I guess people like me, who don't openly convulse from aspartame, are just being silently destroyed, right? Great. Too bad most people don't know this.

Maybe they should put a warning label on NutraSweet-containing products that says, "Warning: As you drink this, your brain is being silently destroyed."
12    Hunter describes Methanol, the third product of aspartame, as having no therapeutic properties. It may even cause cancer. Methanol is regarded strictly as human poison. *And* it is responsible for genetic mutations and defective offspring (24). Well, that did it. I am really scared now. I am still angry that the general public has not been given this information. Some people really use a lot of NutraSweet. It's in over ninety products now. I think they should warn us about more than the phenylalanine. How can they get away with this?
13    Finally, I guess I have to come to a conclusion. Aspartame can be really dangerous stuff if you don't watch it. The FDA should care more about us than to just let this go. I guess I'm caught in a vice. I see the potential problems, but as I read about them I sit back, relax, and enjoy another Diet Coke.

## Works Cited

"A Bitter Dispute Over NutraSweet's Safety." *Business Week* 30 Jan. 1984: 24–25.

Hunter, Beatrice Trum. "Aspartame: The Jury Is Still Out." *Consumer's Research Magazine* Jan. 1986: 22–26.

"Low-Calorie Allergy." *Science News* 28 June 1986: 410.

Stegink, Lewis D. "Aspartame: Review of the Safety Issues." *Food Technology* Jan. 1987: 119–122.

Stern, Judith S. "Sweet Dilemma." *Vogue* Dec. 1984: 214–215.

"The Sweet Taste of Distress." *Science News* 19 Apr. 1986: 248.

---

In Julie's paper we can see clear manifestations of the three characteristic qualities of the essay: its skepticism, anti-scholasticism, and use of chrono-logic. The skepticism of Julie's essay is apparent from the outset. This paper is clearly a true exploration of the subject: she really doesn't know where she stands on the issue as the text begins. "Does the use of aspartame need to be limited? Should aspartame be taken off the market since it could pose health problems?" she asks in ¶1, and replies, frankly, "I don't know." She asks a sincere question in her introduction and spends the rest of the paper struggling and groping toward some understanding. The text's outwardly directed skepticism is evident in ¶4 and ¶5, for instance, where Julie first skewers a statistic provided by the FDA,

> how did the FDA come with 99 percent? They sure as heck didn't survey me! Did they just guess that number? They have no way of knowing how much is consumed per person. You can't tell by looking at the total amount that is sold because you can't tell how many people are actually *consuming* that amount.

and then takes a jab at consumer "paranoia,"

> I think people freak out too much when something new comes out. They need to chill out and realize that too much fruit is just as bad as too much alcohol.

We can also see the essay's inwardly directed skepticism in ¶9, for example, where Julie liquidates her own previously held opinion. "I always thought that people who claimed to be allergic to NutraSweet were full of it," she says. "I thought they were part of the paranoids who won't try anything. I guess I was wrong." But the essay's skepticism is perhaps most apparent in the inconclusion and open-ended equivocation of Julie's final paragraph: "Aspartame can be really dangerous stuff. . . . I guess I'm caught in a vice. I see the potential problems, but as I read about them I sit back, relax, and enjoy another Diet Coke."

Julie's paper also demonstrates the essay's anti-scholastic interaction and integration of heteroglossia. In ¶2, for instance, the "objective" voices of two authorities, *Business Week* and a nutrition professor, collide and contradict one another, which produces a dialogic reaction in a third "subjective" discourse: Julie's. From the juxtaposition and clash of these two opposing orientations, Julie builds her own:

> I feel so cheated. . . . How could she cheat me and the rest of the class like that? She even asked us how many of us had used NutraSweet. Most people in the class had and she made it sound like a good thing. That is just not fair!

We see the same hybridization and dialogic intersection of voices at work in ¶7. Here Julie's consciousness serves as a crossroads where the "objective" voice of a scientific medical study runs up against the quirky "touchy-feely-ness" of her composition instructor, a meeting which requires her to produce a third voice, her own, in both a cognitive and affective counterpoint. Her reaction, incidentally, is one place where the text's inwardly directed and outwardly directed skepticism converge:

> Another study found that consumer complaints about aspartame included headaches, depression, menstrual disturbances, convulsions, confusion, dizziness, visual blurring, and memory loss (Stern 214). The voice of Professor Heilker is pounding in my head asking what I think and *feel* about this. Well, I may be jumping the gun, but these same symptoms are often associated with caffeine, too! I think these complaints are stupid and paranoid. How do they know it's not something else?

Along with its skeptical and anti-scholastic aspects, Julie's text is also a good example of the essay's basis in chrono-logic. In reading her paper, we can see the sometimes messy chrono-logical sequence of Julie's thoughts, her text enacting the way her understanding of the aspartame "problem" developed over time. In ¶8, for example, we watch as Julie's thinking turns strongly against the use of aspartame for the first time after she learns that the phenylalanine levels in the brains of lab rats quadrupled after they had consumed three-diet-sodas-worth of aspartame:

> Wow! I bet that could cause mental retardation. And the neurotransmitter was blocked! It doesn't take a neuroscientist to realize that that is pretty bad. Now I realize that I am changing my whole outlook on this. This research shocks me! How come I didn't know? It's just not fair! I really get startled when I see something like that because, well, it could *kill* you!

We continue to witness Julie's cognition in progress in the next paragraph as she self-consciously considers how and why her thinking is changing:

> I guess I was wrong. I really feel different as I uncover new information. I am beginning to change my mind about this. I guess those people who were complaining did have valid cases. I am starting to realize that this could be pretty dangerous. I guess I didn't realize this before because nothing physically happens to *me* when *I* use aspartame.

I think the best example of her essay's basis in chrono-logic comes near the end, however, when Julie comes to know about the by-products of aspartame. In ¶12, she clearly presents her thought as temporally-based and experienced on the spot:

> Hunter describes Methanol, the third product of aspartame, as having no therapeutic properties. It may even cause cancer. Methanol is regarded strictly as human poison. *And* it is responsible for genetic mutations and defective offspring (24). Well, that did it. I am really scared now.

Just as Julie's paper embodies her cognitive and affective becoming over time, her coming to know about an intimately significant topic, Shannon's paper likewise traces the evolution of her attempts to understand a personally important issue.

---

# To Copyright or Not to Copyright, That Is the Question

## Shannon

1    I'm a graphics design major. I've always been interested in commercial art, but I'm just now beginning to really get into the actual business issues involved. I am a member of Design Focus, a graphic design organization on campus. Last year our club sponsored an ethics panel in which professionals in the field came to TCU and answered student questions. This is where I first heard stories of the immoral goings-on in the real business world. Boy, had I been living a sheltered life! It never occurred to me that stealing designs was a problem. I don't know what I was thinking. I guess I envisioned designers working in their own cubicles creating ads for totally unrelated companies and therefore producing completely dissimilar designs. These professionals opened my eyes to the real world with their disturbing stories.

2    For example, one designer said he had prepared an entire advertising campaign for a client. The client rejected the campaign, saying that his company couldn't afford such an expense in advertising right now. A short time later, the designer ran across a brochure for the company with a makeshift reproduction of what he had proposed. This, of course, infuriated the designer, but there was nothing he could do. He spent a ton of "free" hours creating the ideas, but

then his client plugged those ideas in a Macintosh and did a cheap, in-house job. How can this be prevented? I don't want something like this to happen to me. What about copyright laws? It seems like there ought to be some precaution designers can take to prevent problems like this.

3      As it turns out, however, an extensive graphic design copyright law does not even exist. There are copyright laws for sculptures, paintings, photographs, and most every other type of visual art. There is a Visual Artists' Rights Act of 1990, but it makes no mention of graphic arts. In fact, it explicitly *excludes* "any merchandising item or advertising, promotional, descriptive, covering, or packaging material or container" (Sec. A, ii). The only mention I could find of a graphic arts copyright law was a law for *Copyright for Commercial Prints or Labels*, published in 1974. According to this government document, "prints and labels" are one-page ads with "copyrightable pictorial matter, text, or both." In order for a work to be copyrightable, it has to have a "substantial amount of original text or pictorial material." "Brand names, trade names, slogans, . . . familiar symbols or designs, and lettering and coloring" are not copyrightable according to this law (2–3). Could this possibly be more vague? Who decides what a "substantial amount of original text or pictorial material" is? What in the hell does this law do? The government has done graphic designers a great service by allowing them to copyright all one-page advertisements with a bunch of type and illustrations. Gee, thanks. That does nothing to protect the other 99% of advertising designs.

4      But is it a reasonable preventive measure to allow graphic design to be copyrighted to stop theft? According to Tad Crawford, the difference between graphic design and other visual arts is that graphic design is a combination of other visual arts. Graphic design includes designs for printed media, books, brochures, ads, and so on, as well as product packaging and motion picture visuals. Graphic designers utilize paintings, illustrations, and photographs of other artists that are copyrightable (75).

5      With all of these different elements, you would think that a copyright law would not limit a designer's creativity. There seem to be so many different possibilities in design. Like other artists, graphic designers create interesting images to convey meaning. Unlike other artists, however, graphic designers have to limit their designs to a specific purpose which the client describes and is obvious to the public. In this way, graphic designers are more limited than other artists. They need to communicate certain ideas to the public, so their art has to be aimed at the public, as opposed to the self-fulfilling art produced by other artists for a more individual purpose. Graphic artists also deal with type and layout design. To allow either of these to be copyrightable would be ridiculous. That's like putting a copyright on the ©. Type and composition are two elements that are considered common property and usable by all. So, what would be included in a copyright law? That *Copyright for Commercial Prints*

*and Labels* law of 1974 isn't looking so bad now. I guess the only thing really copyrightable, without limiting designer creativity, is an entire design exactly as it appears. The type and layout could still be used by other designers, just not with the exact same words or illustrations.

6     But what if someone "creates" an ad exactly like another with only a slight alteration? If you alter it, is it even really stealing? It is technically different and has a different effect on the viewer's perception. For example, I found an example of a modern advertisement that closely resembles a historical design. Kalman, Miller, and Jacobs cite this example of similarity in advertising:

MATTER POSTER AND SCHER SWATCH AD FROM KALMAN, MILLER, AND JACOBS

The first is a travel poster by Herbert Matter done in 1934. The second is an ad for Swatch watches done in 1986. Is this plagiarism or using a past design as inspiration and so creating a better ad? Where can the line be drawn? I'm not sure what I think. I guess I'd say that the Swatch ad borders on a cheap imitation, but it also possesses a foreign Swiss quality about it in the skiers in the background, in the block san serif type, and the linear graphic quality. I think this Swatch ad effectively used the travel poster to create an image that sets the tone for imported quality goods, the image Swatch wants. Yet, it has a different purpose than the travel poster—it urges us to buy watches rather than visit Switzerland.

7        What exactly is stealing a design? Obviously, copying a design exactly as it was created is plagiarism. But to what extent does a design need to be altered to become someone else's creation? Designers use many past designs for inspiration and as part of their designs—is this plagiarism? I consider graphic design to be a constantly growing process in which the ideas of past designers are a creative inspiration to modern designers. I think of graphic design as more of an upward spiraling process than a circular one. Because modern designs come from inspirations from past designs, there is often a question as to whether the design is unique or not. It becomes difficult to differentiate between a designer using past elements of design to convey a new meaning and a designer doing a cheap spin-off—just like the travel poster and the Swatch ad.

8        Milton Glaser believes that designers learn from copying and that some never grow up and do it on their own. However, he thinks there should be a code of mutual respect where designers are responsible for knowing the boundaries of copying and don't cross them. If they are crossed, the designer should be flattered and forget about it (qtd. in Shapiro 98).

9        Now I feel like I'm making a big deal out of nothing. I feel like Milton Glaser just told me to stop being so anal retentive about the whole thing. Maybe theft in design isn't an important enough issue to put all this energy into. If designers are supposed to have this unspoken law, then they know what's copying and what isn't and won't take advantage of others. Granted, I know that theft will happen, but that's life. Stuff happens, and there's nothing I can do—so why try? Maybe I need to shift back into the real world and try to be flexible and accept these problems that I have no control over.

10       Yet, in the same article, Tad Crawford suggests that a designer form a contract with a client before any work is done. This contract should: 1) state the nature and intended use (including the type of publication) of the design; 2) specify the number of uses or duration; and 3) define the geographic area for use (qtd. in Shapiro 146).

11       This makes me feel better—like there's something I can do. I don't like feeling helpless. This seems like a logical precaution. My dad always told me, "You can never be too safe." He taught me to look ahead to any possible problems and take steps to prevent them. A contract would only guard against client theft, but I should be able to trust other designers, right Milton?

12       But how effective are those contracts? I'm again thinking of those tricky "slight alteration" cases. Can they present a whole new problem and nullify the contract? I would think with the technicalities of law, even the addition of a stripe of color would render the contract useless. Also, there's the possibility that the client who broke the contract could raise a reasonable doubt that they came up with the idea on their own. Maybe I'm overly wary of legal matters. In my experience, however, anything can happen in court and I would rather not

spend the time and money to leave the verdict up to a jury. I'd much rather prevent the problem from happening altogether.

13   I went to speak with Don Punchatz, an illustrator. He told me of an instance when a design of his was stolen. He had designed a full page ad for the SMU newspaper, consisting of illustrations and type. About a year after the ad ran in the SMU newspaper, he saw the same ad in an underground newspaper to which he had not given the copyright rights. He was obviously disappointed, but chalked it up to experience (Punchatz).

14   This is exactly the type of theft I'm still worrying about. Some people, like Punchatz, don't like to deal with the legal battle, whether it be because of the time and money involved or because they feel that there is no point—things like this happen and all you can do is be flattered, as Glaser said. But that still doesn't make it right.

15   Designers learn from the past, but the question is how far can one go before it's plagiarism and no longer using someone else's ideas as a basis for a new and improved design. There's no fool-proof way to guard your work, but I don't know if I'm trying to do justice by attempting to guard my own work or simply raising a big stink about a relatively unimportant issue. Maybe I should just be flattered and forget it if one of my designs is stolen. Life's too short.

## Works Cited

Crawford, Tad. "Copyright for Graphic Design." *American Artist* June 1980: 74–79.

Kalman, Tibor, J. Abbott Miller, and Karrie Jacobs. "Retro-Spectives: Two Views of Design-er-Appropriation." *Print* Mar. 1991: 114+.

Punchatz, Don. Illustrator. Personal Interview. Fort Worth, 14 Oct. 1991.

Shapiro, Ellen. "Bad Practice." *Print* May 1991: 97–99; 145–149.

United States. Copyright Office. *Copyright for Commercial Prints or Labels.* Washington: GPO, 1974.

———. Congress. *Visual Artists' Rights Act of 1990.* Washington: GPO, 1990.

---

Shannon's paper is a good example of how the essay leaves behind old, inadequate orders in its quest for new ideas, new insights, and new visions of the truth. In ¶1, for instance, with her skepticism directed inwardly, Shannon realizes how inadequate, how naive and simplistic, her view of the profession of graphic design has been:

> Boy, had I been living a sheltered life! It never occurred to me that stealing designs was a problem. I don't know what I was thinking. I guess I envisioned designers working in their own cubicles creating ads for totally unrelated companies and therefore producing completely dissimilar designs.

Then, in ¶2, she details an example from a second inadequate order that must be abandoned—the one that permits and tolerates blatant design theft—and begins her journey beyond the known in search of a more adequate order:

> He spent a ton of "free" hours creating the ideas, but then his client plugged those ideas in a Macintosh and did a cheap, in-house job. How can this be prevented? I don't want something like this to happen to me. What about copyright laws? It seems like there ought to be some precaution designers can take to prevent problems like this.

Next, Shannon's text demonstrates how the essay utilizes a transgressive, inclusive discourse to temporarily bring together incongruous points-of-view in an attempt to more fully address the problem at hand. In ¶3, after wading through the *Copyright for Commercial Prints and Labels* law, she apparently finds the "legalese" sadly wanting from a more fully "human" perspective, a deficit she compensates for with a skeptical, sarcastic, subjective slang:

> Could this possibly be more vague? Who decides what a "substantial amount of original text or pictorial material" is? What in the hell does this law do? The government has done graphic designers a great service by allowing them to copyright all one-page advertisements with a bunch of type and illustrations. Gee, thanks.

A similar occurrence of a more whole, inclusive human discourse can be seen in ¶s 10 and 11, where the "legalese" of a precautionary contract again does not seem to adequately address the problem for Shannon. Again, she counters the sterile and clinical coldness of the "legalese" by adding some homey, more human, familial advice:

> Crawford suggests . . . [t]his contract should: 1) state the nature and intended use (including the type of publication) of the design; 2) specify the number of uses or duration; and 3) define the geographic area for use. . . . My dad always told me, "You can never be too safe." He taught me to look ahead to any possible problems and take steps to prevent them.

Shannon's paper also offers us a nice extended example of the essay's chrono-logically-based, skeptical thinking in progress. In ¶9, a little more than halfway through her text, she comes across the notion of an unwritten code of respect among graphic designers and the possibility of being flattered by someone's close imitation. Her response shows us the progress of the skeptical movements of her mind (underscored by the repeated use of "maybe"), movements which, in this case, are in danger of becoming an intellectual retreat:

> Now I feel like I'm making a big deal out of nothing. I feel like Milton Glaser just told me to stop being so anal retentive about the whole thing. Maybe theft in design isn't an important enough issue to put all this energy into. If designers are supposed to have this unspoken law, then they know what's copying and what isn't and won't take advantage of others. Granted, I know that theft will happen, but that's life. Stuff happens, and there's nothing I can do—so why try? Maybe I need to shift back into the real world and try to be flexible and accept these problems that I have no control over.

Finally, Shannon's essay shows how the essayist's struggle to find a new vision of the truth can sometimes be unsuccessful, her search resulting in no real new ideas or insights other than new appreciations for the complexity of the problem and her own uncertainty. In Shannon's case, she remains baffled by the same question throughout her text. It appears numerous times in various guises:

> But what if someone "creates" an ad exactly like another with only a slight alteration? If you alter it, is it even really stealing? . . . Is this plagiarism or using a past design as inspiration and so creating a better ad? Where can the line be drawn? I'm not sure what I think. . . . What exactly is stealing a design? Obviously, copying a design exactly as it was created is plagiarism. But to

what extent does a design need to be altered to become someone else's creation? Designers use many past designs for inspiration and as part of their designs—is this plagiarism?

Her inability to penetrate this conundrum leads to her groping, tentative, and equivocal "conclusion":

> Designers learn from the past, but the question is how far can one go before it's plagiarism and no longer using someone else's ideas as a basis for a new and improved design. There's no fool-proof way to guard your work, but I don't know if I'm trying to do justice by attempting to guard my own work or simply raising a big stink about a relatively unimportant issue. Maybe I should just be flattered and forget it if one of my designs is stolen. Life's too short.

I find it interesting that while the next student writer addressed an entirely different issue in his essay, Shannon and he both employed appropriations of Hamlet's soliloquy as their titles. There is, I think, something profoundly, emblematically essayistic in Hamlet's famous question, something that seems to have spoken to them both.

---

## To Be or Not to Be (Tested!), That Is the Question

### Bluto

1      The Dentist. That word strikes fear in me, more than Freddy Kruger or a Stephen King novel. The thought of picking, scraping, and drilling causes all of my muscles to tense, yet these are things that I must deal with at least twice annually. The best part of the whole ordeal is finishing the visit. I walk out feeling like a ton of weight has been lifted off my shoulders! I've conquered my fear, won the battle, and also have clean, polished teeth. Recently, though, I read about David Acer, the dentist who died from AIDS and was blamed for the infection of five of his patients ("Disclosure Bill" A9). So now with all the fears I already have, I now have to worry about my dentist's health! AIDS is caused by a virus that I thought was passed on by either sex or by sharing needles, not by dental procedures. Hell, dentures don't sound so bad now.

2     Louis H. Sullivan, the Health and Human Services Secretary, is the first federal official to officially state that Dr. Acer passed the AIDS virus to his patients ("Health Chief" A8). I'm shocked that only one official has acknowledged this! It's been over a year since this problem has been brought to national attention and only one person has officially acknowledged that Acer was responsible?! What's the deal? Sounds like our government does not want to admit to a problem. Why didn't anyone say that Dr. Acer had AIDS and his patients could be at risk? Dr. Acer knew! Our government can dictate at what age a person can drink but can't enact a law to notify a patient if his or her dentist has a transmittable disease?! My health is my livelihood. If I cannot work because of an illness, I do not get paid my full wage on disability benefits. I can't support my family.

3     Mr. Sullivan also brought to my attention the fact that of the five confirmed cases, one of the five has a different strain of HIV. The genetic makeup of the virus is different from the others, yet was passed by Acer somehow. He states that Dr. Acer might have passed the virus from one patient he had already infected to another ("Health Chief" A8). How? There is no explanation given. Is Mr. Sullivan saying that the AIDS virus could be transmitted to a patient and then somehow be given to another patient by some dental procedure? If the Secretary of Health and Human Services doesn't know, that leads me to believe that there are even more possibilities for AIDS transmission. Panic attack. I feel kind of numb. How many ways can this stuff spread, anyway? Ignorance leads to fear. And I find myself doubting all that scientists supposedly "know" about AIDS. So why not test my dentist? If some governing body over dentists knew who is infected, then these dentists could be regulated on certain procedures. I could be informed if there was a risk involved. Even if I didn't know if my dentist was infected, just knowing that the American Dental Association (ADA) (or whoever is the governing body) is aware and monitoring to make sure all precautions and safety procedures are followed would make me feel safer.

4     I'm sure that dentists have the same concerns toward their patients. They are at risk too. In response to that concern, the Occupational Safety and Health Administration (OSHA) came up with recommendations that would protect the dentist:

1. Require that impervious clothing, shoe covers, and head coverings be worn during all invasive procedures;

2. Require employers to pay for Hepatitis B vaccinations for their most exposed employees;

3. And require employees to undergo post-exposure follow-ups and medical monitoring. (*Hearings* 187)

These precautions seem like they would protect the patient as well as the worker. The care and protection taken would be visible to everyone. I always like seeing results more than hearing about them. And with the protective clothing, I could see that the dentist is making an effort towards safety. At my work, Southwestern Bell, we have a motto: "There is no job so important, no service so urgent, that we cannot take the time to do our job safely." Makes sense to me.

5      In response to these recommendations, the Academy of General Dentists (AGD) stated that these additions would cause a decrease in compliance to safety regulations and an increase in patient care costs (*Hearings* 519). The ADA agreed and estimated these costs at around $500 million annually for dentists nationwide (*Hearings* 255). I understand that it will cost more for these procedures, but my safety is worth it. Everything is costing more and I don't mind paying a little extra for my health. I do have a problem with the decrease in compliance, however. The AGD estimates that there is a 95% compliance rate on the current regulations (*Hearings* 520). So why would compliance drop with these additional requirements? Sounds childish to me. In my job, there are always modifications to our quality and safety regulations. Some I agree with and some I don't, but I follow them, regardless. If I have a problem, I can offer an alternative in the form of a suggestion. If I were a dentist, I would voice a complaint and state an alternative, not just say, "I'm not going to do it." Display some professionalism!

6      These concerns I have are more than a personal issue. They are a national issue. Congress has addressed the problem by passing a law that mandates health care professionals follow new federal guidelines. These guidelines state that "those who perform invasive medical procedures should be tested for AIDS and Hepatitis B and inform their patients if infected" ("Disclosure Bill" A9). This sounds great. Only one problem. The word "should." It is a word that allows a loophole. At whose discretion will this be enforced? The dentist or the government? They "should" be tested—but will they? I am left guessing again. If the State of Texas said that drivers should have automobile liability insurance, that does not mean that they must have it or will have it. It just states that they should. My dad always said that saying something and doing it are two different things. I now see what he means.

7      According to R. Scott Hitt, AIDS is the second leading cause of death among men between the ages of 25 and 44. It is the fifth leading cause of death among women in that same age group (B7). I always thought cancer, heart disease, and alcohol were the big ones. I am in this age group, so seeing this fact scares the hell out of me! If this is the case, why doesn't the government demand that everyone be tested? It would not be a solution, but maybe with this knowledge we could reduce the risk of spreading the disease. I never thought that AIDS was a leading killer in my or anyone else's age group! Mr. Hitt

claims that Americans view AIDS as a "gay disease" (B7). I must admit I thought the same thing. Ignorance can be dangerous! Maybe these facts will open some eyes in Congress and wake somebody up to the fact that AIDS is an issue that must be addressed. They opened up *my* eyes!

8    But Laurie Jones says that such congressional legislation would waste scarce health care dollars and needlessly drive HIV-infected workers from the profession. With the Acer case being the only incident of a health care worker infecting a patient, she says, there has been a lot of hysteria generated among the public and our nation's policymakers (10). I personally do not want to read about another case in the future, so if hysteria can bring about reform, then let's get hysterical! Let's get some safeguards in place now and avoid another situation later. Jones calls for strict compliance to universal precautions to be taken instead of legislation (10). That sounds great, but they should already be in place! Testing might not be an answer, but it could be a start. If strict regulations were in place on safety precautions, testing would not be needed. The only problem that comes to mind with testing is "bias." I know that I would not see a dentist that tested HIV-positive and I'm probably not alone. What happens then? The dentist cannot earn a living if nobody comes for his services. Is this fair? Is this acceptable? No. These dentists may have families to support, just like me. I feel like my views are on a seesaw, going up and down. Strict compliance to safety regulations is probably better than releasing test results, but maybe we need legislation to enforce this compliance.

9    My uncertainty here is partially based on the fact that no one is sure how Dr. Acer's patients got infected. According to Dianne Kerr, the Centers for Disease Control (CDC) has suggested three possibilities. Perhaps Dr. Acer cut himself through his gloves during an invasive procedure, or perhaps he contaminated his own equipment, or perhaps a patient whom he had already infected contaminated the equipment. The CDC says the first one is the most likely (184). I realize that everyone makes mistakes. Accidents happen. But how can an individual *not* know that he has been cut or pricked? I feel pain. When I cut myself on the job, I stop and take care of the problem. It's human nature to stop and check yourself out. Why not stop, check it out, change gloves, and then proceed? As a service technician, I am rated on my quality of work and safety observations, two standards most everyone uses. Why can't a dentist be rated the same way? Such regulations would cost more because someone would have to observe and rate, but everything suggested so far will add to the cost. I believe quality work depends on two things: pride in one's work and education on what is required to do a quality job. Could Dr. Acer have done something different to prevent this from happening? I believe he could have or else there would be more cases of this kind of infection than just his.

10    AIDS testing is not a solution, maybe not even an alternative that would reduce the possible transmission of HIV. But I think identifying someone with AIDS would let the person know to take extra precautions. The only problem, of course, is that those safeguards should already be in place. Maybe instead of demanding testing, the public should demand better regulations, improved sterilization, and more education on AIDS. Instead of pointing fingers, we could work together for the common goal of overall safety. I read that the AGD and ADA said that OSHA's guidelines are not the answer, but I never read where an alternative was suggested. The reality is that there is not a cure and ignoring the situation or letting things remain the way they are is not going to bring about a solution. Instead of complaining, start contemplating. I read somewhere that great ideas and causes are lifeless without willing workers. Getting involved, contacting congressmen, and writing the ADA or the CDC would be a start. Because to search for an answer, one must first address the problem.

## Works Cited

"AIDS Disclosure Bill Is Approved." *Fort Worth Star-Telegram* 4 Oct. 1991: A9.

"Health Chief Thinks Dentist Passed HIV Patient to Patient." *Fort Worth Star-Telegram* 7 Oct. 1991: A8.

Hitt, R. Scott. "Ideas of Innocent AIDS Victim Implies Guilt in Others." Editorial. *Fort Worth Star-Telegram* 4 Oct. 1991: B7.

Jones, Laurie. "Don't Let Fear Determine AIDS Policy." *American Medical News* 7 Oct. 1991: 10.

Kerr, Dianne L. "HIV Transmission and Invasive Dental Procedures." *Journal of School Health* 33 (1991): 184–85.

United States. HR. Committee on Education and Labor. *Hearings on OSHA's Proposed Standard to Protect Health Care Workers Against Blood-Borne Pathogens Including the AIDS and Hepatitis B Viruses.* 101st Cong. 2nd. sess. 2 vols. Washington: GPO, 1990.

———

Like Julie's and Shannon's papers, Bluto's text offers us instances that highlight its chrono-logical basis. His essay presents knowledge as a personally and provisionally structured entity. The "present-tense-ness" of chrono-logic is apparent at the end of his first paragraph as he announces how he came upon the topic of dentists and AIDS. Bluto uses four explicit time markers, "recently" and three uses of "now," to indicate the temporal progression of his thought:

> Recently, though, I read about David Acer, the dentist who died from AIDS and was blamed for the infection of five of his patients ("Disclosure Bill" A9). So now with all the fears I already have, I now have to worry about my dentist's health! AIDS is caused by a virus that I thought was passed on by either sex or by sharing needles, not by dental procedures. Hell, dentures don't sound so bad now.

Later, in ¶3, he presents us with another good example of chrono-logic in action, his text enacting the way his understanding is evolving:

> If the Secretary of Health and Human Services doesn't know, that leads me to believe that there are even more possibilities for AIDS transmission. Panic attack. I feel kind of numb. How many ways can this stuff spread, anyway? Ignorance leads to fear. And I find myself doubting all that scientists supposedly "know" about AIDS. So why not test my dentist?

But the best example of chrono-logic in his paper, the instance that most embodies the notion of knowledge as the process of coming to know over time, comes in ¶8 when Bluto stops to consider the negative consequences of AIDS testing for dentists:

> The only problem that comes to mind with testing is "bias." I know that I would not see a dentist that tested HIV-positive and I'm probably not alone. What happens then? The dentist cannot earn a living if nobody comes for his services. Is this fair? Is this acceptable? No. These dentists may have families to support, just like me. I feel like my views are on a seesaw, going up and down.

Like Julie's and Shannon's papers, Bluto's text, in addition to using chrono-logic as its structural basis, also exemplifies the essay's anti-scholastic integration of multiple and dissimilar voices. In Bluto's case, however, one discourse consistently reappears and is repeatedly juxtaposed against a series of other discourses that come and go: the voice of Bluto the Southwestern Bell Telephone technician. The discourse of Bluto's "real world" of work keeps "intruding" into his academic paper. In this way, Bluto is able to encompass and present more of his thinking life as it is really lived, more of his unfragmented, undifferentiated cognitive/affective experience. As his essay unfolds and he attempts to explore the issue, moving from one orientation to another, his repeated returns to the discourse of his workplace allow him to fill out the picture, to give us more of the unsorted wholeness of his experience of the truth. For instance, in ¶4 he approvingly compares OSHA's suggested precautions with some wisdom from work:

> I always like seeing results more than hearing about them. And with the protective clothing, I could see that the dentist is making an effort towards safety. At my work, Southwestern Bell, we have a motto: "There is no job so important, no service so urgent, that we cannot take the time to do our job safely." Makes sense to me.

Likewise, in the next paragraph, in his response to the suggestion that these guidelines might cause some decrease in compliance to safety regulations, his bewilderment and disgust is phrased in words from work:

> So why would compliance drop with these additional requirements? Sounds childish to me. In my job, there are always modifications to our quality and safety regulations. Some I agree with and some I don't, but I follow them, regardless. If I have a problem, I can offer an alternative in the form of a suggestion. If I were a dentist, I would voice a complaint and state an alternative, not just say, "I'm not going to do it." Display some professionalism!

And finally, speculating on how Dr. Acer's patients became infected in ¶9, his insertion of the discourse of work causes Bluto to become exasperated.

> I realize that everyone makes mistakes. Accidents happen. But how can an individual *not* know that he has been cut or pricked?

> I feel pain. When I cut myself on the job, I stop and take care of
> the problem. It's human nature to stop and check yourself out.
> Why not stop, check it out, change gloves, and then proceed? As
> a service technician, I am rated on my quality of work and safety
> observations, two standards most everyone uses. Why can't a
> dentist be rated the same way?

By repeatedly juxtaposing the discourse of his workplace against
that of medicine, government agencies, and editorialists, Bluto is
able to intersect numerous areas of knowledge and so more fully
and deeply address the whole of this human problem.

The quality of these three student papers, as I said before, is
not exceptional, but rather typical of what the better students have
been able to produce in response to this assignment. I am pleased
by the success my students have had in tapping into the characteristic qualities of the essay—its skepticism, anti-scholasticism, and
chrono-logic—in embracing these, for them, alien ways of thinking
and writing. The results of our explorations and adventures in
teaching, learning, and writing are consistently gratifying. My students and I have found that it is not only possible to rehabilitate
the essay, but well worth the effort.

## STUDENT RESPONSES

While my responses to our adventures in teaching, learning, and
writing are consistently and overwhelmingly positive, I am,
nonetheless, always concerned about the responses of my students.
How have they taken to writing essays? Do they like it? Despise it?
Are they indifferent to it? Do they find it challenging? Boring?
Worthwhile? A waste of time? I am always curious to know how
their experience of learning to compose the essay compares and
contrasts with my experience of teaching it. Thus, I administer regular, informal measures of their responses in an attempt to discern
what they think and how they feel about writing essays. In most
cases, I try to make the prompts as open as possible in their phras-
ing, so that students can be free to respond as they see fit. Students
understand that I will not be reading any of these various surveys
until after I have assigned and turned in their final grades for the

term. They also understand that they need not put their names on their responses, that their criticism can remain anonymous. What I have consistently found through these measures is that, on the whole, student response to writing the essay is as positive as my response to teaching it.

The first surveys I administer seek to compare and contrast students' perceptions of typical academic writing with their perceptions of the essay. In our first full class meeting, I ask students to respond by completing the phrase, "School writing is (like) . . . ." In this way, I hope to get some students to respond with similes or metaphors for their experiences with academic writing. I have found that when students compose similes and metaphors for writing and writing processes they often tap into a kind and depth of knowledge about writing they either do not know they possess or are unwilling to share in other ways. While some of the students do provide illuminating tropes, others provide alternative kinds of equally enlightening subjective responses. Seven weeks later, when we have finished our work with the essay, I administer a similar survey, this time asking students to complete the phrase, "The essay form is (like) . . . ." In short, students in my composition classes have described school writing as rigid, static, boring, restrictive, senseless, hard, flavorless, overpowering, engulfing, difficult, unyielding, uniform, stressful, formal, precise, correct, concise, dread-inspiring, constricting, regurgitative, repulsive, puzzling, demanding, tedious, punishing, pointless, intimidating, unimaginative, painful, uncreative, horrible, nauseating, elementary, planned, superficial, and exhausting. In contrast, these same students have characterized the essay as flowing, unintimidating, complex, mysterious, personal, casual, relaxed, philosophical, mixed, conversational, different, distinctive, unique, thoughtful, open-ended, surprising, deceptive, exploratory, revealing, undefined, improvisational, and uninhibited. What follows is a side-by-side representation of what some of these students have said in these surveys:

## School writing is (like) . . .

The essay form is (like) . . .

**a building. It is very structured and precise. There is no free expression in form and in your words. There is no deviation from a set form.**

the flow of a waterfall. It all comes into one place.

—Brian

**being in the jungle. There always seems to be more and more of it. It's hard to see how to get through it sometimes.**

an unmade bed of flowers that's in need of a few trimmings. No particular shape or form to it.

—Delicia

**a structured building; as exciting as reading a blank page; a closed subject; like a Ding-dong with no filling; regurgitated facts; as free as a ball and chain; as senseless as green cows eating pink canaries.**

a picture of my thought; a path with offshoots that go on farther than I can see; a bunch of loose ends; one big question; trying to get to the horizon.

—Shannon

**as hard as a rock. A rock is solid and difficult to break all the way through to the center.**

a woman: you work on it and work on it until you finally think you have it figured out, but then you still don't understand it.

—Jason H.

**directions from a train set. Directions are step by step, with an introduction and a conclusion. An introduction that congratulates you on your new purchase and then gives you some pretty difficult directions, which are supposed to be self-explanatory.**

a diary, as it gives you insight on the personal views of the writer based on the facts presented or known. It gives you the personal aspect of facts.

—Angela

**being a frog dissected by a biology class. Things inside have to be in exactly the same place for every frog. Otherwise the body will be picked apart. Creativity of structure is often looked upon with skepticism.**

wearing casual clothes, play clothes—a relaxed way of expressing yourself.

—Barrett

**as stressful as a paramedic trying to save someone's life. It's like a stutterer trying to pronounce a difficult word.**

philosophy. You can ask all kinds of pertinent questions and have no answers.

—Gerald

**formal. I have never been allowed to write in the first person. It is nothing like normal conversation. It's like a job interview—very precise and correct.**

stew. It has a mixture of facts and feelings, things that usually don't go hand in hand in a paper.

—Julie

**very stressful because I have to do lots of thinking in order to be clear and concise. It's also like studying. I know I have to do it, but I dread it for a long time. Once I actually start, though, I'm fine. I say writing is like studying because I have this dreadful feeling in the pit of my stomach every time I think about it.**

talking to yourself. I seemed to be looking at facts and information, and then I would think to myself what I thought about the info. It was a different kind of writing than I've ever done before.

—Kiernan

**a maze, a puzzle. Sometimes you may get lost and have to work a little harder to make it through. It's also like putting a bike together. In order for the bicycle to function, all the parts have to be in the right places.**

a homemade recipe. In a homemade recipe, a person's own ingredients and special mixtures are put together to form a creation distinct from anyone else's. The essay form includes one's own thoughts and reactions that make it unique from any other.

—Kari

**tedious and sometimes like punishment and many times pointless.**

a form of writing different from anything I've written. It's written the way you might talk about or think about your subject over time.

—Diana

**concrete that is set in place and that is the way it is. It is structured with no deviations. It is like eating. You consume information until your are full, then regurgitate it.**

a train of thought. It keeps going without a visible end in sight.

—Bluto

**boring, intimidating, unimaginative, not creative. Like having teeth pulled.**

a mesa. Looking like a plain piece of landscape, but when you take the time to observe it, it can be beautiful and full of life.

—Sarah

**listening to an opera. It's boring but educational.**

an exploration of your thoughts on a subject.

—Bina

**It's boring—basically like fourth grade writing except longer. It's like eating raw oysters—horrible.**

a paper showing how confused a person really is about a certain topic. It is a way to probe one's mind; the writer's mind, the reader's mind.

—Laura

**as structured as an architect's building plans—a very rigid and structured format. There is little or no room for imagination or creativity. The form is set and change in that form is frowned upon. You follow a preset plan.**

an open lot before a house is placed on it. There are no real defined boundaries. You can build it however you feel at that particular time.

—Matt

**a beauty contest to see who can dress up a topic the most. Hide it behind make-up, and, ultimately, whoever can flatter the judge most wins. It's like packing for school. You're excited to be going, but it's a tiring, tedious, long thing to do, and by the time you arrive at your destination you're too tired to enjoy what you've accomplished and where you are.**

being an honorary disk jockey for a day and not having any rules to follow. You can say whatever you feel and it doesn't matter if people agree with you or not.

—Janell

Next, I use this same procedure in an attempt to better ascertain how students think and what they feel about the *process of composing* academic writing and the *process of composing* the essay. In sum, students in my composition courses have described writing a paper for school as laborious, slavish, alien, ritualistic, interminable, impossible, chancy, risky, puzzling, confusing, repetitive, tiring, disappointing, dangerous, exhausting, distasteful, automatic, disorienting, imprisoning, mindless, and rudimentary. In contrast, these same students have characterized composing the essay as natural, intricate, novel, fun, floating, flowing, irrational, endless, new, scary, challenging, obsessive, easy, strange, likable, difficult, interminable, disorienting, comfortable, awkward, and sweet. Below is a side-by-side representation of what some of them have said:

### Writing a paper for school is (like) . . .

Writing the essay is (like) . . .

**when your mother asks you to do something and you don't want to do it but you do it anyway. It's a chore. You don't have your heart in it because of the strict rules your teacher imposes.**

floating down a slow moving stream toward a waterfall where it all comes together.

—Brian

a lottery game; like a blind man trying to read print; a foreign ceremony; a 24,000 hour day; like hunting an extinct animal.

an intricate search in every crevice of my brain; a natural progression; the end of a tunnel that gets farther away the farther you walk toward it; entertaining the ideas of a mentally insane person.

—Shannon

**opening up a new train set and looking for the directions—and they are in a TOTALLY different language. Trying to decipher those directions and put the train together is what school writing is like. Thinking you know where one part goes—but your directions say another. You end up getting pretty confused and that train gets put together 40 million times before it is exactly right.**

learning a new dance or going to a new place. Each new step relates back to the previous ones.

—Angela

**trying on clothes in a huge department store. Many different outfits have to be tried on before the match is made. The resulting outfit is not appreciated or perceived the same by everyone.**

rappelling. It's scary to think about if you've never done it. But once you get into it and relax, it's fun, and you might even want to do it again.

—Barrett

**finding a good car. They all blow up until you find the right one.**

the average person trying to communicate with Helen Keller.

—Gerald

**an airplane's flight. Once I get past the difficulty of the take-off, I'm soaring high. Then I come to my conclusion and I plunge head on into the ground because I always foul up the end.**

a nervous habit. You can't stop going back to it.

—Chantel

**having a heavy backpack taken off my shoulders. Organizing my thoughts is the hardest part.**

once the research is through, is easy and natural since I am saying what I feel.

—Julie

**a chore because you know you have to do it, so you put it off. I dread getting the research, organizing my thoughts, and beginning the writing.**

I just wrote down my thoughts. I was writing down what I was actually thinking. That was strange, but I think I liked it. Of course, I struggled as I wrote, but I had an easy time giving my own opinion.

—Kiernan

**paying my bills and studying. It is these three things that I put off until the last minute, these three times I would be most likely to light up a cigarette if I had not quit.**

just as difficult as any other kind of writing. I'm not experienced in it, and even if I was, it still wouldn't come easy, just like other papers haven't come easy over the years.

—Diana

**being sick, regurgitating information. Stuffed with facts, you spit it out, and feel good when you're finished.**

putting together a 1000 piece puzzle. Only problem is that a puzzle can be finished, with a clear picture, and an essay can go on and on. Where/when do you end?

—Bluto

**stepping into a black hole, not knowing where to go, how to escape. You must begin structuring your information so you can find light and maybe begin to see the way out.**

being in a hurricane. There is wind coming from every direction. Facts you are supposed to know but can't understand and information is coming at you every which way. But you don't know where to go or what to do with it.

—Sarah

**cleaning up after your parents have a party. You don't want to, but it has to be done.**

speaking to a best friend. You don't have to worry about grammar and punctuation so much. You just write down your thoughts so that the other person feels what you feel! Writing an essay is also like doing sit-ups. It's easy for the first few (paragraphs), and then it gets really hard.

—Bina

**copying a bunch of stuff out of encyclopedias in paragraph form and putting your name on it.**

nothing I've ever done before. It's like a new doorway. I was so set in my ways of writing. This forced me into something new.

—Laura

**the first time a child combines the piano notes they've learned and plays a song. It's choppy and needs much work.**

learning to ride a bike. It was awkward and difficult at first but when I finally got going it was a sweet sensation.

—Matt

---

In addition to the comparison/contrast of students' perceptions I collect at the beginning and ending of our adventures with the essay, I also regularly ask students to provide me with "reality checks." These "reality checks," I explain, are to help me understand what *they* think and feel about the essay since I am pretty clear on how *I* think and feel about it. In other words, the "reality checks" allow me to check my reality against theirs when it comes to working with the essay. Again, I try to leave the prompt as open as possible to allow the students great latitude in their responses. And again, I seek to elicit their views on both the essay as a written product and the process of composing an essay. Transcribed below are extracts from some of these "reality checks." I find them to be fascinating, illuminating, and useful.

---

### To me, the essay is . . .

a lot harder than writing the basic English paper. Even though structure and grammar aren't a necessity in writing an essay, it requires a great deal of thought. I do admit that it's a fun paper—to be able to trace your thoughts over time, but you find your thoughts expanding continuously to the point where there's no end. It's a long thinking process and involves you personally, which makes it harder to write sometimes. In an essay, thoughts have to be followed through and explained, which makes it so time consuming because, like I said, thoughts never end!

—Kari

an informal research paper. The technicalities aren't there and the form is whatever my personality is or how I feel that day. The essay is like a confusing road map when you start but gets easier on the way. I feel that the essay is like a stream-of-consciousness type of writing and comes across as random, thoughtful, and interesting.

—Bina

just written proof or evidence of your thoughts on paper. Not just any thoughts, but a progression of thought as you learn new facts or ideas on some topic. I kind of like writing the essay—it gave me more freedom and I felt like I actually accomplished something through my writing—instead of *having* to support and prove three points.

—Angela

pleasant to read. I like to read how people feel—I think it helps me sort out how I feel—it's more personal, less "facty," and that's probably what keeps me interested.

—Diana

more enjoyable to read. The form allows a person to feel more personal and close to their subject. The essay gives so much freedom to a person. The essay is *freedom of speech* in its truest form. The possibilities are endless.

—Laura

a way to explore your feelings without having to "justify" them. You can analyze others' views on the subject and adopt what you agree with (and toss out the rest). What you finally end up with is an accurate record of how external forces shaped your opinion. Then other people can kind of "see" how you got to where you are now. But you don't have to prove if your view is the right or wrong one. That is nice because you don't feel so much pressure. In one way, I like the essay because you can be creative. But it is also hard because it's so different from all the other writing I've done.

—Michelle

freedom of writing, unrestrictive and personalized. It reminds me of several editorials on the same subject put together. There is not a beginning or end, just continuous thoughts, editorials, linked together. I can't just stop and go—I have to finish each thought. It's endless in length. The only restriction is the due date.

—Bluto

a compilation that reveals the writer's innermost thoughts. It makes the writer give his/her true ideas, perspectives, beliefs, and values. The essay is the writer's true identity in rare form.

—Gerald

was a lot different from anything I've ever done, that is true; however, it seemed to come naturally. I actually enjoyed doing it—scary thought. I prefer it much more than something so "structured"—thesis, topic sentence, etc. When I was researching and actually writing my paper, it wasn't agonizing.

—Chantel

a more interesting way to write. It has to be structured, yet loosely, so there's room for style. It doesn't get weighed down and boring because it's not all facts.

—Janell

a wonderful way to put down onto paper your feelings and how they've changed or been challenged to change while you've gone through an informative learning process. It's like a diary, a documentation of your thoughts and feelings on a certain subject or issue. But it's relaxed and fun.

—Kathleen

I really enjoyed the freedom the essay gave me. It allowed me to work through my ideas on a subject.

—Kim

an excellent form of writing. It is easy and free-flowing. An excellent portal for someone's expressions and feelings to flow through. When reading an essay, it seems as though you relate better to the meaning of the paper and get a better understanding of the information in the document because of the way it is presented.

—Brian

**To me, writing the essay is . . .**

like copying my thoughts. Whatever I feel about my subject, I write it down. As a result, the essay is very simple to write.

—Kiernan

a personal struggle. You really have to concentrate on how you feel about something. It's very difficult to constantly struggle to evaluate how you feel. Sometimes I got frustrated and had to put it down. But when I came back to it, I normally had new insight on my topic.

—Sarah

a lot easier once you get into it. I found out that once I started writing I couldn't stop, unlike other papers where I usually get writer's block every other sentence. I like this way of writing a lot better.

—Karen

revealing. It truly reveals the way you think and feel. New things are learned. I've learned a lot about the way I feel about certain issues—things that I never thought about before. It's certainly a new experience. Even though I feel like it's harder than basic writing, I love it because I can be myself and I love the challenge!

—Kari

hard when I first start out. The hardest thing for me was that I didn't know where I was going with the paper. I must admit I did try to organize my essay and tried to think ahead, but I found that hard too. Essay writing is a lot better than the "technical" kinds of writing I've always done in English.

—Bina

easier than normal writing, I guess. Because it is more of my real self, my day-to-day self, instead of my "formal" self. The essay was a good change and I learned how to do something a little different from the norm. At first I was a little nervous and anxious—but it got better! And I kind of enjoyed it!

—Angela

still difficult. I've spent my whole life ignoring how I feel. Now at least I can think it—but verbalize and write it? Geez—it's like going to some kind of Twelve Step meeting on a particular subject.

—Diana

redundant. Because the form is so casual, items can get repeated. Essay writing develops, certainly, but it is sort of pieced-together. Points that could relate to each other may be scattered.

—Barrett

an extreme challenge. I found it hard to always express my personal viewpoints. It's hard to learn how important your thinking is to the paper.

—Kim

is like being in a room full of beach bums and I'm the only one in a suit. It's hard to get that relaxed. I'm so structured in everything I do, and no matter how hard I try, and I *do* try, I just can't get around it. I really try to be more involved, more personal, in writing my essays, but I really don't feel it's working.

—Delicia

is easier than a conventional paper, because my view is counted, my feelings are documented. I don't feel as if I am coughing up someone's research—rewording it and putting my name on it. It's mine. I like it! Fun/Creative Thinking transferred onto paper.

—Bluto

easier than a lot of other forms of writing. I like being able to voice an opinion in the midst of facts. Not many other forms let you do that. It becomes more personal, almost like writing in a diary.

—Janell

challenging but fun. It uncovers feelings, opinions, and ideas buried that I didn't even know I possessed.

—Kathleen

is fun and productive. You find out a lot of new information and at the same time determine your own view about things you may never have considered before. It is quite an enlightening experience.

—Brian

The last measure I make of my students' responses to working with the essay is a little more narrowly structured. Here I try to see if I can discern some generalizable patterns running through their experiences with the essay in the composition class. While this is hardly scientific research, some intriguing common themes do seem to emerge from their responses.

First, students are asked, "What do you like about the essay form?" Let us take the responses from one class as our extended example. Out of a sample of twenty-three students, thirteen said they liked that the essay allows them to express their own thoughts and opinions. David summed up this sentiment best, saying, "I like being able to talk about what I want and how I feel. For once, my opinion counts for something and I'm not just reporting to the teacher." Ten students said they appreciated the essay's informal style. As Cari said, "I liked that I could write like the columnists do—in fragments, slang, etc. I like the informal, conversational style." Four students remarked that they enjoyed the essay's departure from the typical structure of academic writing. Kim's response speaks well for them all: "I truly enjoyed the chance to deviate from the norm with the essays. I'm not real happy about going back to the structure of the argumentative papers." Three students liked how the essay required them to use different mental processes. Brenda suggested that "Essays are very hard to write, but they do make us think more . . . [and] help make us not so closed-minded"; Leslie said, "I felt I could learn more at my own pace writing this way than sticking with a strict format"; and Kellie was "interested in seeing how I could develop my thoughts differently from the typical five paragraph format which has been engraved in my head." Jason and Leslie noted that the essay made them "actually come to like doing research," while Sangmin and Ya Fang liked that there were "no rules to follow." Tracey thought it was "easy and more enjoyable to write in this form." And Meredith liked that in the essay she could be as "irrational and biased as I want."

Students are then asked, "What do you dislike about the essay form?" Out of our sample of twenty-three students, for instance, three stated that they disliked the simple novelty of the form. Mickey summed up this perspective on the essay succinctly: "It was just different." Chris offered an elaboration, saying "The form of the essay was uncomfortable. It was a new experience and called for much adjustment," while Barrett likewise noted that she disliked the essay because she was "just not used to it." A couple of students disliked the essay's lack of clear, prescriptive, formal guidelines. Leslie, for example, said, "At first, I disliked the feeling of not knowing what I was doing and wondering if I was doing it right. I don't like doubting my abilities." Kellie and David were uncomfortable with other kinds of uncertainty about the essay. "I disliked the uncertainty of not knowing my own stance on an issue for sure," Kellie responded, while David stated, "The essay is so open that I found it difficult to begin and end the paper."

　　After explaining their likes and dislikes of the essay form, students are asked, "What do you like about the process of writing an essay?" In our example class, four of the twenty-three students said they like how the writing of an essay lets them learn about themselves. As Leslie said, "Constantly asking myself 'how and why I think this way' made me analyze myself a lot." Similarly, Dana wrote, "I like the way the essay makes me really evaluate the way I think through the writing process. I realize now how much my thinking really does change over time." And Cari said, "I like seeing how my thoughts change as I am being informed. The essay puts down on paper what I am thinking the whole time." Perhaps Scott said it best when he wrote that the essay "helps me understand some of the things I thought. Instead of just writing an impulse thought, I had to talk about what made me think it." Similarly, two students noted that they liked how writing an essay helped them learn about their topic. Ya Fang stated that the process of writing an essay "really makes me think about the topic," while Laura remarked that in the process of "writing both of the essays I made myself much more educated in a couple of subjects." Two students appreciated the greater degree of procedural freedom the essay affords. David noted that in writing an essay "You don't have to follow the old eleven sentence paragraph form or any of that other stuff that we spent 12 years learning before college. You just get to write." Similarly, John said, "I liked the fact that there was a lot of leeway in the way the essay is put together." Two other students liked the multiple voices they got to work with in writing their essays. For instance, Jason said, "I liked doing the research and combining, comparing, and contrasting what other people said in the essay." Two more thought that the process of writing essays was easier than that of composing other kinds of papers. Andrew suggested that "by using our own opinions it makes the flow come more naturally, thus enabling us to write the paper with greater ease." Finally, Sangmin appreciated the mental freedom allowed in the essay. "Searching through my topic let me wonder and be surprised," he said.

Next, students are asked, "What do you dislike about the process of writing an essay?" Four of the twenty-three students in our example class said they found it difficult to deal with the number of simultaneous ideas generated by the writing of their essays. Marcela felt the essay "is difficult to put together because there are so many ideas coming to our minds at the same time." In like manner, Jenny wrote, "When I was writing my essays, there was so much that I wanted to say right off, but that wouldn't have made for very coherent papers." Similarly, David said that "Because of the lack of format, it's sometimes hard to keep from just rambling along. I always found plenty of stuff to write about. I was having trouble getting rid of information so I wasn't just rattling off ideas." Three other students had difficulty with the self-critique and metacognition the process of writing an essay requires. Chris put it well when he said, "I really found it difficult to truly state why I felt the way I did on many issues. I think that my personal beliefs and 'ideologies' have taken many years to form. In some instances I could remember an incident or think of a reason for my feelings, but it was not easy for me." Students had other dislikes about the process of writing an essay as well. For instance, Leslie said she "just felt like I could go on and on and didn't know when to stop getting information," Brenda felt that "having to do something I have never done before was really hard," and Dana disliked that the process of writing an essay required her to use multiple voices: "I dislike the fact that when I feel like I'm on a roll I realize I need more quotes and stuff from my sources."

Finally, students are asked to complete the following phrase: "Professor Heilker should/should not continue to teach the essay because . . . ." One student of the twenty-three in our example class responded in the negative. "Professor Heilker should not continue to teach the essay," Andrew said, "because someone as advanced as you in the field of writing should not be teaching sophomore composition. I think sometimes this causes you to expect too much from us (the average writers)." The rest of the students responded in the affirmative. Eight of them said I should continue teaching the essay because it made them use metacognitive operations, or as John put it, the essay "gets students to think about *their* thinking which in turn broadens their minds. It helps form opinions and makes students critical, not accepting everything they read." Leslie agreed, saying "it allows people who maybe have never thought about how and why they think to search their mind." Chris put it this way: "Professor Heilker should continue to teach the essay if for no other reason than simply forcing the students to realize some of their beliefs and feelings and put them on paper." Dana and Brenda put it simply: the essay "makes people *think*" and "broadens our minds," they said. Four students argued that I should continue teaching the essay purely because of its novelty in the composition class, because of its pure difference. "We need to be taught new ways and new approaches to things," Mickey said. This is the same Mickey, incidentally, whom I quoted in the first paragraph of this chapter—the same one who was so stridently resistant to these "new things and approaches" at the outset. I should continue to teach the essay, Marcela said, because "it is different from all papers we have been writing since we began school." Allison concurred. "It's a different way of writing than what most people are used to and it makes them learn another way to write. It proves that there's always another way to do something," she wrote. Or, as Leslie put it, "It's different and that makes it fun. A lot of my friends thought it was a cool way of writing." Three other students said I should continue to teach the essay because it is a more comfortable and interesting way of writing. "It helps to get a student to open up and write in a way he or she feels comfortable," Jason said. Scott agreed, saying the essay "makes students feel more comfortable with writing a paper. It makes you more interested in writing because for once you're not writing from the outside. You're actually in it."

In conclusion, my students' experiences with the essay, their adventures in writing, leave them with a rehabilitated appreciation of the form much like my own. In the end, we agree that the essay is, in many ways, a challenging form to teach, learn, and compose, but one that repays handsomely those who accept these challenges. We likewise agree that the difficult endeavor of using the essay in the composition classroom should be continued, that the rewards are worth the hard work and radical rethinking required.

# Chapter 6

# The Essay as an Alternative Form in Composition Instruction

## *OR*

## The King Is Dead, Long Live the King *and* Queen

Radical skepticism. Anti-scholasticism. Chrono-logic. The new unholy trinity of composition instruction? A new trio of god terms to be worshiped by legions of composition teachers? I certainly hope not. I am definitely not suggesting that we remove thesis/support writing from the composition curriculum and replace it with the essay. Thesis/support writing, for better or worse, *is* the standard by which almost all academic writing is judged. Obviously, students need to be able to do thesis/support writing well, and we have a clear responsibility to help them learn to do so. To help us achieve these ends, I *am* advocating that we use the essay as an *alternative* form in composition instruction.

I am referring here, of course, to the essay in a strict and narrow sense of the word, a rehabilitated sense: the essay as a textual attempt to come to some understanding of a problem, however partial, provisional, and ephemeral; a weighing out of alternatives; an experiment in thinking whose outcome is unknown at the outset; a Montaignean exploration of a self and world in flux that leaves the known behind. The word *essay*, in this rehabilitated sense, does not refer to what we called "feature writing" in my undergraduate journalism classes. It does not refer to the primarily narrative and/or descriptive writing, or to the in-depth investigative reportage, or to the essentially autobiographical works, or to the fundamentally argumentative or editorial pieces that are typically and mistakenly gathered together under one rubric and mislabeled as "essays" in most anthologies.

The essay, in this rehabilitated sense, embodies and enacts numerous, marked departures from and contrasts to the "normal school writing" students expect to be doing in composition classes. Through these departures and contrasts, the essay allows students to become critically conscious of the artifice and constructedness of thesis/support writing, which, after many years of uninterrupted and unexamined practice, have become opaque or invisible to them. Working with the essay creates a certain distance between students and thesis/support writing, a distance that allows them a new perspective on what has seemed "natural" and inevitable for years, on what has seemed the only possible way to construct a text of critical inquiry. The departures and contrasts that result in this distance and new perspective demonstrate that the essay is in many ways antithetical to the thesis/support form. The essay embodies and enacts corrective complements to the thesis/support form's developmental, epistemological, ideological, and feminist rhetorical inadequacies, which we traced in Chapter 1.

First, the essay does not thwart students' development, but fosters it. Far from being an internalized "default drive" for writing, an automatic and unthinkingly invoked routine for composing, the essay is foreign, unnerving, and challenging. It invites students to work with alien notions of textuality, to deal with what appears to them to be a slippery and amorphous form, and thus to consciously concentrate on their composing, rather than rely on yet another faithful but mindless slotting-in of information in a rigid, formulaic, and too familiar vessel. In this way, the essay addresses what Durst considers some students' greatest need: "a loosening of some of the formal constraints, the scaffolds they [have] come to rely on at the global level, to lead them toward other, more heuristic forms of writing" (102). Similarly, the essay fosters students' development by urging them to open and complicate their topics, often to the point of paradox and ambiguity, rather than narrow and focus them to the point of obviousness and inconsequentiality. It encourages students to open their minds and move beyond an "objective" disinterestedness in their topics to a consideration of how the subjective half of their experience affects how and why they think as they do about issues. Moreover, the essay opens students' minds by inviting them to address their topics from multiple points of view and with a diversity of voices, rather than mandating that they work from a single, static perspective in a single voice. In contrast to the immobility required by the thesis/support form, the essay fosters student development by allowing them to change their positions relative to their topics, to change their minds. Rather than stopping inquiry by trying to fix an idea in certainty, the essay fosters student development by starting inquiry, by celebrating and embracing uncertainty and inconclusiveness, and thus encouraging the writer to freely explore and learn as much as possible about an idea.

A second inadequacy of the thesis/support form that finds its corrective complement in the essay is its overly simplistic positivistic epistemology. In contrast to the thesis/support form, the essay understands that truth is not immutable, not prior to language, not readily available, not objectively, clearly, distinctly, and univocally communicable, not unproblematic, not certain, not definite, nor knowable from a single point-of-view. Rather the essay embodies and enacts the operations of social epistemology, seeing truth and reality as, at best, multiple, provisional, and tentative linguistic entities that arise from a complex dialogic interaction and transaction among different discourses and voices, from an endless dialectic between the subjective and objective. The essay acknowledges and portrays the world as a complex web of perplexities. It does not pretend to offer our students the same simple, easy, straightforward, and insufficient procedure and answers to the world's problems, as the thesis/support form does. Rather, the essay often ends uneasily, in paradox, ambiguity, and contradiction, which lets students understand that it takes perseverance and the willingness to experiment with a variety of innovative approaches to address the difficult interconnectedness of the problems they will face in the world. It lets them understand that sometimes they just will not be able to neatly solve the problems they will face.

In much the same way that it offers complementary correctives for the thesis/support form's developmental and epistemological deficiencies, the essay also compensates for the essay's ideological inadequacy. While the thesis/support form's convention of "objectivity" on the part of the writer makes the implicit claim that the author can (and, indeed, *should*) be "un-ideological," disinterested and unaffected by the sociopolitical structures operating in her environment, the essay recognizes that subjectivity and objectivity are perpetually mutually redefining and reconstructing each other. The essay embodies and enacts the notion that the writer's discourse is not somehow separated from and immune to the cultural, economic, and political influence of the voices of others around her, but rather formed through interaction and contestation with those voices. The essay recognizes that a writer does not speak in a vacuum, untouched and unaffected by others, but rather can speak only *through* those other voices and in intimate relationships with them. Additionally, unlike the incredibly tight discursive structure of the thesis/support form, the essay's form does not make the ideological claim that the enigmatic wrangles of the world's problems and issues are really, after all is said and done, neat, "slottable," and solvable in a short space using a single point of view and rigidly formulaic thinking. Rather, the essay makes the counterclaim that discord and disagreements are often far more intractable and difficult to resolve than we might like to think, that the road to resolution is often confusing, exasperating, and messy, requiring remarkable heterogeneity and flexibility in our thinking, and often, in the end, leaving us with many loose ends to worry about. The implicit ideological claim of the essay form is that sometimes the very best we can do is to arrive at paradox, ambiguity, and contradiction. Furthermore, rather than mystifying the nature of authority and thus making students unthinkingly revere and replicate the existing hierarchy of power structures in society, as Fort claims the thesis/support form does (633), the essay's radical skepticism constantly interrogates the "hidden omniscience" authorities try to display, constantly underscoring each of their interpretations as the product of the mind of a fallible human being. Rather than inculcating the obeisant and deferent attitude toward authority and hierarchy that can unconsciously reinscribe the extant status quo privileging rich, young, able-bodied, highly educated, scientific, white, Christian, business-minded, materialistic, type-A males, the radical skepticism of the essay form resists, questions, and undercuts all of these privilegings, and critiques the system that presents these privilegings as the obvious, "natural," inevitable order of things. Through its skeptical, social epistemological critique of authority and hierarchy in all its arrangements, the essay supports economic, social, political, and cultural democracy.

Finally, the essay offers a corrective complement for the thesis/support form's overemphasis on the use of masculine rhetoric. While the thesis/support form encourages the use of a primarily masculine thinking and discourse, emphasizing an abstract, logical, impersonal, rational, linear, agonistic, framed, contained, preselected, and packaged thinking and discourse that presses for explicitness and closure, the essay celebrates an opposing feminine rhetoric (sensual, contextual, committed, intuitive, associative, holistic, indirect, open-ended, generative, less processed, and less controlled) that values implicitness, multiplicity, simultaneity, openness, and inconclusion. The essay liberates both the female and male students in a composition class, allowing them to "speak in foreign tongues," to use taboo rhetorics and marginalized voices, and thus to rhetorically reinvent themselves. Using the essay in the composition class undercuts the public-private dichotomy, that two-edged hierarchical structure that empowers men to dominate women by excluding women from positions of epistemological authority, but forces men to throw away half their nature, resources, and potential in the process. While the thesis/support form requires students to use only the father tongue—the discourse that has its power in dividing self from other, subject from object, human writer from human fallibility and emotion—the essay allows them to employ the mother tongue—the discourse that binds and connects self to other, subject to object, human writer to human frailty and feelings. The essay, in short, gives students in the composition course the option of exercising a more fully human discourse.

Students who work with these various corrective complements and compose essays in the composition class, who have the opportunity to negotiate these various antitheses between the thesis/support form and the essay, gain a critical distance and a new perspective on the thesis/support form. They become more aware of aspects of the form that had previously been invisible or opaque, that had seemed natural or inevitable. In other words, composing essays seems to help students compose better thesis/support texts. The overall quality of the arguments my students have composed after first working through the processes and products of essay writing is notably better than the overall quality of those composed by other students in my past who had no experience with the essay. There are a couple of reasons for this, I think. First, in addressing opposition arguments, the students who have had experience with the essay do a far better job of examining, understanding, and fairly presenting the opposition's position. Compared to the performance of past classes, they are much more able to get beyond the surface appearance of their oppositions' positions and thus far less likely to present straw persons to be easily disposed of; they are much more able to elaborate on *why* the opposition holds the positions it does and thus do not too simply and too rapidly sketch out only *what* the opposition believes. Second, the students with essay-writing experience seem better able to examine their own positions. Thus, they are better able to locate and plug the holes in their defenses, to articulate *why* they believe *what* they believe, and so to argue from positions that are far more sophisticated and stable, supported from multiple angles. In both cases, I think, these improved abilities in thesis/support writing are traceable to the willingness to explore alternative views characteristic of successful essay writing. The essay urges the writer to look at what may appear to be simple phenomena from multiple and diverse perspectives, complicating her vision in fruitful ways. The cognitive and textual richness and density characteristic of successful essay writing, I believe, complicates and broadens student writers' visions of the world, gives them a newly problematic and sophisticated perspective which can improve their performance in thesis/support writing tasks.

By rehabilitating the essay, by rehabilitating both our and our students' notions of what this challenging kind of text is and what it can do, by using the essay as an alternative form in composition instruction, we can offer our students new, more expansive ways of seeing and being in the world, new, more complex ways of thinking and using language, and new, more active, engaging, and provocative selves to become.

# Kineticism Incarnate: Motion/Movement and the Form of the Essay

*OR*

## Moving Violation: These Boots Were Made for Walking

*I know you think the question tedious. . . . Yet I believe . . . that all the discussions have barely touched upon the essence of the real question: what is an essay?*

—Georg Lukács

*Is, then, the Essay in literature a thing which simply stands outside classification, like Argon among the elements, of which the only thing that can be predicated is that it is there? Or like Justice in Plato's* Republic, *a thing which the talkers set out to define, and which ends by being the one thing left in a state when the definable qualities are taken away?*

—Arthur Christopher Benson

## INTRODUCTION

While the essay has recently been enjoying a new wave of literary, critical, theoretical, and pedagogical interest, four hundred years after its invention, it continues to doggedly defy our attempts to define it in a way upon which we can generally agree. The consensus is that of all literary forms, "the essay most successfully resists

the effort to pin it down" (Hardison 11); that the essay is distinguished by "a sense of indeterminacy, a deliberate vagueness . . .
[and] seems to want to remain incognito" (Sichtermann 88); that
the essay "is a 'puzzling' genre . . . exasperatingly hybrid and amorphous . . . [the] most protean and elusive of literary forms"
(Chadbourne 133–34); that the essay is "a borderline genre" that
"seems to stretch the fabric of definition at the seams" (Joeres and
Mittman 19; 12); that the essay is "a rogue form of writing in the
universe" (Klaus 160). As Cherica puts it, the difficulties involved in
defining the essay "have usually led to the conclusion that the
essay is either unclassifiable—an anti-genre, that is—or classifiable,
but on the basis of what it is not rather than what it is" (201), a
point seconded by Douglas Hunt: "Ask most people what an essay
is, and they will tell you what it is not: not a whole book, not a
short story, not a poem, not a play" (1). The difficulties involved in
defining the essay result in its being "generally consigned to a
netherworld of something different, borderland, extra-ordinary"
(Joeres and Mittman 12). Furthermore, the slipperiness of the essay
has led to an overapplication of the term *essay*, which only exacer-
bates the problem. As several critics have noted, of all our common
literary terms, "the word Essay is certainly the one that his given
rise to the most confusion in the history of literature (Bensmaïa 95),
is the one with "perhaps the widest field and the most indetermi-
nate content" (Whitmore 551), and so "has almost become a word
that connotes without denoting" (Butrym 2).

As a consequence of these combined factors, a number of commentators have simply despaired of ever defining the form, contending that we "would be hard put to find any definition of the
essay which does not contain the seed of its own refutation"
(Cherica 12), that "no satisfactory definition can be arrived at . . .
[that] classifying the essay has eluded human skill" (Holman and
Harmon 186), and that "no matter how many definitions we consider, we will have to determine that the essay is impossible to
define" (Core 219).

I would argue, however, that our continuing inability to
define the essay results from our consistently looking at the essay
in an unproductive way, one repeatedly highlighted in our discussions of the essay's evasiveness. We continue to insist that "the
essay must be some kind of thing, [even] if not exactly like a but-

tercup or a chair" (Fakundiny 3), all the while acknowledging that such a thing would have to possess seemingly impossible properties, that it would have to be a "shapeless, bottomless, lovely receptacle" (Epstein "Piece Work" 402), a "wondrously formless form" (Epstein, Introduction, xviii), a "baggy, perhaps unwieldy, seemingly (but only seemingly) shapeless . . . slippery, elusive shape" (Atkins "Gardening" 57). This unhelpful perspective on the essay is perhaps best highlighted in Hardison's lament that there is "no genre that takes so many shapes and that refuses so successfully to resolve itself, finally, into its own shape" (12).

Our continuing inability to define the essay stems, I believe, from our assumption that the form of the essay is the form or shape or structure or mold of a thing, when it is not. If we stop thinking about the form of the essay as the form of thing, the form of an object, and reconsider it as the form of an activity or action (as in a dancer's form, or the form of a golfer's swing, or the form of a tennis player's backhand), we can locate a consistent and unbroken line of agreement about the nature and form of the essay running from its originators to contemporary essayists and theorists: the essay is kineticism incarnate—the embodiment of perpetual mobility, motion, and movement.

I will outline here the ubiquity of this concept and trope of the essay's form—the essay as motion/movement, as flying, slithering, flowing, journeying, walking, rambling, wandering, meandering, roaming, exploring, searching, seeking, venturing, following, tracking, hunting, and transgressing—from Montaigne to contemporary American essayists and theorists in order to argue that we can finally come to a generally acceptable (and far more exact) notion of the nature of the essay if we (re)turn to a conception of the essay as *essaying*, with its form being not the form of a thing, but rather the form of an activity, if we redefine the essay as a form of transgressive symbolic action in which intellectual freedom is enacted as a movement across ideological boundaries and borders. Finally, I will address two implications of this reconception and redefinition of the essay: first, that the essay thus represents a remarkably "pure," untamed, and fundamental form of discourse; and second, that the essay thus partially overturns the ancient privileging of speech over writing.

# MOTION/MOVEMENT

At the root of the vast majority of images of the essay is the idea of motion or movement. And it is remarkable how many different ways this perception of the essay's nature has been expressed. Thomas Harrison, for instance, writes that "The essay rejects a fixed perspective and lens" (3), while Pebworth contends that "the essay is essentially passage for its own sake rather than for its destination alone; it exists for the totality of its irreducible motion" (22). In like manner, Pamela Klass Mittlefehldt suggests that essays are often marked by "a sense of movement" (199) and so "create momentum rather than reach resolution" (208). Bensmaïa similarly describes the essay as "an efficacious means to *realize and implement* the mind's 'mobility'" (xxxi), as a "mobile text" (57) whose boundaries are characterized by their "perpetual mobility" (90). Holdheim, moreover, articulates a specific kind of movement *within* the essay, arguing that, in the essay, subjectivism and objectivism are "activated into a dialectic, a spiralling movement of mutual approximation." The "essayistic project," he says, "executes a to-and-fro movement between subject and object" (28). For Newkirk, the essay enacts a "movement into the unknown" (16); Harrison argues that the essay reveals "the movement from truth to metaphor and back again" (186); and Spellmeyer maintains that "the essay foregrounds the speaker's movement from presentation to representation, from experience as 'fact' to experience as invested more fully with personal, and with social, meaning" (265). Robert Scholes and Carl H. Klaus likewise suggest both that the essayist is often "not so concerned to move us in a specific direction" since "he is not always sure where he is going himself" (47) and that the pleasure in reading an essay often "comes from watching the author move around" (58). It has been said that essays "chart the mind's motion" (Howarth 640), follow "the zigzag motions of the inquisitive mind" (Sanders "Singular" 661), embody "the twists and turns of [their authors'] thought" (Chapman "Essay" 95), and convey the qualities of their authors' minds through their "tumbling progression" (Hoagland 225), so that in an essay we see "the image of a structured thought in motion" (Cherica 208). Numerous critics have commented that the essay "turns round and round upon its topic" (Gass 25), that it "cut[s] a circuitous path, approaching truth obliquely" (Kauffman "Path" 223). The structure and unity of an essay have also been figured as a function of motion. Howarth says that thoughts in the essay "take form from their movement, not their mass" (642), while Adorno asserts that "Through their own movement, the elements [of an essay] crystallize into a configuration" (161). Similarly, he says, the essay "gains unity only by moving through the fissure[s]" of fragmented reality (164). And even the static images used to describe the essay contain undeniable elements of movement and motion. Richard Rhodes, for example, writes that the essay "is a spiral rather than a circle, by definition unfinished" (x), while Bensmaïa describes the "shape" of an essay as a "spiral, slant, zig-zag, swivel" (33) and likens "the perpetual drifting that defines it" to "'a staircase that never stops'" (51).

That the essay obeys the laws of "kinetic energy" (Cherica 53) was a fact obviously understood by those present at its beginnings. There are numerous references by Montaigne to the essay and essay writing as embodiments of motion and movement, such as his famous observation that

> The world is but a perennial movement. All things in it are in constant motion. . . . Stability itself is nothing but a more languid motion. I cannot keep my subject still. It goes along befuddled and staggering. . . . I do not portray being: I portray passing. (610–11)

Similarly, he writes, "My conceptions and my judgment move only by groping, staggering, stumbling" (107) and "[M]y understanding does not always go forward, it goes backward too . . . a drunkard's motion, staggering, dizzy, wobbling, or that of reeds that the wind stirs haphazardly as it pleases"(736). Cornwallis, having first described the essay as "a maner of writing wel befitting vndigested motions" (190), then declares his freedom of mobility: "Nor if [my essays] stray, doe I seeke to amend them; for I professe not method, neither will I chaine my selfe to the head of my Chapter" (202). Early dictionary definitions of the word *essay* also foreground the notion of movement or motion as an essential part of the genre's nature. For instance, John Baret's *An Alvearie or Quadruple Dictionary* (1580) defines *essay* as "a groaping or feeling of the way with one's hande" (qtd. in MacDonald 3). Samuel Johnson's famously concise definition of the essay as "a loose sally of the mind" (as a sudden rushing out or leaping forth, an excursion, venture, or jaunt) likewise highlights the perception of the essay as the embodiment of motion or movement.

## FLYING, SLITHERING, FLOWING

The essay and essay writing as motion or movement are general images that lie at the center of a great web of arresting, more specific images. One group of images pictures the essay and essay writing as flying. The essay, it has been said, "is a literary trial balloon" (Hardison 14), "is a kind of stunt flying . . . a sequence of loops, rolls, arabesques" (Kaplan xv), is "thought itself in orbit" (Hardwick xviii). In the essay, it has been said, we can see a "theme arising from nothing . . . then vanishing, like a shooting star" (Cherica 52), even though the essay's "free flight is [sometimes] constrained by the unassailable facts of dry matter" (Lukács 13). In Joyce Carol Oates's observation that some essays are "fast-flying particles" while others "lumber along like becalmed elephants" (xviii), we move from flying to a second group of more specific images for the essay: the motion and movement of animals. The essay has been described as "a wilful eccentric creature in its movements" (Rhys ix). Elizabeth Hardwick writes that the essay is a "slithery form, wearisomely vague and chancy as trying to catch a fish in the open hand" (xv), while Edward Hoagland states, succinctly, "It's a greased pig" (223). And several commentators have discussed "how like an eel this essay creature is" (Kaplan xiv). "The Essay," G. K. Chesterton writes, "is like the Serpent, smooth and graceful and easy of movement, also wavering and wandering" (1), while Hardison suggests that Montaigne's essays use sentences "which slither along from phrase to phrase" (15). A number of extended comparisons are propelled by a third kind of specific image of movement: the essay as flowing like water. Sanders, for example, maintains that, in the essay, the movement of the essayist's mind

> must not be idle movement, however, if the essay is to hold up; it must be driven by deep concerns. The surface of a river is alive with lights and reflections, the breaking of foam over rocks, but underneath that dazzle it is going somewhere. We should expect as much from an essay: the shimmer and play of a mind on the surface and in the depths a strong current. ("Singular" 662)

A pair of similar images can be found in Smith. In the first case, he writes that in an essay, "The language flows like a stream over a pebbled bed, with propulsion, eddy, and sweet recoil—the pebbles, if retarding movement, giving ring and dimple to the surface, and breaking the whole into babbling music" (38). In the second, he observes that even if an essayist takes up "the most trivial subject," it will nonetheless

> lead him away to the great questions over which the serious imagination loves to brood—fortune, mutability, death—just as inevitably as the runnel, trickling among the summer hills, on which sheep are bleating, leads you to the sea; or as, turning down the first street you come to in the city, you are led finally, albeit by many an intricacy, out into the open country. (32)

## JOURNEYING

Smith's observation here leads us to a consideration of a long series of closely related, more specific images of the essay, essay reading, and essay writing as motion and movement: an extended family of tropes which relies, at its core, upon a conflation of physical, mental, and textual journeying. As Howarth has noted, it is striking how often essays "begin with motion, the setting forth on a journey." Essays, he says, "seem to have their own brand of itinerancy. As texts they open doors, take to the road, launch a stream of discourse. Their authors begin and move out, heading for uncertain destinations" (633). Similarly, Mittlefehldt writes that essays often begin "with the effort to map a journey" (199). This central trope of the essay as journey is the one operating in Zeiger's assertion that an essayist makes "a personal tour" of her topic ("Exploratory" 455), in Kaufman's observation that in an essay we can see a "self navigating a world in flux" ("Path" 224), and in E. B. White's famous description of essays as "little excursions," in which "Each new excursion of the essayist, each new 'attempt,' differs from the last and takes him into new country" (vii–viii). The essay is not just *any* kind of journeying, of course, but rather journeying distinguished by its spontaneity. As Lydia Fakundiny puts it, in writing an essay

> the route is not planned beforehand, or if planned, then only in
> a general way. There is room for being dilatory, time for digres-
> sion. There is the prospect, too, of the occasional sally: a spirited
> little foray to some appealing spot ahead or sideways, some
> object or sight that calls for a closer look. The route is mapped in
> the going. And except for a general familiarity with the terrain
> to be walked, there's no anticipating what will come your way;
> you set to see what is out there to be seen. (16)

Thus, as Newkirk says, essay writers need a "patient and compan-
ionable reader who likes the open road and the loose itinerary"
(16). Or as Virginia Woolf describes it, in reading an essay, "We
should start without any fixed idea where we are going to spend the
night, or when we propose to come back; the journey is everything"
(97). In sum, it is common and helpful to think of an essay as the
act of "narrating a journey toward some understanding of a textual,
personal, or political problem" (Atkins "Return" 17).

## WALKING

Upon this notion of the essay as journeying is built a branching
family of closely related images, the most elementary of which is
the image of essay, essay writing, and essay reading as walking.
Numerous critics have commented on the "peripatetic" nature of
the essay. Mittlefehldt, for example, says the essay can be compared
"to a stroll" (197), while Newkirk describes the essay as "an amble,
. . . the kind of walk a bird-watcher might take" (13). Similarly,
Samuel Pickering writes, "the essay saunters, letting the writer follow the vagaries of his own willful curiosity. . . . Whenever writing
time rolls around, it starts ambling along" (9–10). According to
Fakundiny, reading an essay thus engages us in "following the
motions and paces of another mind. . . . Reading essays and writing
them [therefore] have this in common: either way you must 'know
how to take a walk'" (19). Knowing how to take a walk means
knowing how to be comfortable with digressions, because, as
William H. Gass writes of the essay, "What is a stroll without a stop,
a calculated dawdle, coffee in a café we've surprised, some delicious
detour down a doorway-crowded street, the indulgence of several
small delays?" (29). Often a more bucolic setting for this walk is

invoked, one in which "the essay is a garden of forking paths and sets out upon them all at once" (Mowitt 2). Or as G. Douglas Atkins likewise puts it:

> Unhurried, taken by all the flora and fauna fortunately come upon, more interested, in fact, in the journey, in the journeying, than in any destination finally reached, the essay *is* a walk (and at the same time a garden of delights made of its adventures). ("Gardening" 61)

In either case, whether pictured as a walk in the city or the country, the essay, according to Good,

> is *essentially* a peripatetic or ambulatory form. The mixture of self-preoccupation and observation, the role of chance in providing sights and encounters, the ease of changing pace, direction, and goal, make walking the perfect analog of "essaying." (xii)

## RAMBLING, WANDERING, MEANDERING, ROAMING

This changing of pace, direction, and goal are the central aspects of a second more specific image of the essay as journeying: the essay as a ramble and its writing and reading as rambling. Essaying as rambling is perhaps the most well-known and widespread trope for the form. It is, for instance, the basis for White's admonition that serious writers had best "leave the essayist to ramble about, content with living a free life" (vii). Furthermore, contemporary critics have repeatedly noted that the essay displays a "rambling structure" (Chapman "Essay" 80), "rambles easily . . . over a variety of related thoughts" (Zeiger "Exploratory" 460), allows the writer "to ramble in a way that reflects the mind at work" (Lopate 1), and seems to transcribe "a ramble through the basement or the attic of the essayist's mind" (Core 219). Some have suggested that an essayist works by "letting all the possible languages ramble and drift through the text" (Bensmaïa 28), while others have highlighted "the rambling, cat-and-mouse game of contrariety played by the great essayists of the past" (Lopate 48). It is, in short, common to figure both the essay itself and its writer/writing as rambling. As Fakundiny puts it, the essay "takes its characteristic outings, has a look around, [and] rambles on in its multiplicity of voices about this and that" (15), while writing the essay is a matter of "rambling among . . . [one's] store" of "things seen, felt, thought, imagined, learned, understood, tried, [and] believed" (17).

Another common image for essays and essay writing, wandering, like rambling, also emphasizes the unhurried and digressive nature of essayistic journeying. We can follow a long trail of references to the "wandering essayist" (Chesterton 5) and the "wandering mood" (White viii) or "wandering mind" which allows essayists to "wander away from the announced subject" (Pebworth 22), "to accumulate meaning as they wander through a series of anecdotes and observations" (Hunt 2). The essay, it has been said, is "frequently marked by a tendency to wander around a subject, to investigate various paths toward a point" (Joeres and Mittman 17), "is a product of both wander and wonder" (Atkins "Gardening" 67), is "a private path on which the wanderer wanders" (Mowitt 333). The essay's "wandering airs of thought" (Howells 802) have been defended frequently. Clifford Geertz, for instance, believes that

> For making detours and going by sideroads, nothing is more convenient than the essay form. One can take off in almost any direction, certain that if the thing does not work out one can turn back and start over in some other at moderate cost. . . . Wanderings into yet smaller sideroads and wider detours does little harm, for progress is not expected to be relentlessly forward, but winding and improvisational, coming out where it comes out. (6)

Similarly, but more pointedly, Bensmaïa maintains that "What may appear as wandering—a total lack of order—is in fact an *exigency* characteristic of essayistic writing" (6).

Two additional branches of the essay and essay writing as journeying—meandering and roaming—follow in the same vein as rambling and wandering. It is fairly common to hear critics comment on Montaigne's "meandering" essays (Hardison 14) and their "meandering, associative order" (Frame xv). It has been said that in writing an essay, the author follows "the meanderings of his own thought in its attempt to describe a mercurial subject" (Cherica

157), while the pleasures of reading an essay come best to "a meditative mind free to meander leisurely in quiet moments" (Butrym 3). Atkins similarly contends that "The essay not merely allows for but actually celebrates—indeed is characterized by—surprise, interpretation, meandering, and slow discovery" ("Return" 12). And Pickering maintains that the essay rarely sets "out hiking boots afoot and compass in hand; instead it meanders" (7). The image of the essay or essayist as roaming goes back to Montaigne himself who maintained that "My style and my mind alike go roaming" (761). Contemporary critics, however, continue to employ the image, asserting that "the essayist is inclined to let his mind roam free" (Kostelanetz 5) and that the essay "is the record of a mind apparently roaming freely" (Pebworth 18), for instance.

## EXPLORING, SEARCHING, SEEKING, VENTURING

In the next common image, exploring, the uncertainty that marks the journeying images of rambling, wandering, meandering, and roaming takes on a more apparent purpose: searching beyond the known to discover something new. As Harrison puts it, "An essay is an act undertaken in deliberate uncertainty, an experimental endeavor or project" (3). Similarly, Mittlefehldt notes that "The essay is literally a trial, an attempt, an exploration" (196). It is thus a simple matter to locate regular references to the essay as "a literary vehicle for the act of exploration" (Zeiger "Exploratory" 464) or an "individualistic exploration of a complicated issue" (Pebworth 26). Thomas E. Recchio, for instance, writes that "the essay records the track of an individual mind exploring and possibly resolving a problem" (285), while Leslie Fiedler discusses the essay's "essential function of exploring the self" (vii), and Zeiger describes the essay as the record of "a mature, energetic mind exploring avenues to which it is suddenly attracted, as the jungle explorer might turn to follow an exotic bird" ("Exploratory" 454). The essayist is likewise regularly figured as "a kind of explorer, examining himself and his environment in search of truth" (Scholes and Klaus 46), one who "believes that the reader is interested in this process of exploration" (Newkirk 4) and so allows the reader to participate in these "mental processes of exploration" (Newkirk 14). According to Hall, for example, Montaigne is an essayist who "engages the reader in a personal, meditative, journey, an exploration of the nature of the world expressed through the word" ("Drawing" 28–29). Indeed, as Chapman notes, the "idea of exploration is so closely tied to the history of the essay" that some have said "the best definition of the essay historically *is* exploratory writing" (Chapman "Essay" 85). Closely related to the image of exploration are a series of similar figures for the essay and essayist which also invoke some kind of purposeful movement beyond the known. It has been said, for instance: that while reading an essay "We follow . . . a search for truth" (Pebworth 23); that in the essay we see the essayist "searching for his direction as he goes" (Chapman "Essay" 92), "feeling and finding a way . . . [in] the search for form" (Gass 20); and that the essayist's ultimate goal "is not truth in its finality, but wisdom as the sought-after prize of the search for truth" (Cherica 127). Employing similar terms, Hall notes that early essayists tried "to portray in language the actual process of the mind seeking truth . . . in a style which reflected the movements of the author's mind" ("Emergence" 79), while Newkirk maintains that, in the writing of his essays, Montaigne considered the "manner of the seeking . . . more important than the truthfulness of that which was found" (13). Good likewise describes an essay as a "venture" (11), "a foray, physical or intellectual, into an open world where almost anything can be encountered" (10), and notes that the word *essayer* embodies "a feeling of venturing outside the paths of conventional methods" (29). Finally, we should note Robert Musil's wry observation that sometimes essayists "are simply men who have gone out on an adventure and lost their way" (qtd. in Mowitt ix).

## FOLLOWING, TRACKING, HUNTING

In the next subset of images of the essay and essay writing, following or tracking or hunting, the uncertainty of the journeying is the uncertainty if one will indeed capture the quarry one is pursuing. In the first instance, essay writing has been referred to as the "making use of words and following them in a continuous movement of pleasure(s)" (Bensmaïa 24), as a process that requires "the ability to chart and follow . . . truth in all its ambiguous, complex forms" (Anderson 303). Likewise, it has been said that Montaigne the essayist "follows with delighted curiosity the vagrancies of his own mind" (Dawson and Dawson 11). In the second instance, the essay has been described as "A cool tracking of one's thought" (Mittlefehldt 196), as writing that can "track movements of the mind" (Newkirk 28); and essay writing has been described as the "tracking" of a chain of recollections (Hoy 288), as the "act of pursuing knowledge" (Newkirk 12). But perhaps the most striking comparisons, however, are those extended analogies that figure the essay and essay writing as hunting. Zeiger, for example, says that

> The essay casts one loop after another to ensnare the fugitive [concept]. Each attempt falls short, but together they indicate directions and qualities from which the reader comprehends the nature of the quarry. ("Egalitarian" 240)

In like manner, Sanders writes that

> The writing of an essay is like finding one's way through a forest without being quite sure what game you are chasing, what landmark you are seeking. You sniff down one path until some heady smell tugs you in a new direction, and then off you go, dodging and circling, lured on by the songs of unfamiliar birds, puzzled by the tracks of strange beasts, leaping from stone to stone across rivers, barking up one tree after another. Much of the pleasure in writing an essay—and, when the writing is any good, the pleasure in reading it—comes from this dodging and leaping, this movement in the mind. ("Singular" 662)

And, finally, MacDonald, discussing the discrepancy between the titles and the contents of Montaigne's essays, suggests that Montaigne

> goes into the bush loaded for bear, and follows every red squirrel that crosses his track. He invariably gets the squirrel, and by the time the reader has ended the chase he hardly wonders what has become of the bear, or whether there was a bear at all, so delighted is he with the wonderful assortment of squirrel-skins. (14)

# CONCLUSION

Among my Daily-Papers, which I bestow upon the Publick, there are some . . . that run out into the Wildness of those Compositions, which go by the name of *Essayes*. (Addison 186)

[The essay's task] is not to stay within the well-charted boundaries of the academic disciplines. . . . To accept the prevailing divisions and to stay dutifully within them would betray the essay's mission of disciplined digression. . . . Entering the road laid down by tradition, the essayist is not content to pursue faithfully the prescribed itinerary. Instinctively, he (or she) swerves to explore the surrounding terrain, to track a stray detail or anomaly, even at the risk of wrong turns, dead ends, and charges of trespassing. (Kauffman "Path" 238)

To choose deliberately the form of the essay is to step away from a path of obedient submission to the academic world. (Joeres and Mittman 20)

By this point, I hope, the conclusion seems inevitable. We can finally come to a generally acceptable (and far more exact) notion of the nature of the essay if we (re)turn to a conception of the essay as *essaying*—less a noun than a verb. What all these assorted motion and journeying images combine to form is a clear consensus that the word *essay*, as Bensmaïa puts it, "designates less a form than an *activity*" (35). What all these assorted motion and journeying images demonstrate together is that there exists a widely shared but variously articulated comprehension that the essay, as Klaus says, "calls for using and understanding language as a symbolic form of action" (173). What all these assorted motion and journeying images add up to is a composite image of the essay as an action symbolic of intellectual freedom and a composite image of essaying as unhindered, unregulated, untrammeled mental mobility, as an active movement across ideological boundaries and borders. The essay, as Adorno says, "reflects a childlike freedom" in that it "does not permit its domain to be prescribed" (152) and "abandons the main road to the origins, the road leading to the most derivative" (159). The essay, in short, is a form of transgressive action: one by which the writer "transgresses the propriety of discrete communities" (Spellmeyer 268); one through which "pseudonatural hierar-chies and generic frontiers are transgressed" (Bensmaïa 50); one in which we can witness the writer "transgressing epistemological taboos and boundaries" (Kauffman "Path" 231), "transgressing the orthodoxy of thought" (Adorno 171). Thus, the essay can be defined as a transgressive symbolic action, one in which freedom of thought is manifested as freedom of movement, in which intellec-tual freedom is manifested as the ability to move freely, and in which independent thinking is manifested as the willful transgres-sion of ideological boundaries and borders. Thus, as Adorno puts it, since "intellect itself, once emancipated, is mobile," the truth of the essay, the truth in an essay, is to be sought "in its mobility" (168).

This reconception of the essay as a form of transgressive sym-bolic action offers us a better understanding of what the essay is and what it does than the one that comes from conceiving of the essay as a thing. This reconception has at least two important impli-cations. First, since the essay is kineticism incarnate, since its form is a form of transgressive symbolic movement, it represents a form of discourse that is not an unsolvable mystery, an undefinable mess, or a slippery hodgepodge (as we typically lament), but rather a form of discourse that is, in fact, arguably "purer" than most oth-ers, less domesticated, closer to the fundamental, core senses of words such as *interpretation* ["interpretation in its roots sense, as a 'going between' two distinct positions" (Spellmeyer 273)], *writing process* ["in its narrowest meaning a process is motion between two points, from here to there" (Howarth 633)], and *discourse* ["in its root sense discourse means a moving back and forth" (Recchio 279)]. Our continuing inability to understand the essay as some-thing other than a mystery, mess, or a hodgepodge stems, I think, from our continuing unwillingness to recognize that thought and language are far more difficult to control than we would like to admit. What the essay highlights is that thought and language resist domestication, that they resist having their freedom circum-scribed, that they will not sit still, will not be cooped up or cor-ralled, will not allow themselves to be pinned down. While we would like thought and language to be static, to be objects, safe and arrangeable like butterflies on pins in a museum case, what the essay highlights is that thought and language are more wild than we like to acknowledge: that they won't be penned in; that they move; that they, indeed, *need* to move; that they *do* things; that they have agency; that they have as much (if not more) power over us than we have over them; and that they are thus unpredictable and dangerous to some degree. Reconceiving of the essay as kineticism incarnate helps us appreciate that some forms of discourse may not have yet been, may never be, and perhaps never *should* be tamed, that the vehicles which offer us intellectual and discursive freedom may simply, necessarily, *have to be* wild and scary rides.

A second implication of this reconception of the essay as a form of transgressive symbolic action, as kineticism incarnate, is that the essay is thus a form of writing that partially overturns the ancient and influential Platonic privileging of speech over writing. For Plato, truth exists in a transcendent, ahistorical realm of divine forms. According to Patricia Bizzell and Bruce Herzberg, Plato believes the philosopher's task is to help others to approach the transcendent, divine truth "by clearing away the worldly debris that obscures the truth" (55). In Plato's scheme, they say, "the philosopher and his pupil free themselves from the conventional and all worldly encumbrances in the pursuit and eventual attainment of absolute truth" (28). This freeing oneself of encumbrances in order to pursue and approach the truth behind appearances "takes place through verbal exchange" (55), they say, through dialectical discourse, through lengthy sessions of "give-and-take" between an older and younger person in which the more experienced thinker "actually [works] out the truth in his own mind by talking to [the younger person] about it and correcting the less experienced thinker's misconceptions" (28). But most important for our purposes, Bizzell and Herzberg write that dialectical discourse "seeks only . . . to bring the beloved closer to transcendent good" in a mutual "motion toward transcendence" (59). It is this power to move, I would argue, this power to free oneself of encumbrances and so pursue and more closely approach truth, this "motion toward transcendence," that lies at the heart of Plato's privileging of speech over writing. In the *Phaedrus*, Plato (in the guise of Socrates) says that when it comes to written words, "you might think they spoke as if they had intelligence, but if you question them, wishing to know about their sayings, they always say only one and the same thing" (141). The problem with writing, in other words, is that it is fixed, static, that it always says "only one and the same thing," that it always "covers the same ground" and so cannot help us pursue truth, cannot help us move toward the transcendent. As Bizzell and Herzberg put it, for Plato, "Oral dialogue between congenial souls is an intellectual activity far superior to writing because it can lead to truth" (60). The signal advantage of dialectical speech over writing, then, is that speech can lead to truth, can approach truth, can move us closer to truth. While the essay is, of course, writing, the essay as kineticism incarnate—as motion/movement, as flying, slithering, flowing, journeying, walking, rambling, wandering, meandering, roaming, exploring, searching, seeking, venturing, following, tracking, hunting, and transgressing—is writing as anything but fixed. In the act of essaying, we write in a perpetual movement toward wisdom and understanding; in reading essays, we witness writers perpetually moving toward wisdom and understanding. The essay is writing that moves toward truth as dialectical discourse moves toward truth: sometimes obliquely, sometimes circuitously, sometimes retrogradely, sometimes directly, sometimes leapingly, but, in any case, eventually. The essay, then, as a symbolic action, is an intellectual activity on a par with dialectical speech in that it, too, can lead us to wisdom and truth, can allow us to move toward transcendence.

In conclusion, then, the essay is less a thing than it is an action, less an artifact than an activity, less a noun than a verb. And reconceiving of the essay as a form of transgressive symbolic action would allow us to emphasize something that is all too often neglected in our pedagogical discussions of writing: that writing is a *behavior*; that writing is something that people *do*; that writing is form of sociopolitical *action* undertaken to make ourselves better, wiser people and make the world a better, wiser place in which to live.

# Appendix A

# Sources Used in Survey of Recent Composition Textbooks in Chapter 1

Axelrod, Rise B., and Charles R. Cooper. *The St. Martin's Guide to Writing.* 3rd ed. New York: St. Martin's Press, 1991.

Barnet, Sylvan, and Marcia Stubbs. *Barnet and Stubbs's Practical Guide to Writing.* 5th ed. Boston: Little, Brown, 1986.

Crews, Frederick, and Sandra Schor. *The Borzoi Handbook for Writers.* 2nd ed. New York: Alfred A. Knopf, 1989.

Dornan, Edward A. and Charles W. Dawe. *The Brief English Handbook.* Glenview, IL: Scott, Foresman, 1990.

Fergenson, Laraine. *Writing with Style: Rhetoric, Reader, Handbook.* Fort Worth: Holt, Rinehart and Winston, 1989.

Gebhardt, Richard C., and Dawn Rodrigues. *Writing: Processes and Intentions.* Lexington, MA: D. C. Heath, 1989.

Gere, Anne Ruggles. *Writing and Learning.* 2nd ed. New York: Macmillan, 1988.

Guth, Hans P. *The Writer's Agenda.* Belmont, CA: Wadsworth, 1989.

Hacker, Diana. *The Bedford Handbook for Writers.* 3rd ed. Boston: Bedford, 1991.

Hairston, Maxine, and John J. Ruszkiewicz. *The Scott, Foresman Handbook for Writers*. Glenview, IL: Scott, Foresman, 1988.

Heffernan, James A. W., and John E. Lincoln. *Writing: A College Handbook*. 3rd ed. New York: W. W. Norton, 1990.

Hodges, John C., et al. *Harbrace College Handbook*. 11th ed. San Diego: Harcourt Brace Jovanovich, 1990.

Kennedy, X. J., and Dorothy M. Kennedy. *The Bedford Guide for College Writers*. New York: St. Martin's Press, 1987.

Kirkland, James W., Collett B. Dilworth, Jr., and Patrick Bizarro. *Writing with Confidence: A Modern College Rhetoric*. Lexington, MA: D. C. Heath, 1989.

Kirszner, Laurie G., and Stephen R. Mandell. *Writing: A College Rhetoric*. 2nd ed. New York: Holt, Rinehart and Winston, 1988.

Kurilich, Frances, and Helen Whitaker. *Re:Writing*. New York: Holt, Rinehart and Winston, 1988.

Leggett, Glenn H., C. David Mead, and Melinda G. Kramer. *The Prentice Hall Handbook for Writers*. 11th ed. Englewood Cliffs, NJ: Prentice Hall, 1991.

Levin, Gerald. *The Macmillan College Handbook*. 2nd ed. New York: Macmillan, 1991.

Lunsford, Andrea, and Robert Connors. *The St. Martin's Handbook*. New York: St. Martin's Press, 1989.

MacDonald, Kathleen. *When Writers Write*. 2nd ed. Englewood Cliffs, NJ: Prentice Hall, 1987.

Mann, Rebecca C., and Pete M. Mann. *Essay Writing: Methods and Models*. Belmont, CA: Wadsworth, 1990.

Marius, Richard, and Harvey S. Wiener. *The McGraw-Hill College Handbook*. 3rd. ed. New York: McGraw-Hill, 1991.

Mulderig, Gerald P. and Langdon Elsbree. *The Heath Handbook*. 12th ed. Lexington, MA: D.C. Heath, 1990.

Neeld, Elizabeth Cowan. *Writing*. 3rd ed. Glenview, IL: Scott, Foresman, 1990.

O'Hare, Frank, and Dean Memering. *The Writer's Work: A Guide to Effective Composition.* 3rd ed. Englewood Cliffs, NJ: Prentice Hall, 1990.

Rawlins, Jack. *The Writer's Way.* Boston: Houghton Mifflin, 1987.

Reinking, James A., and Andrew W. Hart. *Strategies for Successful Writing: A Rhetoric, Reader, and Handbook.* Englewood Cliffs, NJ: Prentice Hall, 1991.

Sullivan, Sally. *Vision and Revision: The Process of Reading and Writing.* New York: Macmillan, 1988.

Troyka, Lynn Quitman. *Simon and Schuster Handbook for Writers.* 2nd ed. Englewood Cliffs, NJ: Prentice Hall, 1990.

Appendix B

# Works Cited in Essay Assignment in Chapter 5

Anderson, Chris. "Hearsay Evidence and Second-Class Citizenship." *College English* 50 (1988): 300–308.

———. "Introduction: Literary Nonfiction and Composition." *Literary Nonfiction: Theory, Criticism, Pedagogy.* Ed. Chris Anderson. Carbondale, Southern Illinois UP, 1989.

Atkins, G. Douglas. "The Return of/to the Essay." *ADE Bulletin* 96 (1990): 11–18.

Beale, Walter H. *A Pragmatic Theory of Rhetoric.* Carbondale: Southern Illinois UP, 1987.

Brashers, Howard C. "Aesthetic Form in Familiar Essays." *College Composition and Communication* 22 (1971): 147–155.

Chapman, David W. "The Essay as a Literary Form." Diss. Texas Christian University, 1985.

Cherica, J. C. Guy. "A Literary Perspective of the Essay: A Study of Its Genetic Principles and Their Bearing on Hermeneutic Theory." Diss. University of South Carolina, 1982.

Epstein, Joseph. "Piece Work: Writing the Essay." *Plausible Prejudices: Essays on American Writing*. New York: W.W. Norton, 1985. 397–411.

Fakundiny, Lydia. "On Approaching the Essay." *The Art of the Essay*. Ed. Lydia Fakundiny. Boston: Houghton Mifflin, 1991. 3–19.

Gass, William H. "Emerson and the Essay." *Habitations of the Word*. New York: Simon and Schuster, 1985. 9–49.

Hardison, O. B., Jr. "Binding Proteus: An Essay on the Essay." *Essays on the Essay: Redefining the Genre*. Ed. Alexander J. Butrym. Athens: University of Georgia Press, 1989. 11–28.

Harrison, Thomas. *Essayism: Conrad, Musil, and Pirandello*. Baltimore: Johns Hopkins UP, 1992.

Howarth, William. "Itinerant Passages: Recent American Essays." *Sewanee Review* 96 (1988): 633–643.

Hunt, Douglas. "Introduction: About Essays and Essayists." *The Dolphin Reader*. Ed. Douglas Hunt. Boston: Houghton Mifflin, 1986. 1–16.

Kauffman, R. Lane. "The Skewed Path: Essaying as Unmethodical Method." *Essays on the Essay: Redefining the Genre*. Ed. Alexander J. Butrym. Athens: University of Georgia Press, 1989. 221–240.

Kazin, Alfred. "The Essay as Modern Form." *The Open Form: Essays for Our Time*. Ed. Alfred Kazin. New York: Harcourt, 1961. vii–xi.

Lopate, Phillip. "The Essay Lives—In Disguise." *The New York Times Book Review*. 18 Nov. 1984. 1+.

Mittlefehldt, Pamela Klass. "'A Weaponry of Choice': Black American Women Writers and the Essay." *The Politics of the Essay: Feminist Perspectives*. Ed. Ruth-Ellen Boetcher Joeres and Elizabeth Mittman. Bloomington: Indiana UP, 1993. 196–208.

Pickering, Samuel F., Jr. "Being Familiar." *The Right Distance*. Athens: University of Georgia Press, 1987. 1–10.

Recchio, Thomas E. "A Dialogic Approach to the Essay." *Essays on the Essay: Redefining the Genre*. Ed. Alexander J. Butrym. Athens: University of Georgia Press, 1989. 271–288.

Sanders, Scott Russell. *The Paradise of Bombs*. Athens: University of Georgia Press, 1987.

———. "The Singular First Person." *Sewanee Review* 96 (1988): 658–672.

Spellmeyer, Kurt. "A Common Ground: The Essay in the Academy." *College English* 51 (1989): 262–276.

Walker, Hugh. Introduction. *The English Essay and Essayists*. Ed. Hugh Walker. London: J. M. Dent, 1923. 1–4.

Winterowd, W. Ross. "Rediscovering the Essay." *Journal of Advanced Composition* 8 (1988): 146–157.

Woolf, Virginia. "Montaigne." *The Common Reader*. New York: Harcourt, 1948. I. 87–100.

# Works Cited

Addison, Joseph. *The Spectator*, No. 476, Friday, September 5, 1712. *The Spectator*. ed. Donald F. Bond. Vol. 4. Oxford: Oxford UP, 1965. 185–188.

Adorno, T. W. "The Essay as Form." Trans. Bob Hullot-Kentor. *New German Critique* 11 (1984): 151–171.

Anderson, Chris. "Hearsay Evidence and Second-Class Citizenship." *College English* 50 (1988): 300–308.

Annas, Pamela J. "Style as Politics: A Feminist Approach to the Teaching of Writing." *College English* 47 (1985): 360–371.

Atkins, G. Douglas. "In Other Words: Gardening for Love—The Work of the Essayist." *The Kenyon Review* 13 (1991): 56–69.

———. "The Return of/to the Essay." *ADE Bulletin* 96 (1990): 11–18.

Axelrod, Rise B., and Charles R. Cooper. *The St. Martin's Guide to Writing*. 3rd ed. New York: St. Martin's Press, 1991.

Bacon, Francis, Viscount of St. Albans. *Francis Bacon*. Ed. Arthur Johnson. London: B.T. Batsford, 1965.

Bakhtin, Mikhail. "Discourse in the Novel." *The Dialogic Imagination: Four Essays*. Trans. Caryl Emerson and Michael Holquist. Ed. Michael Holquist. Austin: University of Texas Press, 1981. 259–422.

———. *Problems of Dostoevsky's Poetics*. Trans. R. W. Rotsel. Ann Arbor: Ardis, 1973.

———. *Rabelais and His World*. Trans. Helene Iswolsky. Cambridge, MA: The M.I.T. Press, 1968.

Barnet, Sylvan, and Marcia Stubbs. *Barnet and Stubbs's Practical Guide to Writing*. 5th ed. Boston: Little, Brown, 1986.

Bensmaïa, Réda. *The Barthes Effect: The Essay as Reflective Text*. Trans. Pat Fedkiew. Vol. 54 of *Theory and History of Literature*. Minneapolis: University of Minnesota Press, 1987.

Benson, Arthur Christopher. "The Art of the Essayist." *Modern English Essays*. Vol. 5 of 5. Ed. Ernest Rhys. London: Dent, 1922. 50–63.

Berlin, James A. "Rhetoric and Ideology in the Writing Class." *College English* 50 (1988): 477–494.

———. *Rhetoric and Reality: Writing Instruction in American Colleges, 1900–1985*. Carbondale: Southern Illinois UP, 1987.

Bizzell, Patricia and Bruce Herzberg, eds. *The Rhetorical Tradition: Readings from Classical Times to the Present*. Boston: Bedford, 1990.

Butrym, Alexander J. Introduction. *Essays on the Essay: Redefining the Genre*. Ed. Alexander J. Butrym. Athens: University of Georgia Press, 1989. 1–8.

Chadbourne, Richard M. "A Puzzling Literary Genre: Comparative Views of the Essay." *Comparative Literature Studies* 20 (1983): 133–153.

Chapman, David W. "The Essay as a Literary Form." Diss. Texas Christian University, 1985.

———. "Forming and Meaning: Writing the Counterpoint Essay." *Journal of Advanced Composition* 11 (1991): 73–82.

Cherica, J. C. Guy. "A Literary Perspective of the Essay: A Study of Its Genetic Principles and Their Bearing on Hermeneutic Theory." Diss. University of South Carolina, 1982.

Chesterton, G. K. "On Essays." *Come to Think of It*. New York: Dodd, 1931. 1–6.

Core, George. "Stretching the Limits of the Essay." *Essays on the Essay: Redefining the Genre*. Ed. Alexander J. Butrym. Athens: University of Georgia Press, 1989. 207–220.

Cornwallis, Sir William, the Younger. *Essayes*. Ed. Don Cameron Allen. Baltimore: Johns Hopkins Press, 1946. 190–202.

Crews, Frederick, and Sandra Schor. *The Borzoi Handbook for Writers*. 2nd ed. New York: Alfred A. Knopf, 1989.

Croll, Morris W. "The Baroque Style in Prose." *Style, Rhetoric, and Ryhthm: Essays by Morris W. Croll*. Ed. J. Max Patrick et al. Princeton: Princeton UP, 1966. 207–233.

Dawson, William J. and Coningsby W. Dawson. *The Great English Essayists*. New York: H. W. Wilson, 1932.

Didion, Joan. "At the Dam." *The White Album*. New York: Simon and Schuster, 1979. 198–201.

———. "On Keeping a Notebook." *Slouching Towards Bethlehem*. New York: Noonday Press, 1990. 131–141.

———. "On Morality." *Slouching Towards Bethlehem*. New York: Noonday Press, 1990. 157–163.

Dobrée, Bonamy. *English Essayists*. London: Collins, 1946.

Durst, Russel K. "The Development of Analytic Writing." *Contexts for Learning to Write: Studies of Secondary School Instruction*. Ed. Arthur N. Applebee. Norwood, NJ: ABLEX, 1984. 79–102.

Duval, Edwin M. "Rhetorical Composition and 'Open Form' in Montaigne's Early *Essais*." *Bibliotheque d'Humanisme et Renaissance* 43.2 (1981): 269–287.

Ehrlich, Gretel. "Island." *Islands, the Universe, Home*. New York: Viking, 1991. 63–66.

———. "Looking for a Lost Dog." *Islands, the Universe, Home.* New York: Viking, 1991. 3–7.

———. "The Smooth Skull of Winter." *The Solace of Open Spaces.* New York: Viking, 1985. 71–74.

———. "The Source of a River." *Islands, the Universe, Home.* New York: Viking, 1991. 27–31.

Epstein, Joseph. "A Few Kind Words for Envy." *The Best American Essays 1990.* Ed. Justin Kaplan. New York: Ticknor & Fields, 1990. 83–98.

———. Introduction. *The Best American Essays 1993.* Ed. Joseph Epstein. New York: Ticknor & Fields, 1993. xiii–xviii.

———. "Piece Work: Writing the Essay." *Plausible Prejudices: Essays on American Writing.* Ed. Joseph Epstein. New York: W.W. Norton, 1985. 397–411.

———. "Tea and Antipathy." *Once More Around the Block: Familiar Essays.* New York: W.W. Norton, 1987. 265–282.

———. "What Is Vulgar?" *The Middle of My Tether.* New York: W.W. Norton, 1983. 126–141.

———. "What's So Funny?" *Once More Around the Block: Familiar Essays.* New York: W.W. Norton, 1987. 127–146.

Fakundiny, Lydia. "On Approaching the Essay." *The Art of the Essay.* Ed. Lydia Fakundiny. Boston: Houghton Mifflin, 1991. 3–19.

Farrell, Thomas J. "The Female and Male Modes of Rhetoric." *College English* 40 (1979): 909–921.

Fergenson, Laraine. *Writing with Style: Rhetoric, Reader, Handbook.* Fort Worth: Holt, Rinehart and Winston, 1989.

Fiedler, Leslie, ed. Preface to the First Edition. *The Art of the Essay.* 2nd ed. New York: Crowell, 1969.

Fort, Keith. "Form, Authority, and the Critical Essay." *College English* 32 (1971): 629–639.

Frame, Donald. Introduction. *The Complete Works of Montaigne.* Trans. Donald Frame. Stanford: Stanford UP, 1957.

Gass, William H. "Emerson and the Essay." *Habitations of the Word.* New York: Simon and Schuster, 1985. 9–49.

Gebhardt, Richard C., and Dawn Rodrigues. *Writing: Processes and Intentions.* Lexington, MA: D. C. Heath, 1989.

Geertz, Clifford. *Local Knowledge: Further Essays in Interpretive Anthropology.* New York: Basic Books, 1983.

Gere, Anne Ruggles. *Writing and Learning.* 2nd ed. New York: Macmillan, 1988.

Good, Graham. *The Observing Self: Rediscovering the Essay.* London: Routledge, 1988.

Guth, Hans P. *The Writer's Agenda.* Belmont, CA: Wadsworth, 1989.

Hairston, Maxine, and John J. Ruszkiewicz. *The Scott, Foresman Handbook for Writers.* Glenview, IL: Scott, Foresman, 1988.

Hall, Michael L. "'Drawing Myself for Others': The *Ethos* of the Essayist." *Explorations in Renaissance Culture* 7 (1981): 27–35.

———. "The Emergence of the Essay and the Idea of Discovery." *Essays on the Essay: Redefining the Genre.* Ed. Alexander J. Butrym. Athens: University of Georgia Press, 1989. 73–91.

Hardison, O. B., Jr. "Binding Proteus: An Essay on the Essay." *Essays on the Essay: Redefining the Genre.* Ed. Alexander J. Butrym. Athens: University of Georgia Press, 1989. 11–28.

Hardwick, Elizabeth. Introduction. *The Best American Essays 1986.* Ed. Elizabeth Hardwick. New York: Ticknor & Fields, 1986. xiii–xxi.

Harrison, Thomas. *Essayism: Conrad, Musil, and Pirandello.* Baltimore: Johns Hopkins UP, 1992.

Heath, Shirley Brice. "The Essay in English: Readers and Writers in Dialogue." *Textual Voices, Vocative Texts: Dialogue, Linguistics, and Literature.* Ed. Michael Macovski. Manuscript obtained through personal correspondence.

Heffernan, James A. W., and John E. Lincoln. *Writing: A College Handbook.* 3rd ed. New York: W. W. Norton, 1990.

Hoagland, Edward. "What I Think, What I Am." *Eight Modern Essayists*. 4th ed. Ed. William Smart. New York: St. Martin's Press, 1985. 222–225.

Holdheim, W. Wolfgang. Preface and "Introduction: The Essay as Knowledge in Progress." *The Hermeneutic Mode: Essays on Time in Literature and Literary Theory*. Ithaca: Cornell UP, 1984. 11–15, 19–32.

Holman, C. Hugh, and William Harmon. *A Handbook to Literature*. 5th ed. New York: Macmillan, 1986.

Howarth, William. "Itinerant Passages: Recent American Essays." *The Sewanee Review* 96 (1988): 633–643.

Howells, William Dean. "Editor's Easy Chair." *Harper's Magazine*. October 1902: 802–803.

Hoy, Pat C., II. "Students and Their Teachers Under the Influence: Image and Idea in the Essay." *Literary Nonfiction: Theory, Criticism, Pedagogy*. Ed. Chris Anderson. Carbondale: Southern Illinois UP, 1989. 287–300.

Hughes, Langston. "Mellow." *The Langston Hughes Reader*. New York: George Braziller, 1958. 104.

Hullot-Kentor, Bob. "Title Essay." *New German Critique* 11 (1984): 141–150.

Hunt, Douglas. "Introduction: About Essays and Essayists." *The Dolphin Reader*. Ed. Douglas Hunt. Boston: Houghton Mifflin, 1986. 1–16.

Huxley, Aldous. "Music at Night." *Collected Essays*. New York: Harper, 1959. 176–180.

———. Preface. *Collected Essays*. New York: Harper, 1959. v–ix.

Joeres, Ruth-Ellen Boetcher, and Elizabeth Mittman. "An Introductory Essay." *The Politics of the Essay: Feminist Perspectives*. Eds. Ruth-Ellen Boetcher Joeres and Elizabeth Mittman. Bloomington: Indiana UP, 1993. 12–20.

Johnson, Samuel. *A Dictionary of the English Language* [1755]. New York: AMS Press, 1967.

Juncker, Clara. "Writing (with) Cixous." *College English* 50 (1988): 424–436.

Kaplan, Justin. Introduction. *The Best American Essays 1990.* Ed. Justin Kaplan. New York: Ticknor & Fields, 1990. xiii–xix.

Kauffman, Robert Lane. "The Skewed Path: Essaying as Unmethodical Method." *Essays on the Essay: Redefining the Genre.* Ed. Alexander J. Butrym. Athens: University of Georgia Press, 1989. 221–240.

———. "The Theory of the Essay: Lukács, Adorno, and Benjamin." Diss. University of California–San Diego, 1981.

Kennedy, X. J., and Dorothy M. Kennedy. *The Bedford Guide for College Writers.* New York: St. Martin's Press, 1987.

Kirszner, Laurie G., and Stephen R. Mandell. *Writing: A College Rhetoric.* 2nd ed. New York: Holt, Rinehart and Winston, 1988.

Klaus, Carl H. "Essayists on the Essay." *Literary Nonfiction: Theory, Criticism, Pedagogy.* Ed. Chris Anderson. Carbondale: Southern Illinois UP, 1989. 155–175.

Kostelanetz, Richard. "Innovations in Essaying." *Essaying Essays: Alternative Forms of Exposition.* New York: Out of London Press, 1975. 1–9.

Kurilich, Frances, and Helen Whitaker. *Re:Writing.* New York: Holt, Rinehart and Winston, 1988.

Leggett, Glenn C., David Mead, and Melinda G. Kramer. *The Prentice Hall Handbook for Writers.* 11th ed. Englewood Cliffs, NJ: Prentice Hall, 1991.

Lopate, Phillip. "The Essay Lives On—In Disguise." *The New York Times Book Review* 18 Nov. 1984: 1+.

Lukács, Georg. "On the Nature and Form of the Essay." *Soul and Form.* Trans. Anna Bostock. Cambridge, MA: MIT Press, 1974. 1–18.

Lunsford, Andrea, and Robert Connors. *The St. Martin's Handbook.* New York: St. Martin's Press, 1989.

MacDonald, Wilbert Lorne. *Beginning of the English Essay*. University of Toronto Studies; Philological Series No. 3. Toronto: The University Library, 1914.

Mann, Rebecca C., and Pete M. Mann. *Essay Writing: Methods and Models*. Belmont, CA: Wadsworth, 1990.

Mittlefehldt, Pamela Klass. "'A Weaponry of Choice': Black American Women Writers and the Essay." *The Politics of the Essay: Feminist Perspectives*. Eds. Ruth-Ellen Boetcher Joeres and Elizabeth Mittman. Bloomington: Indiana UP, 1993. 196–208.

Montaigne, Michel Eyquemde. *The Complete Works of Montaigne*. Trans. Donald M. Frame. Stanford: Stanford UP, 1957.

Mowitt, John William. "From Montaigne to Nietzsche: Towards a Theory of the Essay." Diss. University of Wisconsin–Madison, 1982.

Neeld, Elizabeth Cowan. *Writing*. 3rd ed. Glenview, IL: Scott, Foresman, 1990.

Newkirk, Thomas. *Critical Thinking and Writing: Reclaiming the Essay*. Monographs on Teaching Critical Thinking 3. Urbana, IL: ERIC/NCTE, 1989.

Oates, Joyce Carol. Introduction. *The Best American Essays 1991*. Ed. Joyce Carol Oates. New York: Ticknor & Fields, 1991. xiii–xxiii.

O'Hare, Frank, and Dean Memering. *The Writer's Work: A Guide to Effective Composition*. 3rd ed. Englewood Cliffs, NJ: Prentice Hall, 1990.

Pebworth, Ted-Larry. "Not Being, But Passing: Defining the Early English Essay." *Studies in the Literary Imagination* 10 (1977): 17–27.

Pickering, Samuel F., Jr. "Being Familiar." *The Right Distance*. Athens: University of Georgia Press, 1987. 1–10.

Plato. *Phaedrus*. Trans. H. N. Fowler. *The Rhetorical Tradition: Readings from Classical Times to the Present*. Ed. Patricia Bizzell and Bruce Herzberg. Boston: Bedford, 1990. 113–143.

Rawlins, Jack. *The Writer's Way*. Boston: Houghton Mifflin, 1987.

Recchio, Thomas E. "A Dialogic Approach to the Essay." *Essays on the Essay: Redefining the Genre*. Ed. Alexander J. Butrym. Athens: University of Georgia Press, 1989. 271–288.

Reinking, James A., and Andrew W. Hart. *Strategies for Successful Writing: A Rhetoric, Reader, and Handbook*. Englewood Cliffs, NJ: Prentice Hall, 1991.

Rhodes, Richard. *Looking for America: A Writer's Odyssey*. Garden City, NY: Doubleday, 1979.

Rhys, Ernest. Introduction. *Modern English Essayists*. Vol. 1 of 6. Ed. Ernest Rhys. London: Dent, 1922.

Richman, Michéle. Foreword. *The Barthes Effect: The Essay as Reflective Text*. By Réda Bensmaïa. Trans. Pat Fedkiew. Vol. 54 of *Theory and History of Literature*. Minneapolis: University of Minnesota Press, 1987. viii–xxi.

Routh, H. V. "The Origins of the Essay Compared in French and English Literatures." *The Modern Language Review* 15 (1920): 28–40, 143–151.

Sanders, Scott Russell. "The Men We Carry in Our Minds." *The Paradise of Bombs*. Athens: University of Georgia Press, 1987. 111–117.

———. *The Paradise of Bombs*. Athens: University of Georgia Press, 1987.

———. "The Singular First Person." *The Sewanee Review* 96 (1988): 658–672.

Scholes, Robert, and Carl H. Klaus. *Elements of the Essay*. New York: Oxford UP, 1969.

Sichtermann, Barbara. "Woman Taking Speculation into Her Own Hands." Trans. Ruth-Ellen B. Joeres and Elizabeth Mittman. *The Politics of the Essay: Feminist Perspectives*. Ed. Ruth-Ellen Boetcher Joeres and Elizabeth Mittman. Bloomington: Indiana UP, 1993. 87–94.

Simic, Charles. "Reading Philosophy at Night." *The Best American Essays 1988*. Ed. Annie Dillard. New York: Ticknor & Fields, 1988. 307–314.

Smith, Alexander. "On the Writing of Essays." *Dreamthorp: A Book of Essays Written in the Country*. London: Routledge, 1905. 26–54.

Spellmeyer, Kurt. "A Common Ground: The Essay and the Academy." *College English* 51 (1989): 262–276.

Tompkins, Jane. "Me and My Shadow." *New Literary History* 19 (1987): 168–178.

Troyka, Lynn Quitman. *Simon and Schuster Handbook for Writers*. 2nd ed. Englewood Cliffs, NJ: Prentice Hall, 1990.

Walker, Alice. "Father." *Living by the Word: Selected Writings 1973–1987*. San Diego: Harcourt, 1988. 9–17.

White, E. B. Foreword. *Essays of E. B. White*. New York: Harper & Row, 1977. vii–ix.

Whitmore, Charles E. "The Field of the Essay." *PMLA* 36 (1921): 551–564.

Winterowd, W. Ross. "Rediscovering the Essay." *Journal of Advanced Composition* 8 (1988): 146–157.

Woolf, Virginia. "Montainge." *The Common Reader*. New York: Harcourt, 1948. I. 87–100.

Zeiger, William. "The Exploratory Essay: Enfranchising the Spirit of Inquiry in College Composition." *College English* 47 (1985): 454–466.

———. "The Personal Essay and Egalitarian Rhetoric." *Literary Nonfiction: Theory, Criticism, Pedagogy*. Ed. Chris Anderson. Carbondale: Southern Illinois UP, 1989. 235–244.

# Index

Paul Heilker earned his Ph.D. in Rhetoric and Composition Studies from Texas Christian University in 1992. He presently teaches courses in the theory and practice of rhetoric, writing, and the teaching of composition at Virginia Tech, where he serves as an assistant professor of English and Co-director of English Department Writing Programs. His work has appeared in such journals as *Rhetoric Review, Composition Studies, The Writing Instructor, Computers and Composition*, and *Issues in Writing*. With Peter Vandenberg, he is currently editing *Keywords in Composition Studies* (Boynton/Cook—Heinemann, 1996), a book tracing the origins, evolution, and contested use of sixty critical terms in composition studies. His next project will examine theories of style in the writing of nonfiction prose and their (lack of) relationship to the teaching of composition.